UNDERSTANDING VIOLENT CRIMINALS

Recent Titles in
Forensic Psychology

David J. Thomas, Series Editor

Psychopathy, Perversion, and Lust Homicide:
Recognizing the Mental Disorders That Power Serial Killers
Duane L. Dobbert

Female Sexual Predators:
Understanding Them to Protect Our Children and Youths
Karen A. Duncan

Police Psychology:
A New Specialty and New Challenges for Men and Women in Blue
David J. Thomas

UNDERSTANDING VIOLENT CRIMINALS

Insights from the Front Lines of Law Enforcement

David J. Thomas

Forensic Psychology
David J. Thomas, Series Editor

OCN 852220684

AN IMPRINT OF ABC-CLIO, LLC
Santa Barbara, California • Denver, Colorado • Oxford, England

Library of Congress Cataloging-in-Publication Data

Thomas, David J.
  Understanding violent criminals : insights from the front lines of law enforcement /
David J. Thomas.
    pages cm. — (Forensic psychology)
  Includes index.
ISBN 978-1-4408-2925-3 (hbk.) — ISBN 978-1-4408-2926-0 (ebook)
1. Criminal psychology. 2. Violent crimes—Psychological aspects. I. Title.
HV6080.T546 2014
364.3—dc23   2014000300

ISBN: 978-1-4408-2925-3
EISBN: 978-1-4408-2926-0

18 17 16 15 14   1 2 3 4 5

This book is also available on the World Wide Web as an eBook.
Visit www.abc-clio.com for details.

Praeger
An Imprint of ABC-CLIO, LLC

ABC-CLIO, LLC
130 Cremona Drive, P.O. Box 1911
Santa Barbara, California 93116-1911

This book is printed on acid-free paper (∞)

Manufactured in the United States of America

This text is dedicated to:
Nicole, David, Erika, and Patricia

Contents

Series Foreword

I start every course that I teach in Forensic Psychology by asking my students to define the term forensic psychology. Technically forensic psychology is defined as the research and application of psychological knowledge to the legal system. Television depicts forensic psychologists as profilers working for the FBI and hunting serial offenders, pitting the profilers' knowledge against the wits of the criminal. The reality is that this opportunity is limited to a select few. However, when I examine the field it is one that is truly diverse and includes specialties where clinicians offer their expertise in such areas as competency to stand trial, police psychology, criminal behavior, criminal responsibility, eyewitness testimony/credibility, victimology, trauma, terrorism, child custody, worker compensation cases, personal injury cases, and cases involving the handicap.

The aforementioned list is far from exhaustive; rather it is a fair representation of the diversity in the field and its many opportunities. It should also be clear that no one specialty is stand-alone, meaning that other fields interact and have an impact on the clinician's findings. One could not make a judgment of criminal behavior or insanity based on an interview and the administration of an assessment instrument. I would compare the role of a clinician to that of a criminal investigator. A criminal investigator must examine the totality of the circumstances before charges can be filed in court. In comparison a clinician must complete a thorough assessment of one's psychological, biological, and environmental histories, which is the totality of an offender/

client's mental health. There is one caveat when dealing with assessments and that is the clinician must be constantly aware of an offender/client's attempts to malinger and manipulate the outcomes to benefit themselves.

This is an exciting time in the field of forensic psychology because of its diversity and the state of the world. We struggle to understand acts of terrorism, school shootings, bullying, murder within families, and the aftermath of such incidents. As series editor, I challenge you to take what you learn from our series and use it as a catalyst for social change.

David J. Thomas, Ph.D., LMHC
Series Editor

Theories of Crime

For years, researchers have attempted to explain both the causes of violence and the fluctuation in crime rates annually, but to date no one has been able to do so convincingly. A number of theories have addressed the issue, but none can be applied universally. The reason is that when we examine criminal behavior, we are examining human behavior, which is highly unpredictable. Many scholars have argued that there is a correlation between rising crime rates and the economy—that crime increases when the economy is bad; and yet, in the midst of a severe economic downturn, violent crime has been on the decline since 2000.

According to a 2011 Gallup poll, 68 percent of Americans believed that the crime rates in the United States had increased during the past year. However, when polled regarding local crime, only 10 percent believed that crime was a serious problem in their communities. In stark contrast to those feelings of being safe in their respective communities, however, 38 percent of the same group believed that it was not safe to walk the streets after dark (Saad, 2011). One of the greatest fears we have in America is that we will become victims of crime while we are out of our homes at night.

Before you start reading this chapter, take a moment and think over the Questions for Reflection. The first two questions focus on those who commit crimes; the last question focuses on how what they do affects the rest of us.

> **Questions for Reflection:** What causes crime? What allows a human being to commit acts of violence so egregious that he or she shakes the psyche of even the most seasoned police officers? In the average person's perception of the world as a dangerous place, is there a disconnect between perception and reality, or is little paranoia a good thing?

CAUSES OF CRIME

Everyone wonders what the causes of crime might be. When I propose this question to my students, some argue that it stems from a psychological disorder and use the American Psychiatric Association's *Diagnostic and Statistical Manual of Mental Disorders, IV-TR* (DSM-IV-TR; APA, 2000) to defend their answers. Others argue that crime is caused by the economy and poverty; however, this argument is not logical because we have just experienced the worst economic downturn in the United States since the Great Depression, and yet crime rates have fallen each year for the past ten years.

What do you believe is the cause of crime? To establish a foundation of the causes of violent crime, we must examine theories from the fields of criminology, biology, sociology, and psychology. After you have read about these theories, you will have the opportunity to apply them to acts of violence presented in the case studies at the end of the chapter and in the remaining chapters of the book.

CRIMINOLOGY AND SOCIOLOGY

The study of criminology is one of the many avenues by which scholars have attempted to explain the causes of crime and predict violent criminal behavior. Criminology first attempts to explain the etiology of violent crime. Early theories identified criminal behavior as being biological in nature, but a recent shift in criminological theory has involved a more sociological perspective.

The origins of attempts to understand the criminal mind are found in the nineteenth century with the research of Cesare Lombroso, who is considered the father of criminal anthropology. *Criminal anthropology* is defined as "dealing with the natural history of the criminal, because it embraces his organic, psychic constitution, and social life just as anthropology does in the case of normal human beings and different races" (Brown, Esbensen, & Geis, 1998, p. 229). Lombroso viewed cranial depressions found on the skulls of violent criminals and noticed they were similar to those found on the skulls of primates whose development is primitive. He classified these biological abnormalities as belonging to an atavistic person, or a born criminal.

A second classification was of minor law violators, known as criminaloids (Lombroso, 1876/2006).

The theories of Lombroso spawned a new era in criminology known as *eugenics*. The father of eugenics in the United States was Dr. Harry H. Laughlin, who authored the book *Eugenical Sterilization in the United States*. Laughlin (1922) argued that the success of a democracy depends on the quality of its citizens and that the goal of America is to protect itself from immigrants, criminal degenerates, and racial suicide (p. v). He also argued that America, if short of being pure, would fall into chaos and become a dictatorship. His beliefs were widely accepted in the United States until the 1930s. Until that time, twenty-seven states allowed forced sterilization of the mentally ill, feeble-minded, and chronic offenders (Buchanan, Brock, Daniels, & Wikler, 2000).

William Sheldon developed another biological theory called *somatotyping*, which involved identifying and predicting criminal behavior based on an individual's body type. Sheldon (1949) argued that the body is an object, a tangible record, of the most long-standing and deeply established habits that have been laid down during a long succession of generations. Sheldon believed that there were three distinct body forms, which he called somatotypes. He identified these three body types, which could determine one's behavior and intelligence, as: endomorph, the subject is soft and round; mesomorph, the subject is muscular; and ectomorph, the subject is tall and lean. The body type that was found to be involved in criminal activity most often was mesomorphic, as compared to a matched group of nondelinquents. Sheldon's initial findings were supported in a later study (Sheldon & Glueck, 1951) comprised of 500 juvenile delinquents and nondelinquents.

Today we would question whether there is any validity to such research, but Greenberg (1995) reported that such research was believed to be valid until the 1960s. In fact, freshmen who sought admission to Ivy League and other prestigious colleges were required to pose for nude photographs from the 1940s through the 1960s. This was a direct result of Sheldon's research, which asserted there was a correlation between body type and intelligence, as well as other traits. The nude photographs of Hillary Rodham Clinton, George Bush, and Diane Sawyer are a part of Sheldon's historical archives, which are housed at the Smithsonian Institute. The photos and research have been sealed (Greenberg, 1995).

It is here that criminological theories began to change and the focus became sociological in nature. In essence, criminology of this type examines crime from a cause-and-effect perspective, with the goal being to establish links between crime and the external environment. The first major body of works that emerged using the sociological perspective is known as the *Chicago school of criminology*. This school, beginning in the 1920s and 1930s, produced many theories and principles regarding causes of crime, but none that identifies criminals. Although the Chicago school's theories are numerous enough to be the subject of an extensive literature review, these researchers' ideas can be grouped under three main headings: ecological theories, cultural conflict theories, and differential association theory.

Ecological Theories

The prevailing premise from which the Chicago school operated is that crime is the result of social disorganization. The Chicago school was responsible for the development of many of the methods used in the study of crime and criminals, including official statistics, life histories, and ethnography (Short, 2002). Of all the theories and subgroupings included in the Chicago school, however, only one addresses the cause of violent crime: the subculture violence theory.

The *subculture violence theory* was introduced by Marvin Wolfgang and Franco Ferracuti in 1967. The theory was designed to explain spontaneous assaults and homicides. Subculture violence draws not only from criminology but also from the medical, biological, and psychological disciplines. Wolfgang and Ferracuti (1967) theorized that subculture violence is only partly different from the parent culture—that it is, in fact, an integral component of the parent culture. The act of violence is learned and facilitated by positive reinforcement. Since violence is learned and positively reinforced, controls such as interpersonal conflict or guilt are obviated. This theory is supported by Gray's behavior inhibition system discussed later in this chapter in the section on neuropsychology.

Two researchers performed studies to test the theories of Wolfgang and Ferracuti, but came up with two different results. Ball-Rokeach (1973) completed the first empirical study of the subculture violence theory and came to the conclusion that the values established by the subculture play little or no role as determinants of interpersonal violence. Bernard (1990) tested a variation not rooted in violence and suggested that angry aggression develops among the truly disadvantaged as a consequence of racial discrimination and low social position, that is, the parent culture, as first theorized by Wolfgang and Ferracuti in 1967.

An extension of the subculture of violence theory was presented by Elijah Anderson in 1999 in a book titled *Code of the Street*, which is a narrative ethnographic exploration of a low-income African American neighborhood in the city of Philadelphia. The basis for Anderson's research was rather simple: He wanted to know why inner-city youth are willing to perpetrate violence and acts of aggression toward each other (p. 90). Anderson (1999) defined the *code of the street* as a set of informal rules that govern relationships, behavior, and specifically violence (p. 33). Interestingly, those who have adopted middle-class values and live in these communities have to adopt a duality in their personality: one that allows them to address their contemporaries in the neighborhood and the other that allows them to be accepted by mainstream America.

Anderson (1999) argued that being treated with respect is central to the code and the violence, with respect described as an external entity, "one that is hard-won, easily lost, and must constantly be guarded" (p. 31). The concept of respect, along with the idea of credibility, is about safety and security; disrespect is a challenge to one's sovereignty. This need for self-preservation grew out of distrust of police and the criminal justice system, so the same code extends to "stop snitching campaigns," where those who have adopted the street code are willing to die or kill to resolve their own conflicts.

Cultural Conflict Theories

Another school of thought is referred to as conflict theories. Within this school, Emile Durkheim (1933/1984), a French sociologist often identified as the father of sociology, first introduced a theory called *anomie* or *strain theory* in 1892. The term *strain* is used to refer to the idea that problems are created due to society's structure: The structure creates a strain on certain groups, resulting in a push toward deviance (Durkheim, 1933/1984). Robert Merton continued research regarding anomie/strain theory in 1938. Merton (1938/1968) conceptualized that at the center of a disorganized society is too much emphasis placed on common cultural success. Goals and the opportunity to reach those goals are not equal or fair, so in essence, the emphasis on cultural success creates a society that is stratified and in conflict.

Following anomie/strain theory, another theory emerged in criminology known as the labeling theory. The *labeling theory* was spawned by the civil rights movement, protests, and the question of inequality. Becker (1963) argued that deviance and crime are not innate, but rather, criminality is defined by one's social environment. In fact, society defines how one will be judged by establishing a set of rules and applying the label based on the infraction. An extension of the labeling theory is the conflict theory presented by Quinney (1977), who asserted that those most likely to be labeled are powerless.

Conflict theories offer many different approaches; however, there is one common denominator: conflict, which is described as a natural state of human society. In conflict theory, there are two schools of thought: one that is conservative and a second that is radical. The conservative view offers that society itself is the basis of conflict, while the radical approach offers power as the basis of conflict.

Social control is the final sociological theory to be discussed. Conger (1976) stated that there are many theories regarding social control, and they all assert: "In control theory, there is little interest in what motivates the individual to deviate. Rather, the basic assumption of the theory is that most individuals would deviate if their bonds to conformity were loosened deviance" (p. 19).

Differential Association Theory

The theory of differential association asserts that all behavior is learned and takes place while we interact with other individuals or groups, primarily family, peers, and school (Sutherland, Cressey, & Luckenbill, 1992). Bandura (1973) argued that except for elementary reflexes, all behavior is learned, and that responses are acquired through direct experience and/or observation (p. 16). Learning through direct experience is nothing more than the concept of reward and punishment.

In the case of criminal behavior, positive reinforcement and inducements include the satisfaction of committing the crime, not being apprehended by the police, increased self-esteem, increased stature within a respective peer group, and the financial and other benefits as they relate to the commission of the crime. The negative consequences are just the opposite: apprehension by the police, loss of self-esteem, being considered a failure by peers, and loss of any gains that might have been acquired through success.

When it comes to the commission of a violent felony, one has to wonder if the rewards could be greater than the possible consequences. Based on data from the Federal Bureau of Investigation's 2011 *Uniform Crime Reports* (FBI, 2012), nationally, only 47.7 percent of all violent crimes are cleared by arrest. The categories of violent crime and their respective clearance rates are as follows:

- Murder: 64.8 percent
- Rape: 41.2 percent
- Robbery: 28.7 percent
- Aggravated assault: 56.9 percent
- Arson: 18.8 percent

Unfortunately, based on these statistics, the odds of success remain in the criminal's favor.

PSYCHOLOGY AND BIOLOGY

If we were to examine every theory in psychology, each would describe environmental conditions associated with a child's family and the love and nurturing a child receives from the family unit. Three interrelated theories that stand out in the field are Maslow's (1968) hierarchy of needs, Bowlby's (1940) attachment theory, and Rothbart's (2007) temperament model. All three theories explain the importance of a safe and secure environment in the development of personality and temperament from birth. Safety and security provide a platform for a child to explore and learn through support and nurturing. Human beings are social creatures, and failure to provide such an environment has a direct impact on a person's overall well-being.

The concept of development is directly related to each of the aforementioned theories. Bandura (1973) argued that aggression is a learned behavior through either modeling or practice and that, if not addressed through some form of control, then it will be reinforced (p. 68). In the discussion of psychology, however, one also has to consider the individual's cognitive processes. When speaking of cognition, what we are attempting to understand are a person's attitudes, beliefs, thoughts, and values and how they influence social interaction. In a much simpler form, the cognitive process defines our perception, and our perception is our reality.

Ellis (1994) argued that humans are both rational and irrational and that we learn to construct self-preserving and destructive thoughts, feelings, and behaviors (p. 53). From a purely psychological perspective, it is an illogical or distorted thought process that allows criminals to interact and commit crimes of violence, independent of feelings.

Yochelson and Samenow (1976) described this type of thinking or logic as distorted thinking errors. These authors believed so firmly in the concept of distorted thought patterns that they did not use the term *criminal* in the legal sense but instead classified criminals based on their cognitive processes. They used two categories to describe either end of what they saw as a continuum of criminality: responsible and irresponsible (p. 253). In their view, the *responsible person* accepts the social contract that is prescribed by society, meaning that the responsible person is law-abiding. The *irresponsible person,* however, is the criminal; and criminals fall into three categories:

- *Nonarrestable:* someone who is not reliable, abuses benefits, lies to get ahead, and is not a criminal as classified by statute but looks to benefit themselves
- *Arrestable:* a person who possess all the thinking patterns of the hardcore criminal, yet engages in petty offenses such as shoplifting, and does not cross over into violent crimes because of fear of the consequences
- *Extreme criminal:* the person who develops the distorted process at an early age, is prone to violence, and looks at the law and consequences as the cost of doing business

Neuropsychology

Neuropsychology, one of the many disciplines in the field of psychology, is the study of the functioning of the brain as it relates to behavior. It appears that this field may provide some insight into violent crime and aggression and their connection to the mind and the brain.

Frontal lobe syndrome (FLS) is a mental disorder wherein there is a correlation between impulsive violence and frontal lobe damage. The frontal lobes are the focal point of memory, cognition, abstraction, concentration, and judgment. The clinical and empirical evidence linking impulsive violence to frontal lobe damage was significant enough to lead the American Medical Association to classify FLS as an organic mental disorder in the 10th edition of the *International Classification of Diseases* (ICD-10-CM; AMA, 2012). The symptoms of FLS are an identifiable injury to the brain or a congenital defect. The manifestations of FLS include impairment of self-control, lack of foresight, loss of creativity, and spontaneity. Other deficiencies of FLS include increased irritability, selfishness, restlessness, lack of concern for others, boastfulness, and temper outbursts.

Feldman and Quenzer (1985/1997) conducted a study with rats to determine if impulsive violence is a by-product of "nature or nurture." The results of the study were uniform. There were two groups of rats, those that were trained aggressively and those that were peaceably raised. The frontal lobe of one group of rats was intentionally damaged. When another rat was introduced into the experimental space of the rats with frontal lobe damage, the attacks were aggressive and described as abnormal. The rats kept biting and gnawing at their victims even after death.

Pallone and Hennessy (1998) theorized that there is a short step between the frontal-lobe-damaged rat's unnatural activity and the crime scene of a sadistic murderer. These researchers conceptualized a criminal aggression theory they termed the *tinder box theory*. In developing this theory, the authors collated the studies of adjudicated offenders reported for forty years. Each of the offenders was evaluated by an accepted neurological examination: an electroencephalogram (EEG), the Luria-Nebraska instrument, or a Reitan instrument. In this study, there were nineteen offender groups with a total of 2,100 subjects. The results of the study were remarkable. The authors noted the following observations:

> Neuropathology is found in very high incidence among those offenders who have committed the most serious of aggressive offenses and among those whose offense histories reveal persistently aggressive patterns. At the extremes, the relative incidence of neuropathology among homicide offenders (94 percent) exceeds the estimated incidence in the general population (3 percent) at a ratio of nearly 32:1 or, phrased differently, the incidence of neuropathology among the murderers studied exceeds the estimated incidence in the general population by nearly 3,200 percent. Among the offenders studied, the mean incidence of neuropathology exceeds that in the general population by some 2033 percent. (Pallone & Hennessy, 1998, p. 6)

Another aspect of this complex puzzle is examined in Gray's (1981) two-factor theory in regard to antisocial behavior. Gray's theory offers two behavioral systems, both of which have a neural basis. The two systems are described next:

1. *Behavioral activation system (BAS):* The BAS is believed to activate behavior in response to cues of reward and punishment. A physiological response to the underactivation of the BAS is a low heart rate and the secretion of low amounts of dopamine.

2. *Behavior inhibition system (BIS):* The BIS is believed to inhibit behavior in response to cues of punishment or frustration due to nonreward. A physiological response to the underactivation of the BIS is low skin conductivity and secretions of low amounts of norepinephrine and serotonin.

Gray's BIS model suggests that antisocial behavior may occur due to an individual's decreased ability to learn to inhibit behavior from cues of punishment, which reflects decreased anxiety, decreased heart rate, decreased skin conductivity, and decreased amounts of serotonin and norepinephrine.

The indices developed by Gray are similar to those that are associated with the frontal lobe syndrome and Bandura's theory of social learning. Simply, a desensitization that inhibits the fear associated with punishment or consequences occurs.

To this point, the literature seems to indicate that criminality is a process of influences from an early age. Scott and Stenberg (2008) support this notion, noting that juveniles who know and understand right from wrong and yet continue to make poor decisions do so because their emotional and psychological development lag behind their cognitive processes. Gur (2004) has noted that, despite their size and/or appearance, teenagers are not mature cognitively; people reach cognitive maturity only in their mid-twenties. Gur describes the maturation process as peeling away layers of gray matter until the brain is fully matured. This lack of maturity is why juveniles are easily influenced by peers and act without fear of consequences. Ultimately, the decisions are made by the amygdala, which is responsible for the human survival instinct and for processing fear, anger, and pleasure. The frontal lobe provides balance and allows humans to process information and not act on impulse.

Hormones and Neurotransmitters

Any discussion regarding neuropsychology and the effects of brain damage to particular regions of the brain would be incomplete without a discussion of the most prominent neurotransmitters and their role in aggressive behavior. Raine (1993) asserted that neurotransmitter activity within the regions of the brain known as the prefrontal cortex modulates impulse control, sensation-seeking or novelty seeking, cognitive functions, and aggressiveness. It follows, then, that alterations to one or more of these systems might predispose an individual to display impulsive violent behavior.

The studies of neurotransmitters and aggression have focused on three systems and their role in the modulation of impulse/aggressive behavior control: the serotonergic system and the neurotransmitter *serotonin,* the dopamine system and the neurotransmitter *dopamine,* and the norepinephrine system and the neurotransmitter *norepinephrine.* These neurotransmitters form the basis for information processing within the brain and are considered neural forms of communication that occurs rapidly when they are released within the brain.

Raine and Screbo (1991) theorized that research on neurotransmitters may have genetic implications. Analysis of their data shows that there is no difference in central serotonin and norepinephrine between children and adults. The results also suggest that whatever the cause of the reduction in serotonin and norepinephrine, they are in place at some point during childhood and are stable across time. However, it is unclear if neurotransmitter alterations are caused by genetic or environmental factors.

Hormones are the second form of communication that the body uses to transmit information. Hormones have the same effect on the body as neurotransmitters. The distinction between neural and hormonal transmitters is that hormones are biochemical substances that are released into the bloodstream by endocrine organs, while neurotransmitters are electrical impulses originating in the brain that carry messages of action. The reaction time with hormones is much slower in regard to the cause and effect of communication within the body than it is with neurotransmitters.

Some of the most recent research indicates that there is a relationship between hormones and aggression. Gowin (2011) studied a juvenile's predisposition to violence by examining the following variables: child abuse, impulsivity, and psychopathy. Gowin determined that base levels of cortisol can predispose a child to future acts of violence. In an earlier study, McBurnett and colleagues (2000) studied boys between the ages 7 and 12 and determined that boys with low cortisol concentrations exhibited triple the number of aggressive symptoms and were named as the most aggressive by their peers as compared to boys who had higher levels of cortisol at the time of sampling (p. 42).

Cortisol is a hormone that is released in response to fear of the possible consequences of one's actions. It is not mentioned in either of the studies produced by Gray or Raine, which focused on neurotransmitters. Although cortisol is not a neurotransmitter, the possible effects of the lack of cortisol may be reflected in Gray's theory of the behavior inhibition system. McBurnett and colleagues (2000) asserted that this lack of fear is resistant to traditional forms of treatment, and stated that there is a strong correlation between a lack of cortisol and childhood-onset conduct disorder.

When discussing hormones and aggression, the one hormone that stands out is testosterone because it is associated with men and aggression. With that said, there is conflicting research in regard to this issue. Stevens (1995) examined testosterone levels in female hyenas for ten years. The results of the study indicated that there is a clear correlation between aggression in female hyenas and testosterone. Because female hyenas are a unique female species, however, one should be cautious when examining these data. The female hyena is larger and more ferocious than her male counterpart and, unlike any other female species, gives birth through a pseudo-penis.

The evidence in regard to humans is less exacting than that obtained with animals. Studies correlating hormone levels with aggression in the normal population have produced weak or insignificant findings (Boyd, 2000). There is one population, however, where hormone levels have been shown to be different from those in the general population; in inmates who have been incarcerated for acts of violence, researchers have found a moderate correlation between high levels of testosterone and the acts of violence the offenders committed (Brooks & Reddon, 1996; Dabbs & Morris, 1990).

In the final analysis, the commission of a violent crime is a very personal act, meaning that in many instances we are uncertain about what need is being met. Is it psychological, emotional, or both? Is the need based on something that is intrinsic, or is it an effort to correct a perception that others have of the individual? Is the act of violence a result of learned behavior, or does it stem from some other deficit in the personality? Criminologists, sociologists, psychologists, and others have made much progress in answering these questions, but it may be that different theories need to be applied to different cases.

Questions for Reflection: Since there are no absolutes, can you envision a scenario where a suspect is arrested, prosecuted, and convicted—and then rewarded, either publicly or in prison, for his or her acts of violence? Or, conversely, can you envision a convicted criminal who would be considered the scourge of society both on the outside and within the prison population? What would set these two apart?

CASE STUDIES

This section presents three case studies involving violence. Read the case studies with the theories discussed in this chapter in mind, and consider this question in regard to each case study: Which of the theories presented in this chapter do you believe explains the subject's actions?

CASE STUDY 1.1   SUSPECT KILLS THREE FRIENDS AFTER BEING PUNKED AT GUN RANGE

Suspect Andrew Lobban shot three of his friends after being punked at a local target range. Lobban and three friends went to a local target range for practice. One friend, who was responsible for loading Lobban's firearm, set the weapon up so that there was no round in the chamber, which meant that when Lobban attempted to fire the gun, the firing pin would fall on a dead chamber and the gun would not fire. As Lobban attempted to fire the gun, one of the friends videoed the misfire by Lobban and shared it with the other two friends. Two days later, Lobban apologized to another friend, stating, "I am sorry for what I am going to do later today." That night, as the local bar closed and the three friends exited the bar, Lobban shot one in the back of the head and the other two in the forehead, killing all three (Thompson & Miller, 2013).

CASE STUDY 1.2   SUSPECT BREAKS INTO HOUSE AND ATTEMPTS TO MURDER 80-YEAR-OLD WOMAN

Suspect Vertrice Robinson knew the victim personally. He had just completed some work on her house approximately one week before the incident. Robinson arrived at the victim's house on foot; he did not see the victim's car and broke into her home. Robinson stated in his interview that he had every intention of robbing the victim and stealing her car. He laid in wait until the victim returned home. Upon entering her home, the suspect struck the victim over the head repeatedly in an attempt to render her unconscious. The victim was able to fight back, striking the suspect several times with pots in the kitchen. During the struggle, the victim fell unconscious; the suspect robbed the victim and fled by stealing her car.

Robinson stated in the interview that he had not expected the victim to fight and that he thought she was dead after he had struck her in the head repeatedly with a bottle. He admitted to knowing the victim and confirmed the victim's story that he had worked at her house the previous week. Both Robinson and the victim noted that the victim was a close friend of the Robinson family. When Robinson was asked why he did this, he replied, "Because I saw it as an opportunity to get money and a car. I could care less about the victim or anyone else" (Marion County Sheriff's Office, 2005).

CASE STUDY 1.3   SEVENTEEN-YEAR-OLD BREAKS INTO HOUSE AND TERRORIZES QUADRIPLEGIC DURING BURGLARY

Suspect 17-year-old Roger Thomas waited outside a local man's home until the victim's wife left. The suspect lived in the neighborhood and was aware that the victim was quadriplegic. Thomas entered the house through a rear basement window where the burglary was almost undetectable. The victim could hear Thomas rummaging through items in the house when the victim called out. Thomas told the victim to be quiet or he would kill him. In fact, Thomas, armed with a knife, entered the victim's bedroom and stated, "I know that you have no legs and arms; that's why I am here. Now shut up, or I will cut your throat." Thomas put the knife to the victim's throat, demanded money, and then fled the scene.

Thomas was caught three days later and stated in his interview: "I needed the money for child support and this was the easiest way. I knew the old man was by himself so it was easy. Jobs don't pay enough, and I have needs; so I robbed, big deal. Now that you have me and I confessed, can I go home? I am still a juvenile." The detective replied, "Roger, you are a juvenile, except this is Michigan, and you turned 17 two weeks before you committed this crime. That makes you an adult in criminal proceedings, so, no, you can't go home" (Grand Rapids Police Department, 1981).

REFERENCES

American Medical Association (AMA). (2012). *International classification of diseases, 10th revision, clinical modification (ICD-10-CM) 2013: The complete official draft code set.* Chicago: Author.

American Psychiatric Association (APA). (2000). *The diagnostic and statistical manual of mental disorders, IV-TR,* 4th ed. Arlington, VA: Author.

Anderson, E. (1999). *Code of the street: Decency, violence and the moral life of the inner city.* New York: W. W. Norton.

Ball-Rokeach, S. J. (1973). Values and violence: A test of the subculture of violence thesis. *American Sociological Review, 38*, pp. 736–749.

Bandura, A. (1973). *Aggression: A social learning process.* Englewood Cliffs, NJ: Prentice-Hall.

Becker, H. (1963). *Outsiders: Studies in the sociology of deviance.* New York: Free Press.

Bernard. T. J. (1990). ANGRY Aggression among the "truly disadvantaged." *Criminology, 28*, pp. 73–96.

Bowlby, J. (1940). The influence of early environment in the development of neurosis and neurotic character. *International Journal of Psychoanalysis, 25*, pp. 154–178.

Boyd, N. (2000). *The beast within: Why men are violent.* Vancouver, BC: Greystone Books.

Brooks, J. H., & Reddon, J. R. (1996). Serum testosterone in violent and nonviolent young offenders. *Journal of Clinical Psychology, 52*, pp. 475–483.

Brown, S. E., Esbensen, F. A., & Geis, G. (1998). *Criminology: Explaining crime and its context*, 3rd ed. Cincinnati, OH: Anderson.

Buchanan, A., Brock, D. W., Daniels, N., & Wikler, D. (2000). *From chance to choice: Genetics and justice.* New York: Cambridge University Press.

Conger, R. (1976). Social control and social learning models of delinquent behavior: A synthesis. *Criminology, 17*, pp. 17–40.

Dabbs, J., Jr., & Morris, R. (1990). Testosterone, social class, and antisocial behavior in a sample of 4,462 men. *Psychological Science, 1*, pp. 209–211.

Durkheim, E. (1984). *The division of labor in society* (L. A. Coser, Trans.). New York: Macmillan. (Original work 1933).

Ellis, A. (1994). *Reason and emotion in psychotherapy: A comprehensive method of treating human disturbances.* New York: Carol.

Federal Bureau of Investigation (FBI). (2012). *Crime in the United States 2011, Table 25.* Washington, D.C.: Department of Justice.

Feldman, R. S., & Quenzer, L. F. (1985/1997). *Fundamentals of neuropsychopharmacology.* Washington, D.C.: American Psychological Association.

Gowin, J. L. (2011). *The role of cortisol in the cycle of violence.* Unpublished doctoral dissertation, University of Texas, Houston.

Grand Rapids Police Department. (1981). *Burglary and armed robbery: 81-20536.* Grand Rapids, MI: Author.

Gray, J. A. (1981). A critique of Eysenck's theory of personality. In H. J. Eysenck (Ed.), *A model of personality* (pp. 246–276). New York: Springer.

Greenberg, B. (1995, January 21). Nude posture studies of students create stir. *Johnson City Press*, I A.

Gur, R. C. (2004). *Patterson v. Texas*. Petition for Writ of Certiorari to U.S. Supreme Court.

Laughlin, H. H. (1922). *Eugenical sterilization in the United States*. Chicago: Psychopathic Laboratory of the Municipal Court of Chicago.

Lombroso, C. (2006). *Criminal man* (M. Gibson & N. H. Rafter, Trans.). Durham, NC: Duke University Press. (Original work 1876).

Marion County Sheriff's Office. (2005). *Attempted murder and burglary: Case report number 05057946*. Ocala, FL: Author.

Maslow, A. (1968). *Toward a psychology of being*. New York: Wiley.

McBurnett, K., Lahey, B. B., Rathouz, P. J., & Loeber, R. (2000). Low salivary cortisol and persistent aggression in boys referred for disruptive behavior. *Archives of General Psychiatry, 57*(1), pp. 38–43.

Merton, R. K. (1968). *Social theory and social structure*. New York: Free Press. (Original work 1938).

Pallone, N., & Hennessy, J. J. (1998). Brain dysfunction and criminal violence. *Society, 35*(6), pp. 21–27.

Quinney, R. (1977). *Class, state, and crime: On the theory and practice of criminal justice*. New York: McKay.

Raine, A. (1993). *The psychopathology of crime: Criminal behavior as a clinical disorder*. San Diego: Academic Press.

Raine, A., & Screbo, A. (1991). Biological theories of violence. In J. S. Milner (Ed.), *Neuropsychology of aggression* (pp. 1–26). Boston: Kluwer.

Rothbart, M. K. (2007). Temperament, development, and personality. *Current Directions in Psychological Science, 16*(4), pp. 207–212.

Saad, L. (2011). *Most Americans believe crime in the U.S. is worsening*. Retrieved May 21, 2013, from http://www.gallup.com/poll/150464/Americans-Believe-Crime-Worsening.aspx

Scott, E. S., & Stenberg, L. (2008). *Rethinking juvenile justice*. Cambridge, MA: Harvard University Press.

Sheldon, W. H. (1949). *Varieties of delinquent youth: An introduction to constitutional psychology*. New York: Harper and Brothers.

Sheldon, W., & Glueck, E. (1951). Unraveling juvenile delinquency. *Cambridge Law Journal, 11*, pp. 168–169.

Short, J. F. (2002). Criminology, the Chicago school, and sociological theory. *Crime, Law, and Social Change, 37*, pp. 107–117.

Stevens, J. (1995). Hyenas yield clues to human infertility, aggression. *Technology Review, 98*(2), pp. 20–21.

Sutherland, E. H., Cressey, D. R., & Luckenbill, D. F. (1992). *Principles of criminology*, 11th ed. Lanham, MD: General Hall.

Thompson, B., & Miller, A. L. (2013, June 1). Man killed 3 in revenge for humiliation, Ocala police say. *Ocala Star Banner*, A1.

Wolfgang, M. E., & Ferracuti, F. (1967). *The subculture of violence: Towards an integrated theory in criminology.* London: Tavistok.

Yochelson, S., & Samenow, S. E. (1976). *The criminal personality. Volume I: A profile for change.* Lanham, MD: Rowman & Littlefield.

Murder

Everyone is capable of committing murder. From the perspective of the police, many officers have already determined in what situations they will use deadly force. A soldier in the military has made the same kind of determinations. In both cases, however, this process goes against people's teachings and belief systems, and as a result, those in both professions are prone to experiencing *posttraumatic stress disorder* when they have to act in such a manner (Thomas, 2011). The members of the police and military, who have taken an oath to protect the citizenry, are involved in situations where they encounter the worst of the worst. As a result of the need to protect society, laws that allow those who take the oath of office to use deadly force as justifiable under certain conditions have been created.

Murder is one of many classifications under the broad term *homicide*. Homicide is defined as the taking of another human being's life. There are two classifications of homicide:

- Murder, which has many degrees. Here, the state assesses a case and charges an individual based on what is believed to be the suspect's motive or responsibility in the case.

- Justifiable or excusable homicide. Here, a person acts under the color of law, usually in defense of self or another. These cases are assessed by the state examining the totality of the circumstances, and if they meet the criteria, the cases are closed. If the standard of excusable homicide is not met, then the case will be moved to criminal court (Florida State Legislature, 2013a).

> **Questions for Reflection:** Considering the first sentence of this chapter, which reads "Everyone is capable of committing murder," ask yourself under what conditions you could take the life of another. Could you kill someone in self-defense? Could you do it in defending another? Are there other circumstances under which you could take someone's life?

When we examine the concept of murder, it is difficult for many to comprehend how an individual can take the life of another without there being some form of special circumstance. The reality is that murder is closely associated with human emotions and human needs such as jealousy, revenge, money, sex, insanity, anger, during the commission of other crimes, fear, just because, or any combination (Falk, 1990; Ghiglieri, 1999; Wille, 1974; Wilson, 1993). It would be impossible to write a book that detailed every motive for homicide; however, in this chapter, we will dissect some of the emotions associated with murder, and we will apply these concepts to case studies dealing with two different murders that were committed in the same building seven years apart. At the end of the chapter, we will compare the motives of the suspects in these two case studies as well as some psychological theories that could be applied to them.

ANGER AND FEAR

Anger is a human emotion that can be caused by the simplest transgression or misunderstanding; and if it is not checked, it can fester and metastasize like a cancerous lesion, leading someone who is normally reserved to commit an act of violence. For example, a driver shoots another driver because he was cut off, or one man shoots another while arguing over a basketball game. Ghiglieri (1999) has argued that rage is central to what he described as the human passions of violence and that the triggers of rage vary (p. 35). Beck (1999) has asserted that aggressive, manipulative people generally believe that their entitlements and rights override those of others. Hostility, be it from a group or an individual, stems from the principle of seeing the adversary as wrong or bad, and perceiving the self as right or good. The aggressor construes the facts in his or her favor, exaggerating the transgression, whether imagined or real, and retaliates violently (pp. 125–128). Beck's description is nothing more than rationalizing one's action in the cognitive process known as destructive entitlement.

Bandura (1973) argued that anger and aggression cannot occur in a vacuum void of some form of instigation. In Bandura's view, there has to be a cause and effect. Violent triggers can come in the form of insults, status threats, posturing, unfair treatment, disrespect, or a perceived loss of value. It does not matter whether the triggers are imagined or real; we must understand that one's perception is one's reality. In addition, any response, positive or negative, is based on one's ability to address any of the triggers in a way that may or may not be socially and psychologically appropriate. Finally, when speaking of anger, it is important to note that anger is just an emotion; although it is closely associated with aggression, anger by itself is not harmful.

Donovan (2001) has argued, much like Bandura, that anger and violence do not occur in a vacuum but are interrelated, noting that shame is a key ingredient and that people vacillate between shame and anger until it finally erupts into an act of violence. Researchers describe these acts as if they are on a progressive continuum: The violence may begin with the destruction of inanimate objects such as doors and furniture; then become personal with attempts to harm oneself by drinking, driving fast, or self-mutilation; and then progress to violence against others, usually those in intimate circles such as partners, children, colleagues, classmates, surrogates, institutions, organizations, businesses, or government entities, causing serious injury and/or death (Covin, 2011; Donovan, 2001; Meloy, 2000; Yochelson & Samenow, 1976).

Gilligan (1996) argued that there is a dependency in America and that violence is dependent on shame. He noted that for men to show that they want to be loved is to be passive or, more importantly, unmanly—and that in itself is shameful (p. 237). He postulated that when one suppresses one's needs, it impacts one's subconscious, and those repressed feelings will manifest themselves in the form of a psychopathology or acts of violence (p. 238).

MOTIVES FOR HOMICIDE

Anger and fear are but two of many different motives for committing murder. Douglas, Burgess, Burgess, and Ressler (2006) list forty-one types of murder, and each type is unique in that it involves a different motive. These types can be put into the following four categories:

- *Criminal enterprise homicides:* murders committed for some sort of personal gain
- *Personal cause homicides:* associated with interpersonal relationships, such as intimate partner violence
- *Sexual homicides:* where a sexual sequence is performed before, during, or after the homicide, or in any combination of these times
- *Group cause homicide:* where a group of two or more sanctions a homicide and it is carried out by one or more members of the group (pp. 93–260)

These authors recognize, however, that no one classification or type of murder is etched in stone and that murders may have multiple motives, as seen in Case Study 2.1.

CASE STUDY 2.1 MULTIPLE MOTIVES FOR MURDER

The police received a call of a burglary with injury where the suspect just fled the scene. Upon their arrival, they found the homeowner, John Barringer, who appeared to have been the victim of an assault. He was dazed and confused and had minor lacerations on his face and two bumps on his head. Upon checking the house further, police discovered the body of a nude female lying on the bedroom floor. Mr. Barringer identified the body as his wife, Mary, and became hysterical. Upon further examination of the body, it was determined that Mrs. Barringer had been sodomized with a hot curling iron and severely beaten. The autopsy revealed that the cause of death was strangulation.

Mr. Barringer stated that he worked night shift at the local hospital and that when he arrived at the house on the morning of the incident right after work, he entered the house through the kitchen door and was met by a flurry of punches and struck over the head and knocked unconscious. He called the police to report the incident but did not check the house because of his injuries. Mr. Barringer denied that he and his wife were having problems and stated that they had not had problems in the past. He described them as having an occasional argument over normal things like dishes, money, or laundry. When questioned about domestic violence or abuse, he stated confidently that there had been none.

The police investigated the case, starting with Mr. Barringer, first offering a polygraph and explaining to him that the goal was to eliminate him as a suspect. Mr. Barringer refused, stating that he did not trust them, and provided a long story about a friend who went to jail for a crime he did not commit. The police investigated Mr. Barringer and found several things:

- He had been having an affair for the past year with a nurse at the hospital where he worked. On several occasions, the nurse had mentioned to her friends that she and Mr. Barringer were going to get married.

- There had been accusations of domestic violence; however, no one had ever seen any evidence of physical abuse, nor had the police ever been to the Barringer residence.

- The Barringers were in debt and one step away from filing bankruptcy because Mrs. Barringer had been spending money faster than they could make it. Their house was in foreclosure.

- Mr. Barringer had asked for a divorce on several occasions, but his wife had refused, noting the affair with the nurse.
- Mr. Barringer had an insurance policy valued at $300,000 on Mrs. Barringer, and it was purchased around the same time he began having his affair.
- At the time of the murder, Mr. Barringer claimed he was at work, which was confirmed by video cameras at the hospital, the time clock, and conversations with co-workers.

Questions for Reflection

1. Was this murder part of a criminal enterprise, or was it personal or sexual? Or are all three of these possible motives that should be investigated collectively?
2. Why was Mrs. Barringer sodomized?
3. If Mr. Barringer killed his wife, why would he sodomize her with a hot curling iron? Was it to throw the police off and make them think there was another suspect?
4. If Mr. Barringer did not sodomize his wife, was the act committed to send a message or humiliate Mrs. Barringer?
5. Since Mr. Barringer was at work during the time of the murder, who are the other potential suspects and what are their possible motives?

FAMILY: THE SEED OF FUTURE ACTS OF VIOLENCE

Familial homicides are crimes that occur within the family or between family members. For years these crimes were associated with those happening between spouses, most often with a husband killing his wife. Occasionally, a mother who suffered from postpartum depression killed an infant. Today the potential exists for any member of a family to kill another, and for various and often unexplained reasons.

Questions for Reflection: Why would one family member kill another? Isn't the family unit a place where love and nurturing take place? Is the traditional family, as it was depicted in the 1950s and 1960s, a myth or reality?

In contemplating why family members kill one another, we might wonder about how the family is defined today, and whether that is part of the problem. For many years in America, a traditional family was defined as a husband, wife, and 2.5 children. Today that definition and the images that went with it have been changed drastically because of the recognition of same-sex marriages and unions, the high divorce rate, and single-parent households, and situations in which extended family members live under one roof.

To address the changing definition of a family, the law and researchers recognize that a family may include two or more people who are related by birth, marriage, or adoption as well as any extended family members such as grandparents, cousins, and uncles who usually live under the same roof. Because state statutes dealing with family violence have had to change the definition of a family to extend beyond the nuclear family, most state legislatures, in defining a family and authorizing the police to make an arrest, now provide a definition similar to this:

> A family or household member means spouses, former spouses, persons related by blood or marriage, persons who are presently residing together as if a family or who have resided together in the past as if a family, and persons who are parents of a child in common regardless of whether they have been married. With the exception of persons who have a child in common, the family or household members must be currently residing or have in the past resided together in the same single dwelling unit. (Florida State Legislature, 2013b)

Note that this definition is void of gender and age, meaning that any family member child or adult who meets the criteria can be held responsible for acts of family violence. The definitions of familial violence provide the framework for understanding all acts of violence within and outside the family.

Part of the problem in understanding the nature of family violence is that it has been compartmentalized, meaning that a police investigation determines the outcome. When patrol officers are sent to investigate an act of spousal abuse, rarely will the investigation extend beyond the original call for service. Flowers (2000) has argued that domestic violence, child abuse and neglect, child sexual abuse, elderly abuse, and sibling violence coexist, are interrelated, and are intergenerational—and yet they are not investigated in the context of the family (p. 7). It is important to note that for years the laws forbade police from making arrests for domestic violence or spousal battery, classifying the crime as a misdemeanor without exception, meaning that the actual battery had to be committed in the presence of an officer.

It has been argued that children are our most precious treasure, yet as a country we have been at a loss when it comes to protecting them. The first federal legislation that recognized children was not enacted until 1935. The legislation provided grants to states funding welfare services for children where their environment would impair their physical and social development, and services for maternal and child health (Seventy-Fourth Congress, 1935). This 1935 legislation did nothing to protect children from acts of violence. It was not until 1962 that battered child syndrome became recognized as an official form of abuse in an article published by Dr. C. Henry Kempe and colleagues in *The Journal of the American Medical Association* (Kempe, Steele, Droegemueller, & Silver, 1962). The term *battered child syndrome* is all-encompassing, describing every form of abuse that a child might experience, including emotional, physical, and sexual abuse; malnourishment; and death. Despite Dr. Kempe's efforts, it was not until 1967 that forty-four states passed legislation protecting children from abuse (De Cruz, 2010; Myers, 2006). In contrast, the first animal abuse laws in the United States were enacted in 1828 (Schlueter, 2010).

When reviewing the history of implementation of laws to protect family members from abuse, it is easy to see a certain irony in that fact that U.S. law valued animals long before there was a value placed on children, women, and the family. In my years as a law enforcement officer, I have conducted numerous interviews of males who committed domestic violence, child abuse, and murder of their spouses, and there has been one constant: the lack of value that they placed on their victims. In almost every case, the suspect failed to take responsibility for the attack, but instead blamed the victim or someone else as being responsible, as did the suspect in Case Study 2.2.

CASE STUDY 2.2   DOMESTIC VIOLENCE HOSTAGE TAKER

Two officers who were on patrol in an unmarked car at 2:00 A.M. observed a car pass with no lights on, turn left at the next street, and park. The driver exited the car, dragging a female by the arm from the driver's side and leaving the driver's door open. The male dragged the female by the arm across the street and entered the corner house. The officers ran the tag; it came back to the name John Ford and an address where one officer recalled having been called on three separate occasions for domestic violence. In each of the previous incidents, the officer had to threaten the husband with arrest if he attempted to interfere while his wife was getting a few items to leave for the night. In each of the previous incidents, there was no probable cause to make an arrest.

On this night, the officers were parked out of sight, and just as the tag information came back, the suspect dragged the victim from the house. As the victim and suspect arrived at the vehicle, the suspect punched the victim in the head several times and she collapsed. The suspect threw the victim's unconscious body into the car. The officers blocked the suspect's exit with their car. As the officers exited their vehicle, the suspect grabbed the victim, using her as a shield, and placed a gun to her temple. The suspect yelled, "I will kill this bitch if you don't move your car and let me past."

In the excitement, the victim became conscious, wrestled out of the suspect's grasp, opened the passenger door, and crawled out of the vehicle. The victim ran from the suspect's car and collapsed unconscious in the middle of the street. During the struggle, as the suspect attempted to hold onto the victim, his foot slipped off the brake and he struck the officers' vehicle. The suspect exited his vehicle, holding a gun at his side, but after several verbal challenges from the officers, he dropped the gun.

After being read the Miranda rights, the suspect made the following statement:

> You have been at my house before, and every time, it's the same thing. You guys are protecting that bitch; she is no good. Tonight I brought her to her mom's house for one reason—to get them to admit or deny that the bitch was having an affair. Her mom, brother, and sister were all in the house; each denied the existence of an affair. I got angry, pulled my gun out, and fired into the ceiling, but they stuck to their story. Tonight my plan was to take the bitch out in the country and shoot her in the back of the head. Then I was going to rip her clothes off so it would appear that she had been murdered and raped by someone else. Her family is responsible for this because in the past they have never called the police, even when I beat the shit out of her. They have always told my wife that what happens in our house is nobody's business and that it is between a husband and wife. In fact, every time she left, they encouraged her to come back. Her mom told me on more than one occasion that I was the best thing that ever happened to her daughter. Then you fuckin' guys showed up out of nowhere. I put the gun to her head to get you to back off. I knew if I shot her there that you would kill me. After she got away, I had to make the decision if I could shoot both of you. I couldn't, since both of you had your guns pointed at me. Then, I thought, is that bitch worth dying for, and I decided that I value my life more than that. This ain't over; I will see her again, and then I will finish it.

Case Notes

1. The suspect was held without bond until trial. He refused to accept a plea deal where he would have been released in five years.

2. Because he failed to accept the plea, he went to trial on the following charges: battery, aggravated battery, aggravated assault (four counts for

threatening the victim's family as well as the victim with the firearm),
possession of an unregistered handgun, carrying a concealed weapon
in a motor vehicle, and discharging a firearm within the city limits.

3. The suspect was convicted and sentenced to twenty years. The judge
noted the violence and the statement the suspect made to the police
at the close of the interview: "This ain't over; I will see her again, and
then I will finish it."

Questions for Reflection

1. Do you believe that the suspect felt he had a right to abuse his wife?

2. In your analysis of his statement, do you believe the suspect thought
his wife's family gave him a pass to do whatever he wanted to the
victim, and that the violence was acceptable because they did not
intervene?

3. When reviewing the statement, do you believe the suspect acted in a
cowardly manner in dropping his gun?

4. How would you interpret the suspect's final statement, "This ain't
over; I will see her again, and then I will finish it"?

Gelles and Straus (1979) made the following observation concerning family violence:

> With the exception of the police and the military, the family is perhaps the
> most violent social group, and the home the most violent social setting, in our
> society. A person is more likely to be hit or killed in his or her home by another
> family member than anywhere else or by anyone else. (p. 15)

In examining this quotation, I am struck by the fact that the family also
appears to be the basis of learned behavior. Remember, behavior is not learned
in a vacuum; there are many contributing factors. I would also argue that the
family may well be the foundation for all other acts of violent behavior, or
how one responds to perceived transgressions coupled with the lack of coping
mechanisms. Since family appears to be the genesis of violence, let's examine
the categories associated with family violence.

Filicide

Filicide is defined as the murder of a child by a parent or caregiver, and there
are two subcategories: *neonaticide,* which is the killing of infant within the

first twenty-four hours of birth, and *infanticide,* which is killing a child older than twenty-four hours (McKee, 2006; Schwartz & Isser, 2000). Fujiwara, Barber, Schaechter, and Hemenway (2009) completed an analysis of data concerning infanticide of children less than 2 years of age. The authors examined seventy-two homicides and determined that 93 percent of all infanticides were committed by caretakers. Fujiwara and colleagues noted that there were striking differences between men and women perpetrators, and hence created two distinct categories:

- *Type 1 incidents* are classified as beating/shaking committed by a caretaker. In 83 percent of the cases examined, the suspects were men, either the father or the mother's boyfriend. In the majority of Type 1 cases, the infant was transported to the hospital with a false story explaining the nature of the injuries.

- *Type 2 incidents* are classified as all other infant-related homicides, including neonaticide, intimate-partner problem–related homicide, or crime-related death. Seventeen percent of the Type 2 cases utilized such methods as poison, stabbing, drowning, and starvation. In contrast to Type 1 victims, these victims were never transported to the hospital. (p. 210)

Neonaticide

The issues associated with neonaticide or any other form of filicide is that there are really no accurate statistics or databases from which to access data. In fact, no state has enacted laws to address the murder of an infant because these cases are treated like any other murder. In almost every case involving murder of an infant, you will find additional charges of some form of child abuse or aggravated child abuse in addition to the murder charge. Malmquist (2013) has argued that with neonaticide, not only do we lack laws that specifically address it, but we also are given no psychiatric designation for it in the *Diagnostic and Statistical Manual of Mental Disorders, IV-TR,* which classifies such acts as a mood disorder with onset criteria.

Since neonaticide addresses the murder of a child within the first twenty-four hours, researchers describe neonaticide as *denial of pregnancy,* which has many meanings. No matter the definition, it should be looked upon as detachment from the fetus or a delusional state based on postpartum depression. Oberman (2003) noted that in the United States, perpetrators of neonaticide have been females in their mid- to late adolescence biologically and cognitively, single, living with a parent, isolated, secretive, and living in poverty. In contrast, Vellut, Cook, and Tursz (2012), in their examination of thirty-two French women who were convicted of neonaticide, provided the following description of the French offenders: average age 26, two-thirds already had children before the incident, ten lived with a significant other, not physically isolated, and five unemployed.

Infanticide

Infanticide is defined as the murder of a child beyond the first twenty-four hours. Resnick (1969) determined that mothers who committed filicide suffered from depression, psychosis, and had a prior mental health history and/or suicidal thoughts. Friedman, Hrouda, Holden, Noffsinger, and Resnick (2005) noted, in their review of thirty filicide cases, that psychologically parents exhibited symptoms and/or were treated for depression, psychosis, and paranoid delusions, which supports Resnick's findings.

CASE STUDY 2.3   CHILD ABUSE AND THE FUTURE

Tom was a 14-year-old juvenile. By all accounts and on face value, he was a handsome kid—the type most would believe to be the all-American teenage boy. However, when he was 10, his mother discovered that Tom had been torturing the cat and had killed the neighbor's dog. In school Tom had severe behavioral problems with acting out, committing acts of violence against fellow students and teachers. By the age of 12, he had raped a local 7-year-old girl.

Tom was evaluated and diagnosed with *early onset conduct disorder,* with a severe designator. In addition, because of his behavioral problems in school, he was classified as *severely emotionally disturbed* and placed in a school that specialized in treating students with behavior problems.

Before Tom entered the school, the staff psychologist and principal interviewed Tom's mother, and she related the following: She had tried to abort Tom while she was pregnant through the use of illegal drugs, specifically, prescription pain pills, cocaine, and alcohol. She stated on more than one occasion during the interview that she did not want Tom and that being pregnant interfered in her life and plans. She also stated that Tom's dad did not want a child, and as soon as he found out that she was pregnant, he left. Tom's mother said that she had no use for Tom and that she abused him on a regular basis. In fact, she disliked Tom so much that she allowed her boyfriends to abuse him as well. Even at that point, she blamed Tom for losing the love of her life. When Tom raped the 7-year-old, tortured the cat, and killed the neighbor's dog, it only confirmed for Tom's mother that Tom was useless and a pain in her ass. She felt the best place for Tom was jail; that way, he could be punished for what he did.

Questions for Reflection

1. If a child were born into such an environment and survived the first 24 hours, what would be the quality of his or her life?

2. Would the mother likely to change and provide love and nurturing, or would the child most likely be abused like Tom?

3. If the child endured years of abuse, how would that manifest itself in the future?

4. Would the manifestations of the abuse ever go away?

Let's revisit the observations of researchers Gelles and Straus (1979) concerning the family. Keep in mind that suppression of abuse, coupled with the inability to respond accordingly, sets the stage for the perfect storm where violence becomes the norm:

> With the exception of the police and the military, the family is perhaps the most violent social group, and the home the most violent social setting, in our society. A person is more likely to be hit or killed in his or her home by another family member than anywhere else or by anyone else. (p. 15)

The model and discussion of the family was used for several reasons, primarily because it is where we first learn several behavioral cues, controls, responses, and most importantly coping skills. If we think of child abuse in light of the terminology developed by Kempe and colleagues (1962), that is, the *battered child syndrome*, we have to wonder how that affects an individual in the long term.

My own belief is that violent behavior is learned, and, without the proper controls, it manifests itself (as seen in Case Study 2.3) and provides a platform for acts of violence that include murder, robbery, rape, and arson. Gilligan (1996) supports this assertion, arguing that violence is a contagious disease that is psychological in nature and spread through environmental, economic, and cultural interaction (p. 104).

To comprehend the magnitude of child abuse, let's examine the statistics. The Children's Bureau (2011) reported that there were 676,569 substantiated cases of child abuse in the United States. Twenty-five percent of the victims were less than 3 years of age, and 20 percent were between the ages of three and five. The types of abuse the victims experienced were: neglect (78 percent), battering or physical abuse (17 percent), and sexual abuse (9 percent) (pp. 19–21). The Children's Bureau noted that many victims suffered more than one form of abuse, and each form was counted separately.

SITUATIONAL MURDER

Murder must be considered in terms of a situation or cause and effect. In most cases of murder, the offender and victim have had some form of relationship, and each of the actors (offender and victim) contributed to the escalation of the incident (Canter & Youngs, 2009; Luckenbill, 1977; Wolfgang, 1958). Roberts, Zgoba, and Shahidullah (2007) examined 336 homicide offenders and created the following classification system:

- Altercation- or argument-precipitated homicide
- Felony homicide
- Domestic violence or intimate partner induced homicide
- Accident homicide (p. 500)

We look at each type more closely in the following sections.

Altercation- or Argument-Precipitated Homicide

The classification of altercation- or argument-precipitated homicide represents those cases in which the homicide occurred following an argument or altercation. Often the disputes begin over insignificant amounts of money or property and/or disrespect. These arguments usually start as verbal disagreements, escalate to fighting, and are ultimately resolved through shooting or stabbing, with murder being the end result (Roberts et al., 2007, p. 500).

As one of my clients stated in a therapy session: "I had no choice but to kill him. He disrespected me, and everyone knew it. If I did nothing, I would spend my remaining time in prison fighting everyone off. This way I get respect." My client pounded the victim's head into the floor until he was dead, and my client had ten years added to his thirty-year sentence for the murder of a drug dealer on the street. When I asked my client whether either murder was worth it, he replied yes, stating that in each case it was about respect (Thomas, 2001).

Felony Homicide

In felony homicide cases, the homicide is committed during the commission of another crime such as robbery, rape, burglary, kidnapping, or theft (Roberts et al., 2007, p. 500). In some instances, the homicide may be the primary crime and another crime is committed in addition to the intended homicide. Other times the homicide occurs when the victim attempts to intervene in the offender's actions; the victim surprises the offender while the offender is committing a felony; the victim refuses to comply with the offender's demands; or the offender kills the victim and/or witnesses because they are considered a liability and can identify the offender.

Here is an offender's statement from a case in which the victim was considered collateral damage:

> It was fate. The old bitch was going to die whether we killed her or not last night. Look, we broke in her house, to steal her money and whatever else we could find. We figured that she would be there, but she is an old lady so she wasn't a threat. Once in the house we found the old bitch asleep, so Tommy suggested we have some fun, so we decided rape her. Man, could that old bitch scream. Once we both had our way with her, we took turns beating her until she was dead. Think about it, she was going to die last night whether we killed her or God took her life naturally. (Thomas, 1981)

Domestic Violence or Intimate Partner–Induced Homicide

In domestic violence or intimate partner–induced homicides, where murder occurs due to familial relationships, the offenders and victims may include intimates, family members, current or ex-spouses, and current or ex-boyfriends and girlfriends (Roberts et al., 2007, p. 500). In this type of incident, often there is no logical reason for the murder in the eyes of an outsider.

An example of the lack of logic is apparent in this excerpt from a 911 call made by a 14-year-old boy named Noah Crooks after he shot and killed his mother: "I shot my mom and I don't know why I did it. I tried to rape her, but I couldn't. She took my *Call to Duty* video game, and something just came over me. My life is over and it all goes down the drain now. I have to move and I'm going to jail" (Senzarnio, 2013). Noah had fired more than twenty rounds into his mother's body after his mother took his video game because he had received bad grades on his report card.

Accident Homicide

In accident homicides, offenders cause death through the use of an automobile (Roberts et al., 2007, p. 500). We understand that drinking and driving do not mix, and yet millions of Americans still partake in both activities at the same time. Drunk driving is responsible for a large number of fatalities annually.

Here is a statement made by a drunk driving suspect after an arrest: "I was driving home minding my own business. I heard a thump and my car went up and my car shook like I hit the curb and ran over something in the road like a dog. I didn't think anything of it until you came to my house and told me that I killed someone. I had no idea it was a person that I hit. Now I understand that I was driving on the sidewalk and hit the guy. Come on, I could not have been that drunk" (Thomas, 1979).

THE PSYCHOLOGY OF HOMICIDE

Questions for Reflection: Since there are so many different motivations for murder, do you believe that there is a particular psychology associated with homicide suspects? Do the suspects suffer from a specific form of psychopathology?

Given the many different types of homicides and motivations for murder, I would argue that there is no definitive psychological profile of a typical murder suspect. With that said, there may be an exception when it comes to special types of murderers such as the sexual serial killer, hit man, or assassin. These types of killers often can be profiled into particular psychological types. At the same time, nonmurderers may have some of the same psychological illnesses that murderers have, and yet they do not commit murder.

Wille (1974) studied forty subjects and found the following: ten murderers with psychosis, ten murderers without psychosis, ten nonmurderers with psychosis, and ten nonmurderers without psychosis. Within this population, there were distinct differences in the patterns for handling anger, fear, and overt aggression of the murderers versus the nonmurderers (p. 28). In Wille's analysis of the data, he determined that psychologically the murderers overall spent less time thinking about anger, fear, and aggressive behavior, meaning that a great deal of their energy was spent on repressing these thoughts and feelings. However, if provoked, there was an expectation that the response would be sudden, violent, and destructive. Finally, Wille described two syndromes in every murderer:

- *Syndrome of repression and intense thought,* which allows the subject to function normally in his or her world, with one exception—the syndrome of expectancy
- *Syndrome of expectancy,* which can be described as the subject being always on edge and ready (pp. 33–34)

I interpret the syndrome of expectancy to mean that the person's body is always in a state of "fight or flight," ready to respond with aggression to the slightest provocation. In such a constant state of hypervigilence, the body is never able to relax.

The term *biphasic personality* best describes Wille's syndromes, meaning that a murderer's personality is only two-dimensional and shallow. Keep in mind that a healthy personality is multidimensional and can adapt to changing situations (Mischel & Shoda, 1998). In contrast, the biphasic personality is limited, forcing the person to be defensive about his or her shortcomings and to exist in a constant state of paranoia or expectancy.

CASE STUDY 2.4   THE PIMP WHO BECAME INFAMOUS

State of Michigan v. Ronald Crawford, Kent County Court File No. 81-27714 FY.

Background

Ronald Crawford (also known as Ronnie Crawford) was a pimp in Grand Rapids, Michigan, in the late 1970s and early 1980s. Crawford was notorious for being brutal with his girls and hating the police. The relationship was so bad that on numerous occasions, the police looked for any reason to stop Crawford while he was driving his car. It was so bad that the Michigan State Police who were assigned the freeway would come on South Division Avenue and stop Crawford for minor traffic violations. The goal was to make his life as uncomfortable as possible, and if drugs or guns were found, he would be arrested.

Crawford had been arrested numerous times for assault and battery, carrying a concealed weapon, illegal possession of a firearm, possession of controlled substances, aggravated assault, and aggravated battery. The problem was that Crawford was like Teflon—none of the charges had stuck. Often the victims recanted their stories. The victims usually fell into one of two categories: prostitutes who had failed to bring in money, had lied to Crawford, or had been caught talking to other pimps; or "johns" who had shortchanged Crawford's girls or injured them in some way. The criminal charges against Crawford were always dismissed, primarily through threat and intimidation.

One of the local prostitutes who was serving as an informant advised the police that there was a subculture that was a microcosm of society as a whole. Members of the subculture were pimps, prostitutes, drug dealers, robbers, and thieves. She described Crawford as being at the top of this group because he had a reputation of beating all the criminal charges and of being violent, and it was because of this he gained the respect of his peers.

Here is an example of Crawford's brutality and intimidation: One night one of his girls decided that she wanted to stop prostituting. After she advised Crawford of her intentions, he told her that everything would be okay and that he did not have a problem with her leaving. Crawford returned later that night as the victim was packing her bags. He beat the victim until she was unconscious, tied her to four bed posts so that she was lying on her stomach, ripped off her clothes to expose her naked back and buttocks, and beat her for approximately two hours with a wire hanger. Crawford made the victim pledge her allegiance and told her that if she ever tried anything like that again, he would kill her. It was not until the victim convinced Crawford that she would never leave him that he allowed her to be transported to the hospital. When we arrived at the hospital to take the report, neither the victim nor her friend would discuss what had happened. In fact, they both claimed that the victim had been beaten by one of her "johns."

The witness and driver, who was an informant, told police the story after completing the initial interview at the hospital. She also refused to testify, and it was clear that she feared Crawford would do the same to her, if not worse, if he ever found out that she was giving information to the police. After this incident, it was not long before the story made it to the streets, which enhanced Crawford's street credibility, especially since the police did not have a victim or witness who was willing to testify.

The Bloody Week

In December 1981, Crawford was in a feud with another pimp who was challenging his authority. The police received information in January that Crawford was wanted by another jurisdiction for throwing a female victim from a moving car onto a freeway. Police looked for him for several days and could not locate Crawford anywhere.

In the meantime, his feud with the rival pimp had escalated to the point where he wanted to kill his rival. In talking to his inner circle, Crawford became aware that an acquaintance had a special handgun that was used for hunting. The handgun was an 8-inch-barrell 357 magnum single shot with a scope. On January 6, 1981, Crawford and one of his associates went to the house of the acquaintance, Mark Clark, and demanded the gun. Clark refused to relinquish the gun, at which time Crawford pulled a gun from his pocket and continued to demand the gun. Clark refused even under threat of death to his girlfriend and 2-year-old son. Crawford forced Clark into the bedroom, threw him on the bed, and shot him in the forehead with a .25-caliber pistol. Crawford then confronted Clark's girlfriend, who scratched Crawford on the side of the face for shooting Clark. Crawford knocked Clark's girlfriend to the floor, took a butcher knife from the counter, and attempted to cut her fingers off with the knife. When that was unsuccessful, Crawford used the knife to stab the victim in the chest. He stabbed the victim with such rage and force that the knife was impaled in the wood floor beneath the victim. Crawford then turned to the 2-year-old who had just witnessed the brutal murder of his mother and threatened to kill him. It was at this time that Crawford's associate stepped in, reminding him that Crawford had a son of the same age.

Clark, who had survived the incident, called the police and provided the name of the suspect: Ronnie Crawford. Clark was shot with a small-caliber bullet that entered the skull and traveled on the right side between the brain and the skull, lodging at the back of the head and causing no permanent injury or impairment. However, Crawford eluded police for three more days.

On January 9, 1981, at approximately 3:30 P.M., Ronnie Crawford entered the Hall of Justice armed with a .38-caliber handgun because one of his prostitutes was on the witness stand in an unrelated charge. His intent was to kill her; and as she was on the witness stand testifying, Crawford entered the courtroom, drew his gun, and pointed it at the prostitute. As Crawford drew the gun, the judge pushed the panic alarm, but it had been disconnected because there had never been an incident in the courtroom to date. In addition, the judge grabbed the phone and found that it had been disconnected as well. However, vice detectives were aware that Crawford was in the courtroom and were there to arrest him on a warrant for murder from the other jurisdiction in which he had thrown the female from the car. Interestingly, at that time officers were not allowed to carry firearms in the courtroom because prosecutors believed that the weapons could be used against the police, such as by the defense arguing that they were intimidating and coercive.

The vice detectives confronted Crawford and attempted to get him to stop and put the gun down. One was a black female whom Crawford hated because she had gone after him with a vengeance whenever she could because of his history. He shot her in the face, in the left cheek just under the eye, and fired a second round that struck her in the chest. Her partner tried to get to Crawford but was shot in his collarbone. Crawford ran from the courtroom. Two off-duty officers who were at the front desk of the police department heard the shots, and they shot Crawford twice in the stomach. The courthouse and police department lobby was full of citizens that Friday afternoon. At that time, the courthouse and police department shared the same lobby and deputies did not screen for weapons.

Analysis of Ronnie Crawford's Bloody Week

1. Crawford was untouchable; no matter what law enforcement did, he had a strong hold on the criminal community and was noted as the top dog. He was respected by his peers because he was ruthless and they feared him.

2. Crawford functioned in a subculture where members were drug dealers, pimps, prostitutes, thieves, burglars, and robbers. As a rule, this subculture was not known of, but an informant had shed light on how the group functioned. In essence, it was a secret society that was hidden from police.

3. Crawford maintained his stranglehold over the group and members of the community with his acts of brutality. One such act was the beating of a prostitute with a wire hanger on her buttocks and back. Both the community and the subculture were aware of his actions and became more afraid.

4. Besides being untouchable when he committed a crime, Crawford had the ability to go underground and hide from police until he had contacted his attorney or forced a witness or victim to recant his or her story.

5. When Crawford threw the prostitute from his car and she died, he was never arrested; he felt comfortable with the idea that law enforcement was unaware that he was a suspect in that case.

6. The feud Crawford encountered with the other pimp fueled his anger to the point that he wanted to kill him in a special way from a distance. He felt that if he did that, no one would be able to pin the murder on him.

7. When Crawford entered the Clark residence, his intent was to rob Clark and his girlfriend and kill them both. By killing them both, there would not be any witnesses to the crime and he would go free and clear.

8. Crawford was shocked and angered that Clark and later his girlfriend refused to give him the weapon even when threatened with death. Clark stated in an interview that he believed Crawford was going to kill him no matter what.

9. When Crawford shot Clark with the .25 automatic, he believed that he had killed him. Little did he know that by shooting Clark in the forehead, the thickest part of the skull provided the greatest protection to the brain.

10. Crawford was not used to anyone defying his commands or orders, and when Clark's girlfriend scratched Crawford, he became enraged. He attacked the very thing that hurt him, her fingers. When that attack was unsuccessful, he stabbed her.

11. Even after the murder at the Clark residence, Crawford was still a free man. What did this do to his ego? What was he thinking about when he walked into a courtroom and shot two police officers?

12. Today Crawford sits in a Michigan prison, serving six life sentences: three counts of assault with intent to commit murder, one count of armed robbery, and two counts of first-degree murder.

CASE STUDY 2.5   THE COP AND THE JUDGE

State of Michigan v. Clarence D. Ratliff, Kent County Court File No. 88-46542 FC

Suspect

Clarence Ratliff was a decorated gunnery sergeant in the Marine Corps Reserves and a full-time police officer with the Grand Rapids Police Department with twenty-one years of service. Ratliff was a divorced father of three who had a history of alcohol abuse and domestic violence. His first wife divorced him because of the alcohol abuse and domestic violence. In 1975, he broke into his first wife's house while on duty, and pistol-whipped her with his duty weapon. His punishment for the beating was a five-day suspension and no criminal changes. After his first divorce, he lived a rather modest life, living over a local store and paying child support. He owned a cabin and a boat on a lake where he would go to get away with friends.

Ratliff was a street cop and, by all accounts, a "cop's cop." When he worked the midnight shift, he would get off work and stop at the local bar where he would drink with fellow midnight-shifters, which was a midnight shift tradition. At one point in his career, he was assigned to the neighborhood patrol unit (NPU), which was a fancy name for a street crimes unit. The unit had two functions: to stop crimes in progress and to serve as a S.W.A.T. team. He was the senior statesman and the unit's bomb technician.

Victim

Judge Carol Irons was a 40-year-old attorney who was the first female judge in Kent County, Michigan. Judge Irons was highly respected by her peers and was considered a pioneer for women's rights in the West Michigan area because of her judgeship.

The Relationship

Ratliff and Irons began dating in the early 1980s. Ratliff was rather quiet about the relationship until team members noticed the couple out on several dates, having a good time drinking together. Team members applauded Ratliff and admired him because he was dating a judge, was in a good place in his life, and was no longer paying child support. Ratliff and Judge Irons married, and by all accounts it was a great marriage. However, two years into the marriage, Judge Irons decided to stop drinking. Apparently drinking had been the glue that held her and Ratliff together; after Irons quit, she and Ratliff began taking separate vacations.

Ratliff was getting teased by his close inner circle of friends because Irons won their arguments with her attorney's wit and clarity, she picked up his paycheck, and he suffered from sexual dysfunction. Ratliff became paranoid and thought that Irons was cheating on him with an old boyfriend from school. Ratliff verified the relationship with a review of the telephone bill and later bugged the home phone where Irons's conversations with her new boyfriend were explicit. In 1987, at the time Ratliff determined Irons was having an affair, they were still living together; but in early 1988, Irons filed for divorce and agreed to pay for the cabin.

On the morning of October 18, 1988, Ratliff ended his midnight shift at 7:00 A.M. and went to the Westside Bar. There he had several shots of Jim Beam. Then he went to another bar and had several more shots. He went to his attorney's office to discuss the divorce and was advised that Irons refused to pay for the cabin and wanted Ratliff to buy her out.

Ratliff left his attorney's office, entered the Hall of Justice where the Grand Rapids Police Department and the Kent County Courts were located, entered Judge Irons's chambers, pulled his 9-mm pistol from his belt, and pointed it at Judge Irons. Judge Irons pushed the silent alarm, and dispatch called to confirm the alarm. The dispatcher asked if everything was all right, and Judge Irons replied: "Nothing is all right. My husband is pointing a gun at my head as we speak." Ratliff fired one shot, striking Judge Irons in the throat, and she died moments later. Ratliff attempted to leave but encountered two officers that he had served with for twenty years on the department. Ratliff fired two shots, one at each officer, and retreated to the judge's chambers where he held up for several minutes, contemplating suicide or suicide by cop, before he surrendered.

Analysis of the Ratliff Murder

1. Ratliff admitted under oath that when his first marriage failed and he broke into his ex-wife's house, his plan had been to shoot and kill her and then commit suicide. Since no criminal charges were filed, he only received a five-day suspension; the law and the department reinforced his behavior.

2. All of Ratliff's friends and acquaintances knew he abused alcohol, and yet no one attempted to intervene. In fact, Ratliff's blood alcohol at the time of the murder was .25, which was 2.5 times the legal limit of .10 at the time. Ratliff appealed his conviction because of his blood alcohol level, stating that he was too drunk to know or understand what he had done. However, each of the witnesses at the bar, including the bartenders, noted that Ratliff had appeared to be just fine when he left the bar, which indicated that he was an alcoholic. A newspaper

described him as a hard-drinking cop. In fact, drinking was a part of the cop culture at the time, and it remains so today.

3. Ratliff was a failure at marriage, and the loss of Judge Irons was devastating to his personality as well as his machismo. The cabin was all that he had left, and it appears that Ratliff had blackmailed Judge Irons to get her to pay for the cottage or her reputation and image would be destroyed publicly. When Judge Irons refused to pay for the cabin, it was the last insult.

4. Although Ratliff was a "cop's cop," he was a coward because in each attack, both the one on his first wife and the one on Judge Irons, he allegedly wanted to die; yet police always intervened to keep him from taking that step.

5. To add insult to injury, Ratliff was convicted of manslaughter for the murder of his wife, which carried a fifteen-year maximum sentence. In contrast, he received two life sentences for the shots he fired at fellow police officers for attempted murder. Members of the jury stated in no uncertain terms that Judge Irons contributed to her death because of the way she treated Ratliff.

6. On that same note, members of the jury were not allowed to hear about the assault and abuse with his first wife because it would have been prejudicial and might have influenced their decision. Nor was the jury allowed to hear the documented accounts of abuse that Judge Irons described to family and friends because that would have been hearsay evidence.

7. Ratliff shot Judge Irons in the same courthouse in which Ronnie Crawford shot the two Grand Rapids Police Officers.

8. Ratliff contracted cancer while in prison, and his relatives along with several officers attempted to submit a petition for his release, noting that he should be allowed to die in dignity.

9. Ratliff died in June 2011 while still incarcerated.

HOMICIDE CASE STUDIES: PSYCHOLOGICAL COMPARISONS

This section makes psychological comparisons between the two homicide case studies presented in this chapter. It examines the motivations associated with the subject of Case Study 2.4, Crawford, and the subject of Case Study 2.5, Ratliff, as well as some of the psychological theories that might apply to these two subjects.

Case Study 2.4: Crawford's Motivations

By all accounts, Crawford was a bad man. He reveled in his reputation for being brutal and did whatever he could to earn street credibility and the respect of other criminals. He never worked an honest day in his life; instead, he made his living off the misery of others. He believed that women were scum and that they lived to serve him.

Crawford was a typical pimp. Pimps are low on the scale of criminals because of how they make their money. In the criminal world, those at the top of the food change are the ones who are violent, such as armed robbers or murderers. Crawford was unusual in that he had his hands in every form of crime besides prostitution: narcotics, dealing in stolen property, extortion, armed robbery, and fencing of stolen goods.

As noted, Crawford had multiple interactions with police, and in almost every instance, he never did much time. Most, if not all, of the time he served was for traffic violations, which did nothing more than enhance his ego, support his belief that he was entitled, and enhance his power and street credibility. Crawford had such a powerful network that whenever he committed a crime, he could go underground, establish an alibi, threaten victims or witnesses, and contact his attorney before turning himself in. The end result was that he always walked free. To secure his position among his peers, he exemplified his brutality through such incidents as beating the prostitute with a wire hanger to instill fear in those who might be willing to challenge him.

When I asked my informant how she and other prostitutes ended up in a life of prostitution, she stated that it was easy. Almost all of them did not finish high school and were single mothers on welfare. Someone like Crawford would take them out, buy them things, introduce them to powder cocaine, and give them attention that they never had from a man. After receiving the goods, money, and drugs, it was easy to make the transition to prostitution. The key part of the picture that I never understood is: Each of these women loved Crawford and would do anything for him. When I asked my informant whether she could see that he was using her to get money, she wanted me to understand that Crawford took care of their every need and sex was nothing more than a tool to get what they wanted: money and to please Crawford. In return for their efforts, they had a place to stay as well as food and drugs; their kids were taken care of; and if they went to jail, Crawford was there to get them out. She also noted that all of the women had been abandoned by everyone else in their lives, including parents and their babies' daddies, and that none of them could find a decent job.

Crawford had never been challenged before. A pimp who did that very thing was new to the game. Crawford warned him, fought him, and then had him beat up, and yet nothing deterred the new pimp's challenges. Finally, Crawford abducted one of the new pimp's girls and took her for a ride. As they drove southbound on U.S. 131 in Wyoming, Michigan, he threw the prostitute from his car. Wyoming police identified Crawford as the suspect, but he could not be located.

From a psychological standpoint, at this time Crawford had stepped up his game. This was the first time he had committed murder. Prior to this incident, his reputation was based on threat, fear, and intimidation. With the murder, his anxiety level rose as well as his hatred for the other pimp. Crawford realized that this was the crime that would put him away for life.

While hiding out, Crawford ruminated about the crime, his life, and the new pimp. His thoughts were fueled by cocaine and alcohol consumption, with the anger and rage rising to a level where he developed the plan to rob Clark of that special handgun. When Clark refused, Crawford shot him. When Clark's girlfriend refused, Crawford responded brutally by attempting to cut her fingers off. His rage and frustration culminated in his stabbing of Clark's girlfriend so hard that the knife went through her body and was impaled in the wood floor below. Crawford thought he was home free because he left no witnesses.

When the news was released that Clark had survived, Crawford decided he would rather be dead than go to prison. His focus became the Hall of Justice; his statement makes it clear that he felt he had chosen the greatest stage the city had to offer. Crawford could demonstrate his disgust for everything he despised most in life, that is, the courts and the police. By taking this route, he also proved that he was a coward, because he was incapable of committing suicide.

When Crawford pulled the gun and attacked the police officers, he knew from his past experiences in the court that neither would be armed. He also knew that the courthouse and police department shared a lobby and that he would be met by the police in a running gun battle. Crawford got everything he wanted except death; today he is serving three life sentences with the Michigan Department of Corrections.

Case Study 2.4: Psychology Associated with Crawford

Based on Crawford's history, he would be diagnosed with *antisocial personality disorder,* the criteria for which are failure to conform to social norms, deceitfulness, impulsivity, irritability and aggressiveness, reckless disregard for the safety of others, irresponsibility, and a lack of remorse coupled with the ability to rationalize hurting others (American Psychiatric Association, 2000, p. 706). Although it is not a diagnosis in the *Diagnostic and Statistical Manual*

of Mental Disorders IV-TR, he would truly be classified as a psychopath. However, if we go back and compare Crawford's murder spree to Wille's (1974)
description of murderers, Wille's analysis fits Crawford perfectly. Crawford's
personality was two-dimensional and inflexible, meaning that he exhibited
the following traits: the *syndrome of repression and intense thought* and the
syndrome of expectancy (pp. 33–34).

Case Study 2.5: Ratliff's Motivations

Unlike Crawford, Ratliff began on the side of the law. By all appearances, he
was a "cop's cop," or, in the vernacular, a "man's man." However, he turned
out to be an illustration of my belief that when cops are flawed, have a tendency to abuse the rules, and act as if they are entitled, they are on a slippery
slope—and committing criminal acts can be much easier than one would like
to believe.

The first case that was publicized was the beating of Ratliff's first wife in
1975. Think of the rage and anger that it took to kick in the door, take his
duty weapon from the holster, and strike his ex-wife in the head three times,
causing three lacerations. Interestingly, this was not done while he was drunk;
through his own admission at his later trial for murder, he had every intention
that the attack would be a murder-suicide. The department's response was a
five-day suspension without pay. The department failed by not demanding a
psychological examination and by taking him back with open arms. The message was that such acts are condoned.

There was another unrecorded violation of public trust and department
policy that was discussed only in the small circle of the Neighborhood Patrol
Unit. Ratliff needed to get a part for his boat to his cottage before winter set
in. Since he was working the street crimes unit and was not responsible for
taking calls for service, he and his partner took an unmarked patrol car fifty-
three miles outside the city to deliver the part. Ratliff did not feel guilty about
this at all; in fact, he joked that the worst that would happen is that he would
get sent back to midnight shift or get a day off. He never once thought about
the integrity of the unit or the other officers.

An interesting side note that is not directly related to Ratliff: His partner
who rode with him that night was later fired for stealing ammunition from
the police pistol range and selling it at gun shows. Today that person has had
multiple arrests for theft, embezzlement, and, most recently, stealing gas in a
gas drive-off.

When Ratliff began dating Judge Irons, he was the envy of every officer. In
fact, they considered him to have taken a step up socially. The key here is that
everyone only spoke of them and only saw them at drinking establishments.

At that point in their lives, alcohol was the only thing they had in common. Once the alcohol was removed from the equation and Judge Irons stopped drinking, they had nothing in common. The very trophy that brought Ratliff pride and joy was the very thing that would destroy him.

If we look at the issue of one's ability to adapt, this is where Ratliff failed miserably. A cop's job, and his or her personality, is centered on exercising control. If a cop cannot control a situation or his or her own behavior, then the officer's hemostasis is threatened. An inability to adapt in such situations can lead to disaster.

Case Study 2.5: Psychology Associated with Ratliff

Ratliff would have been diagnosed with *depressive personality disorder,* the symptoms of which are mood dominated by dejection and unhappiness; self-concept of low self-esteem, inadequacy, and worthlessness; negative and critical of others; and pessimistic and prone to feeling guilty (American Psychiatric Association, 2000, p. 789). In addition, Ratliff abused alcohol and was constantly teased by his friends regarding Judge Irons's superiority in winning their augments, her picking up his paycheck, and the fact that Ratliff suffered from erectile dysfunction. The teasing fueled the depression and need to regain control. Ratliff felt that he was no longer a "cop's cop" but rather Judge Irons's "bitch" and that Judge Irons was "wearing the pants."

Ratliff became suspicious that Judge Irons was having an affair because he could not believe that the judge would stop drinking; he thought there had to be a reason for the change, and in his mind, that meant there was another man. This is when the acts of domestic violence began. In addition to the physical violence, Ratliff threatened to kill Judge Irons's new boyfriend by blowing him up. Ratliff was the agency bomb technician and had access to explosives.

The mistake that Judge Irons made is that she did not report the acts of domestic violence and the threats because they were embarrassing. She believed that reporting them would somehow damage her image as a judge. Failing to report the acts of domestic violence provided Ratliff with a stronger sense of entitlement and security, especially since he had only been suspended for pistol-whipping his first wife. The only ones who were aware of Ratliff's abuse and threats were the judge's friends and family.

Throughout the situation, what Ratliff failed to realize is that people change. In this case, Judge Irons chose to stop drinking because her brother was a recovering alcoholic and she did not want to travel down that road, especially since she was the first female judge in Kent County and a role model.

It was the combination of all these issues that led to the murder of Judge Irons. Ratliff lost all control, and with it his self-esteem. The last bit of control that he had was in the original divorce settlement in which Judge Irons agreed to pay for the cottage. When Judge Irons took a stand on this issue, Ratliff lost the last of his self-esteem and standing with his peers. He lost the ability to boast to his friends, "The bitch had to pay me; she is paying for the cottage."

Oddly, Ratliff chose the same stage that Ronnie Crawford used for his final act—the Hall of Justice, although in this case it was Judge Irons's private chambers. The goal was to kill the judge and commit suicide by cop, but, like Crawford, Ratliff was a coward and was unable to complete the task and let himself be murdered. In this case, it would have been Ratliff's friends who would have killed Ratliff had he not retreated back into the judge's chambers. Also like Crawford, Ratliff fits Wille's (1974) description of murderers perfectly. Ratliff's personality was two-dimensional and inflexible, meaning he exhibited the following traits: the *syndrome of repression and intense thought* and the *syndrome of expectancy* (pp. 33–34).

CONCLUSION

Murder has many motivations, and there are a number of classification systems for murderers. Research indicates that we learn acts of violence as we develop from infants to adulthood and experience a number of disappointments. Those of us who do not murder usually acquire coping skills and learn how to manage disappointment, anger, rage, jealousy, and resentment. Murderers, however, are often void of those coping skills; their behavior is inappropriate in social settings such as school.

It would be wonderful if every murderer fit into a certain category and they all fit into Wille's analysis; however, when dealing with human behavior, such certainty is impossible. The Crawford and Ratliff homicides were chosen at random before any analysis was completed, and yet in the final analysis, they are similar. To really understand any act of murder, it is important to understand the psychology associated with the incident, breaking down every aspect of the crime and the suspect's behavior prior to the incident. It is really important to understand the stressors, substance abuse, failure, disappointments, and losses, and whether psychosis exists.

REFERENCES

American Psychiatric Association (APA). (2000). *The diagnostic and statistical manual of mental disorders, IV-TR*, 4th ed. Arlington, VA: Author.

Bandura, A. (1973). *Aggression: A social learning process.* Englewood Cliffs, NJ: Prentice-Hall.

Beck, A. T. (1999). *Prisoners of hate: The cognitive basis of anger, hostility, and violence.* New York: HarperCollins.

Canter, D., & Youngs, D. (2009). *Investigative psychology: Offender profiling and the analysis of criminal action.* West Sussex, United Kingdom: Wiley.

Children's Bureau. (2011). *Child maltreatment 2011.* Washington, D.C.: Department of Health and Human Services.

Covin, R. (2011). *The need to be liked.* Montreal: Author.

De Cruz, P. (2010). *Family law, sex and society: A comparative study of family law.* New York: Routledge.

Donovan, F. (2001). *Dealing with your anger: Self-help solutions for men.* Alameda, CA: Hunter House.

Douglas, J. E., Burgess, A. W., Burgess, A. G., & Ressler, R. K. (2006). *Crime classification manual: A standard system for investigating and classifying violent crimes,* 2nd ed. San Francisco: Jossey-Bass.

Falk, G. (1990). *Murder: An analysis of its forms, conditions, and causes.* Jefferson, NC: McFarland.

Florida State Legislature. (2013a). *Homicide, Florida State Statute 782.* Tallahassee, FL: Author.

Florida State Legislature. (2013b). *Marriage, domestic violence, Florida State Statute 741.* Tallahassee, FL: Author.

Flowers, R. B. (2000). *Domestic crimes, family violence and child abuse: A study of contemporary American society.* Jefferson, NC: McFarland.

Friedman, S. H., Hrouda, D. R., Holden, C. E., Noffsinger, S. G., & Resnick, P. J. (2005). Filicide-suicide: Common factors in parents who kill their children and themselves. *Journal of the American Academy of Psychiatry and the Law, 33*(4), pp. 496–504.

Fujiwara, T., Barber, C., Schaechter, J., & Hemenway, D. (2009). Characteristics of infant homicides: Findings from a U.S. multisite reporting system. *Pediatrics, 124*(2), pp. 210–217.

Gelles, R. J., & Straus, M. A. (1979). Violence in the American family. *Journal of Social Issues, 35*(2), pp. 15–39.

Ghiglieri, M. P. (1999). *The dark side of man: Tracing the origins of male violence.* Reading, MA: Perseus Books.

Gilligan, J. (1996). *Violence: Our deadly epidemic and its causes.* New York: Putnam.

Kempe, C., Silverman, F. N., Steele, B. F., Droegemueller, W., & Silver, H. K. (1962). The battered child-syndrome. *Journal of the American Medical Association, 181*(1): pp. 17–24.

Luckenbill, D. F. (1977). Criminal homicide as a situated transaction. *Social Problems, 25*(2), pp. 176–186.

Malmquist, C. P. (2013). Infanticide/neonaticide: The outlier situation in the United States. *Aggression and Violent Behavior, 18*, pp. 399–408.

McKee, G. R. (2006). *Why mothers kill: A forensic psychologist's casebook.* New York: Oxford University Press.

Meloy, J. R. (2000). *Violence risk and threat assessment: A practical guide for mental health and criminal justice professionals.* San Diego: Specialized Training Services.

Mischel, W., & Shoda, Y. (1998). Reconciling processing dynamics and personality dispositions. *Annual Review of Psychology, 49*, pp. 229–258.

Myers, J. E. B. (2006). *Child protection in America: Past, present and future.* New York: Oxford University Press.

Oberman, M. (2003). A brief history of infanticide and the law. In M. G. Spinelli (Ed.), *Infanticide/psychosocial and legal perspectives on mothers who kill* (pp. 3–18). Washington, D.C.: American Psychiatric Publishing.

Resnick, P. J. (1969). Child murder by parents: A psychiatric review of filicide. *American Journal of Psychiatry, 126*(73), pp. 73–82.

Roberts, A. R., Zgoba, K. M., & Shahidullah, S. M. (2007). Recidivism among four types of homicide offenders: An exploratory analysis of 336 homicide offenders in New Jersey. *Aggression and Violent Behavior, 12*, pp. 493–507.

Schlueter, S. (2010). Law enforcement perspectives and obligations related to animal abuse. In F. R. Ascione (Ed.), *The international handbook of animal abuse and cruelty: Theory research, and application* (pp. 375–392). West Lafayette, IN: Purdue University Press.

Schwartz, L. L., & Isser, N. K. (2000). *Endangered children: Neonaticide, infanticide and filicide.* Boca Raton, FL: CRC Press.

Senzarnio, P. (2013, May 2). First deputies on scene testify in Crooks trial. *Waterloo Cedar Falls Courier*, A1.

Seventy-Fourth Congress of the United States. (1935). *The social security act, title IV-B.* Washington, D.C.: Author.

State of Michigan v. Clarence D. Ratliff, Kent County Court File No. 88-46542 FC. *State of Michigan v. Ronald Crawford*, Kent County Court File No. 81-27714 FY.

Thomas, D. J. (1979). *DWI traffic investigation.* Grand Rapids, MI: Grand Rapids Police Department.

Thomas, D. J. (1981). *Homicide case files.* Grand Rapids, MI: Grand Rapids Police Department.

Thomas, D. J. (2001). *Inmate case files.* Gainesville, FL: Author.

Thomas, D. J. (2011). *Police psychology: A new specialty and new challenges for men and women in blue.* Santa Barbara, CA: Praeger.

Vellut, N., Cook, J. M., & Tursz, A. (2012). Analysis of the relationship between neonaticide and denial of pregnancy using data from judicial files. *Child Abuse and Neglect, 36*, pp. 553–563.

Wille, W. S. (1974). *Citizens who commit murder.* St. Louis, MO: Warren H. Green Publishing.

Wilson, A. V. (1993). *Homicide: The victim/offender connection.* Cincinnati, OH: Anderson.

Wolfgang, M. E. (1958). *Patterns in criminal homicide.* New York: Wiley, Science Editions.

Yochelson, S., & Samenow, S. (1976). *The criminal personality, Volume I: A profile for change.* Lanham, MD: Rowman & Littlefield.

Rape and Sexual Serial Homicide

Rape, a crime with many monikers, is defined by state statute. Each state may have a different way of defining it. In the state of Michigan, it is called *criminal sexual conduct* and has four degrees, which include behaviors ranging from something as simple as touching to sexual penetration. The state of Florida calls it *sexual battery,* which by its very nature describes the crime as touching, union with, and penetration of sexual organs.

When you think of rape, it is important to understand the relationship between the victim and offender as well as the way society views each. The question that we in the United States have struggled with for many years is: When a victim says "no," does that equate to forcible rape? With that question in mind, consider the following: There is no particular profile of a victim. Victims range in age from infant to senior citizen; they are not of a specific gender but may be either male or female (rape is not limited to females and children); and, finally, victims come from every socioeconomic background.

Although society often questions the legitimacy of rape victims' claims, sexual serial homicide is truly a crime that gets the attention of everyone. The public is fascinated by the gruesome details that leave little to the imagination. Sexual serial killers act out their darkest fantasies, leaving a trail of victims. The one thing that we know is that sexual serial killers are predators seeking to satisfy a compulsion and a drive that are unique to their psychological makeup. The act is usually a ritual that fulfills a psychological need and, in most instances, a paraphilia (discussed in more detail shortly).

This chapter will examine rape, serial rape, and sexual serial homicide. It will provide several case studies and, in the end, compare the etiology of the cases in an attempt to determine if there are any differences between those who rape and those who commit sexual serial homicide.

> **Questions for Reflection:** Why does one commit violent sexual crimes? Are there any similarities between rapists of any kind and sexual serial killers?

SOCIETAL PERCEPTIONS OF RAPE

For many years, rape has been viewed as taking place in a situation in which the victim was in control and that created an environment that was conducive to the act of rape. During my early years as a police officer, and even before I retired, I heard these excuses from police and citizens alike: The victim was wearing provocative clothing; she was by herself and everyone knows that to be alone is asking for it; she got what she went there looking for; and, finally, since she did not resist, then she was not raped. I have even heard the claim that the woman was a whore and got what she deserved. Think about how each of these statements places the blame on the victim, leaving the perpetrator's conscience free and the attacker absolved of responsibility. However, remember what we noted earlier: There is no particular victim profile; victims are of all ages, genders, and socioeconomic backgrounds.

To further complicate the issue of rape, even our politicians continue to perpetuate myths that cannot be substantiated, as in the case of Congressman Todd Akin, who made this claim concerning "legitimate" rapes: "First of all, from what I understand from doctors, [pregnancy from rape] is really rare. If it's a legitimate rape, the female body has ways to try to shut that whole thing down" (Blake, 2012). These statements were made by Akin in an interview on KTVI-TV Fox News in Kansas City. Just think: This was in 2012, not 1960, that politicians were discussing what would be considered a "legitimate" rape!

The problem of rape, as well as the misperceptions surrounding it, is not only part of society as a whole but also has been a major problem in specific areas of society. For example, the U.S. military ignored the problem for years until it was brought to the forefront in 2012 by former secretary of defense Leon Panetta, who provided the following data in a press conference: In 2011, there were 3,191 sexual assaults reported in the military, but this number is only a fraction of the actual crimes committed. Panetta reported that he believed the true number of sexual assaults to be closer to 19,000 for that same year, and that 56 percent of the victims were men (Parrish, 2012).

Anyone can become a victim of sexual assault. Groth and Birnbaum (1979) note that any discussion of provocation is ridiculous, since the assaults can and do happen in every conceivable location, at all times of the day, and no person is immune from becoming a victim (p. 7). If you consider the data regarding male soldiers who have been victims, it is clear that anyone has the potential to become a victim in any circumstance.

THE ETIOLOGY OF RAPE

In Chapter 2, I argued that the family is the genesis for murder, and I will contend that is the case with all crimes of violence. Rape and serial homicide are unique in that they are acts that are very personal and brutal.

> **Questions for Reflection:** Where do you believe that a person learns brutal behavior? Where does one become so disconnected from the human race that all one can see is one's own needs and wants, and not care whether fulfilling them will destroy the life of another?

When you think of child development, everyone's personality development is based on six core areas that allow us to move from one stage of development to the next. The six core areas are described by Roys (2005) as follows:

- *Dependence versus independence:* If children are not taught to be self-reliant, then their personalities will place them in a position where they will depend on others for the rest of their lives (p. 2-4). This is often seen in victims of domestic violence, who many times are seeking a mate to validate them and their self-esteem. The same dynamic can be seen in the prostitute–pimp relationship.

- *Pleasure seeking versus delayed gratification:* Here is where children learn coping skills and understanding that often they will have to wait to get what they want (pp. 2-4 to 2-5). If the concept of delayed gratification is not mastered, what develops over time are people who are used to having their needs met at the drop of a hat. With such behavior, there is a sense of entitlement that I describe as destructive entitlement, meaning they will get what they want at all costs.

- *Ignorance versus information:* In this stage, children move from knowing nothing to the process of information gathering and logically defining their world (p. 2-5). This is where the cognitive processes are central to development. Attachment and creating a loving environment for children are important from birth. However, it is here where children understand the environment and begin to define their environment as either cold and detached or interactive and supportive.

- *Incompetence versus competence:* In this stage, children learn to control their emotions (i.e., delayed gratification), problem-solve, identify roles, and pattern sexual responses (p. 2-5). If this development is interrupted or interfered with through a series of negative events, the result will be children who cannot control their emotions, who demand instant gratification, who are void of appropriate sexual relations or roles, and who are incapable of developing meaningful relationships.

- *Diffusion of identity versus self-identity:* This stage is where children grow into themselves (p. 2-6). Think about personality development as taking pieces of others that we like and do not like and incorporating them into one personality. Many people say, "I will never be like my dad/mom," and yet if they reflect and compare their behavior to that of their parents, they often find that they are more like their parents than they want to admit.

- *Amorality versus morality:* This is children's awareness of good and evil (p. 2-6). Central to this concept are the influences that guide them to make sound decisions. In addition, there is a social contract, which is an unwritten code to which everyone in the culture subscribes. Within the moral contract, we agree to abide by society's laws, rules, and values for protection, and in so doing we give up free will (Hobbs, 1886). The acceptance or rejection of the social contract begins at birth, with our caregivers having the greatest amount of input; later, we also are influenced by our peers.

I recall my first psychology course where I learned that Freud theorized that our development was poised in what he described as the five phases of psychosexual development. If each stage was successfully completed, one would grow to have a healthy personality. However, if our personality development was stunted at any of the stages, then we would become fixated at that stage (Frick, 1995). What I came to understand from that first class is that Freud was not so far off the mark. Freud associated our development with the environment, but, more importantly, he recognized the role that nurturing, love, and support mean in the development of a healthy personality.

Contrary to Freud, Adler theorized that if we as humans examine our feelings of inferiority, we will strive for superiority. Adler did not believe that human behavior and faulty cognitive processes are associated with repressed sexual conflict and destructive urges as Freud theorized (Lundin, 1989). Rather, Adler argued that children's positions are based on their perceptions and interpretations, and that the road they take is determined by educability.

Furthermore, I have argued—and Adler supports this view—that our perception is our reality. Thus, if children determine that their position is inferior, to use Adler's term, and that they are in a place where they cannot find peace and some form of homeostasis, then they will strive to control their environment (Frick, 1995; Lundin, 1989). Most notably, they will become problem children because every experience is interpreted as a form of defeat.

If we take a moment and go back to Chapter 2, where we examine Wille's (1974) description of the two components of a murderer's personality, there is very little difference between the rapist and the murderer:

- *Syndrome of repression and intense thought* (pp. 33–34). This syndrome allows the subject to function normally in his or her world, with one exception: the syndrome of expectancy.

- *Syndrome of expectancy,* which can be described as the subject being always on edge and ready (pp. 33–34). I would interpret this to mean that the subject's body is in a state of fight or flight at all times, and ready to respond with aggression. In other words, the subject's body is always in a constant state of hypervigilence, and does not have the ability to relax.

Questions for Reflection: How would child abuse create a constant state of hypervigilence? Is child abuse a contributing factor in rape or serial sexual murder?

IMPACT OF CHILD ABUSE AND CHILD SEXUAL ABUSE

Widom (1992) argues that a childhood history of physical child abuse predisposes the survivor to violence in later years and that the victims are more likely to engage in violent behavior. After examining and following 908 cases, Widom noted that childhood victims of sexual abuse were not at greater risk of being arrested for rape or sodomy. In contrast, however, those who were physically abused showed a greater tendency toward the crimes of rape and/or sodomy (p. 6). It is important to note the limitation of Widom's study in that it was based on official arrest records and, therefore, addressed only the cases where an arrest was made.

THE CYCLE OF VIOLENT SERIAL OFFENDING: THOUGHTS, FEELINGS, EMOTIONS, BELIEFS, AND BEHAVIORS

There are a number of templates that describe some form of serial offending. The reality is that any form of violence that is repeated multiple times is based on some cycle of violence. Terry (2005) explains an offense cycle as "the interaction of the offender's thoughts, feelings, and behaviors" (p. 52). This offense cycle holds true to every violent offender be it a murderer, rapist, serial rapist, serial murderer, or arsonist.

Rarely can one disconnect thoughts, feelings, and behaviors. I will argue, however, based on my experiences during police and forensic interviews, that there is a disconnect in that the thoughts, feelings, and behaviors most closely associated rape and murder are part of a distorted, flawed cognitive process that allows the offender to minimize and rationalize the incident. This rationalization is frequently fueled by some form of substance abuse that lowers the offender's inhibitions and enhances the perception that the victim was responsible or that the act was consensual.

Contrary to my argument, the literature provides another explanation, noting that violent offenders such as rapists and serial murders mentally move to a dissociative state in order to complete the act (Yochelson & Samenow, 1976). This mechanism allows the offender to push fears away from conscious consideration, and it is a critical psychological defense. This mechanism has been discussed by the likes of Freud, Egger, and Lifton, all of whom described what appears to be some out-of-body experience or a dissociative state.

The primary difference between the distorted cognitive process and the dissociative state is that the distorted cognitive process uses critical thinking, as well as rationalization, to minimize the impact, which allows the offender to discuss the incident without guilt or emotional baggage, and without accepting responsibility. The dissociative state, on the other hand, allows the offender to place the act in an emotional box where he or she never has to visit the incident or feelings again. Both are coping mechanisms used to control the emotional impact on the offender's psyche.

Thoughts

Central to the concept that the cycle of violence begins with an offender's thoughts is the concept of paraphilias. In most circles, paraphilias are defined as deviant sexual thoughts or fantasies. The American Psychiatric Association (2000) defines paraphilias as recurrent, intense sexually arousing fantasies, sexual urges, or behaviors that involve one of the following: nonhuman objects, the suffering and humiliation of one's self or partner, or children or other nonconsenting persons (p. 586). Researchers have reported that rapists have three or more paraphilias associated with each rape (Abel & Rouleau, 1990; Freund, 1990).

Keep in mind that paraphilias are unique to individuals; every human being on earth who has such thoughts could have different ones. Common to rapists and sexual serial killers, however, are the following paraphilias: voyeurism, an activity where an offender watches unsuspecting strangers who are naked, disrobing, or engaged in sexual intercourse; exhibitionism, the exposure of one's sexual organs, which may well include masturbation; and frotteurism, the act of touching, or more specifically rubbing, a penis against an unsuspecting party, usually in large crowds (American Psychiatric Association, 2000, pp. 569–575). To help the reader appreciate the complexity and the uniqueness of paraphilias, here is a quotation from Gray (1998), who provides the following description of how the Marquis de Sade found pleasure:

> Incited by what psychiatrists call "coprophillia," a neurotic pleasure derived from the smell of feces, [Marquis de Sade] wished, above all, to stimulate the prostitutes' intestinal functions and have them produce a maximum of gases. So he covered large doses of Spanish Fly with a coating of anise, equally known to increase flatulence. (p. 128)

There is no way to provide a detailed list of all of the paraphilias, since they are based on each individual's experiences and imagination, and thus theoretically the list could be limitless. Following is a small sampling from Milner and Dopke (1997) of some of the more unusual ones:

- *Formicophilia:* The focus is on small creatures, such as snails, frogs, ants, or other insects, creeping, crawling, or nibbling on the body, especially the genitalia or nipples.
- *Klismaphilia:* This refers to receiving an enema. Historically, erotic enemas were provided in specialty brothels and in enema spas.
- *Olfactophilia:* The sexual focus is on the smells and body odors of a sexual partner, especially odors from the genital area.
- *Mysophilia:* The sexual focus is on smelling, chewing, or otherwise utilizing sweaty or soiled clothing or articles of menstrual hygiene.
- *Urophilia:* This refers to the use of a urinary stream, which may or may not include a partner.
- *Coprophilia:* The focus is the ingestion or the act of elimination of feces.
- *Vampirism:* This refers to sexual arousal attained through blood extraction. There are four types: (1) complete vampirism, defined as necrosadism involving death; (2) vampirism without ingestion of blood, called necrophilia; (3) vampirism without death being involved; and (4) autovampirism, which is ingesting one's own blood.

The paraphilias that are unique to rape, sexual sadism, and sexual serial homicide are hybrids that include power and control, and in most if not all instances the victim experiences humiliation, torture, and possibly mutilation.

Groth and Birnbaum (1979) state that in every act of rape, there are two entities: aggression and sexuality. Sexuality becomes the act through which the offender releases feelings of rage, frustration, and resentment. The aggression is eroticized so that the offender derives pleasure from the control, domination, and pain imparted on the victim.

Feelings, Emotions, Beliefs, and Behaviors

How are feelings, emotions, and beliefs related? Pettinelli (2008) describes the difference between emotions and feeling in the following terms: Feelings are immediate and usually associated with one individual thing, whereas emotions are something that affect your entire being, are much more complicated, and are a combination of feelings and thoughts (p. 17). Frijda, Manstead, and Bem (2000) argue that emotions are a result of how one perceives and believes the world to be, and beliefs are one of the major components of emotions (p. 1). Frijda et al. also note that emotions influence the content and strength of our belief system. The influences of emotions on one's belief system serve as a gateway and stimulate one to action. The concepts are simple, and every component is interrelated.

The actions of a rapist, serial killer, or violent criminal are built on a faulty foundation. This faulty foundation is developed early in life and forces the individual to find a form of escape, which is most often bound in fantasy. As Leo Boatman, the fledgling serial killer, stated in his interview with police after his arrest:

> When I was growing up my life was miserable and I had no control. The state of Florida is responsible for raising me and I escaped the abuse in foster homes and juvenile detention by reading murder mystery books and placing myself in the role of the killer. It was there that I was in control and it was there that I learned to manipulate others to get what I wanted. (Marion County Sheriff's Office, 2006)

The cycle of sexual offending offered below best describes a sexual offender's cognitive process:

- *Stimulus:* The stimulus could be a stressor, misperceptions, miscommunication, or any event that activates the offender's distorted or irrational thinking. To the offender, this distorted thinking is logical and rational; however, to an outsider, the thoughts would be deemed irresponsible, illogical, and irrational.
- *Rationalization:* Here the offender ties up all the loose ends in the thought process so that his or her decision can be defended and explained. This process may be fueled by some form of substance abuse and/or a series of fantasies that

make the process of rationalization that much easier. What is most interesting here is that the decision is made in a vacuum, without consideration or empathy for the victim; it is all about the offender.

- *Choice:* Here the offender has made a conscious decision to attack the victim, although in the offender's mind it may not be seen as an attack. Keep in mind that this choice is usually made after a great amount of thought, which might include: mental rehearsal and/or fantasies about the act, victim selection, and/ or selection of location (depending on the nature of the attack). Although this is a choice, it is made without consideration of the potential consequences. The need and drive of the offender outweigh any potential consequences. Offenders who have been successful in the past tend to believe that they are invincible.

- *Commission of the act:* Here the offender commits the act. The offender will feel a sense of exhilaration much like that of a "crack addict" experiencing the first high. Or the offender might find the act disappointing because the victim was not a willing participant, meaning the victim's behavior was not what the offender had expected. I find this most interesting because, since this is the offender's fantasy, how would the victim know or understand his or her role?

- *Minimizing:* This provides the offender with a tool that allows him or her to catalog the incident without damage to the psyche. The act of minimizing reduces the psychological aftermath to the offender's psyche, meaning the offender will not repress the memory but can relive the rape or sexual murder over and over without intrusive negative thoughts. Again, there is a total lack of empathy for the victim; the emphasis is on the offender and his or her needs.

MODELS FOR RAPE AND SEXUAL SERIAL HOMICIDE

As with theories on all subjects, there are multiple models on why one becomes a rapist or serial killer. In examining the models, we find slight differences and the same end result. I believe, however, that it is important to understand the many schools of thought to enhance one's knowledge base.

The first model of sexual serial killers to be discussed is the *sexual homicide motivational model* as it appears in the text entitled *Sexual Homicide: Patterns and Motives* (Ressler, Burgess, & Douglas, 1995). This is the model used by the Federal Bureau of Investigation (FBI).

In the sexual homicide motivational model, the social environment of the child is one that offers an ineffective atmosphere. In it the child's behavior is ignored, the parents are nonintervening, family support is distorted, and the family is nonprotective. This concept is the same as Bowlby's discussion regarding attachment theory. Simply put, a child who receives love and nurturing will develop healthy relationships; but abuse and distorted family processes plant the seed for violent behavior, as noted by Ressler and colleagues (1995, p. 70).

If there is physical and sexual abuse during the child and adolescent years, it may well exacerbate the problems the child experienced from birth to early childhood, resulting in developmental failure, the development of negative social attachments, diminished emotional responses, and poor performance in school. Critical personal issues that occur as a result of this kind of environment manifest as follows: The child experiences social isolation and begins to fantasize; the fantasies place the child in a position of power and control. The end result may be preferences for autoerotic activities, pornography, and fetishes. Behavior problems manifest themselves in the form of aggressiveness, angry outbursts, lying, and a sense of destructive entitlement.

These behaviors lead to the development of distorted thinking and cognitive processes, including the development of absolutes in thinking, as noted by Wille. The themes of this distorted cognitive process are dominance, revenge, violence, rape/molestation, power/control, death, torture, mutilation, and inflicting pain on others/self.

The second model of sexual serial killers to be discussed is that of *clinical anger* as it appears in the text *Signature Killers: Interpreting the Calling Cards of the Serial Murderer* (Keppel & Birnes, 1997). In Keppel's theory of clinical anger, the anger displayed is totally abnormal and constant, rather than transient or situational. Wille notes this type of anger in his discussion. Beck (1999) also notes that such anger is based on perceptions or misperceptions and is the result of interaction between the individual and the social environment (p. 125).

In the clinical anger model, the child and adult perceive the anger as beyond his or her control, and it may include an entity (Keppel & Birnes, 1997, p. 327). The concept of an entity means that the offender hears voices, as a psychotic or schizophrenic would, or believes a presence (another personality) is guiding the offender through the event. Ted Bundy described each of his murders in this fashion, and in fact Dan Rolling attempted to use this concept in his defense in the Gainesville student homicides case. The subject may never understand the source of the anger because of the environment in which he or she grew up: one that was lacking in the development of social bonds and that involved exposure to amoral values and distorted cognitive processes, all of which appeared to be normal. The anger increases progressively and exponentially as the subject matures through adolescence to adulthood (p. 327). Beck (1999) notes that even when we attempt to intervene or change behavior through punishment, it only serves as a temporary deterrent because it reinforces the subject's beliefs that he or she is weak and vulnerable (p. 125).

Because there is no permanent relief from the intense feelings of anger, violence offers temporary relief as the offender seeks to achieve some form of homeostasis. If you look at those who are addicted to drugs or self-medicate, you will find that they are seeking relief by ingesting the substance. Keppel and Birnes (1997) note that in order to maintain the level of homeostasis, the acts of violence may include sexual crimes and murder; this is the beginning of the cycle of violence (p. 328).

Since none of the theories are all-encompassing, I will offer a theory as to the etiology of rapists and those who commit sexual serial homicide. What differentiates this model from the ones previously discussed is that this model is inclusive, containing the biological, environmental, and psychological components.

NEW PARADIGM

The subject at birth has some predisposing factor that allows him or her to be susceptible to psychopathology. The factor may be neurological, such as damage to the frontal cortex of the brain or a failure of the neurotransmitter communication system within the brain, or possibly hormonal, such as an imbalance that influences aggression. This predisposition is exacerbated when the infant is ignored and becomes the victim of physical abuse or neglect. The infant develops early emotional frustration (EEF), and as the infant transitions to early childhood, he or she develops a dissociative system that allows him or her to escape or fantasize.

As development continues, the child's frustration evolves into "clinical anger." The signs of this anger are ever-present in the acts of violence that the child commits: fire-setting, killing of animals, acts of bestiality, and acts of violence committed against other children. The fantasies become more intense as development continues. The adolescent begins to develop the characteristics of a predator: prowling at night, window peeping, acts of burglary, and the indiscriminate rape of smaller children and other adolescents.

The offender learns through trial and error, even after multiple arrests, that the juvenile justice system is ineffective, and the fantasies become more intense, more perfect—and hence the bi-phasic personality is developed along with the offender's cycle of violence. The offender finds that petty crime and acts of rape are no longer satisfying and progresses to the ultimate paraphilia, sexual homicide. To continuously satisfy the anger, the cycle becomes repetitive.

INCIDENTS OF RAPE AND SEXUAL ASSAULT ANNUALLY

In 2011, according to the FBI's *Uniform Crime Reports* (UCR), there were 64,382 reported incidents that were classified as forcible sex crimes committed in the United States. Of those reported incidents was a total of 69,356 offenses and 69,356 victims, and 67,550 of the offenders were known (FBI, 2011). The FBI's UCR uses the term *offenses known* to refer to the number of offenses that are reported to law enforcement. When the UCR refers to *known offenders,* that does not mean that the offender was identified by an arrest or by law enforcement, but rather that law enforcement has some distinguishing characteristic of the offender(s) who committed that offense.

There are four categories of forcible sex crimes: rape, sodomy, sexual assault with an object, and fondling. In addition to the forcible sex offenses, there are a number of nonforcible sex offenses that fall into two categories: incest and statutory rape. In 2011, under the category of incest, there were 1,034 reported incidents; of those, 1,152 offenses were committed and there were 1,071 known offenders. In the category of statutory rape, there were 5,343 reported incidents, 5,613 incidents, 5,613 victims, and 5,662 known offenders (FBI, 2011). One cautionary note as you view the FBI data: Keep in mind that these are only the incidents reported to the police.

Bert and Stein (2008) state that 20 to 25 percent of all adult women will become victims of sexual assault; 15 percent of all college women and 12 percent of adolescent girls report that they have been victims of sexual assault or sexual abuse in their lifetimes (p. 1512). The most common victim profile is a white female, 15 and under, and in many of categories the rate of incidence is on average two times greater than that for black females. However, in the areas of forcible rape and forcible fondling, white female adolescents 15 and under were victimized at a rate four times that of black females in the same age group (FBI, 2011). One thing not noted in official reports are the cultural differences: Members of the black community do not report acts of rape or violence as often as whites for a number of reasons: shame and embarrassment, a lack of trust in the police, and a belief that the matter is personal.

VICTIM–OFFENDER RELATIONSHIPS

In 2011, the most common offender for forcible rape was between the ages of 16 and 30; for forcible sodomy, age 15 and under and 16 to 20 years; for rape with an object, age 15 and under and 16 to 20 years; for forcible fondling, age 15 and under and 16 to 20 years; for statutory rape, ages 16 to 25 years; and for incest, age 15 and under, 16 to 20 years, and 31 to 40 years (FBI, 2011). As with the victims who are white, white males commit sexual assault crimes twice as often as black males, the next closest group. Again, the same assertion regarding cultural differences must be made; as with the black female victim, the black male offender profile issue is cultural, based on the same dynamics.

In understanding the motivations of offenders, it is important to understand the offender–victim relationship. These relationships can be classified in many ways; however, the simplest categories are: familial relationships, friend or acquaintance, and stranger. In examining the data from the *2011 Uniform Crime Reports,* we find the following victim–offender relationships:

1. *Forcible sex crimes* are classified as rape, sodomy, sexual assault with an object, and forcible fondling.

    - Familial relationships accounted for approximately 24 percent or 17,287 of all the sex crimes reported in 2011 and 26 percent of all the forcible sex crimes reported in 2011.

    - Friend or acquaintance relationships accounted for approximately 49 percent or 35,557 of all the sex crimes reported in 2011 and 54 percent of all the forcible sex crimes reported in 2011.

    - Stranger, where no relationship was known or present, accounted for approximately 18 percent or 12,600 of all the sex crimes reported in 2011 and 19 percent of all the forcible sex crimes reported in 2011.

2. *Nonforcible sex offenses* are classified as incest and statutory rape.

    a. Incest familial relationships accounted for approximately 2 percent or 1,637 of all the sex crimes reported in 2011 and 25 percent of the nonforcible sex crimes committed in 2011.

    b. Friend or acquaintance relationships accounted for less than 1 percent or 33 of all the sex crimes committed in 2011 and less than 1 percent of all the nonforcible sex crimes committed in 2011.

    c. Stranger, where no relationship was known or present, accounted for less than 1 percent or 21 of all the sex crimes committed in 2011 and less than 1 percent of all the nonforcible sex crimes committed in 2011.

    d. Statutory rape

        - Familial relationships accounted for less than 1 percent or 578 of all the sex crimes reported in 2011 and 9 percent of the nonforcible sex crimes committed in 2011.

        - Friend or acquaintance relationships accounted for approximately 6 percent or 4,234 of all the sex crimes committed in 2011 and 84 percent of all the nonforcible sex crimes committed in 2011.

        - Stranger, where no relationship was known or present, accounted for less than 1 percent or 563 of all the sex crimes committed in 2011 and 8 percent of all the nonforcible sex crimes committed in 2011.

In the final analysis, one is most likely to be victimized by a friend or an acquaintance, and the second most likely suspect is a family member.

As I reviewed the data, I was struck by the quotation from Gelles and Straus (1979), introduced in Chapter 2, concerning the family:

> With the exception of the police and the military, the family is perhaps the most violent social group, and the home the most violent social setting, in our society. A person is more likely to be hit or killed in his or her home by another family member than anywhere else or by anyone else. (p. 15)

I would argue that this quotation should include friends, with the understanding that it is through close familial and friendship relationships that violence is experienced. In other words, those who we trust and allow close to us will more than likely be the source of violence in our lives. Yet, if we go by news reports, it is apparent that the greatest fear of most Americans is that they will be victimized by a stranger.

VIOLENCE MODELS

Traditionally, many models and classification systems have been used to explain violent behavior. In examining each of the classification systems, however, we find they can be placed into two categories: reactive violence models and predatory violence models.

- *Reactive violence* is violence that is spontaneous in reaction to what is perceived to be an immediate threat. The goal of reactive violence is to stop a threat. Note that reactive violence does not have to be in response to an act of violence; it may be in response to denial and committed spontaneously in a fit of anger and rage. This is often the case in date rape. Another example is where a couple is attempting to reconcile and the offender becomes frustrated and views the victim as leading him or her on. In either instance, the offender feels that he or she has done everything possible to please the victim, playing to the victim's emotional side. When the victim shuns the romantic advances of the offender, it results in acts of violence: date rape or murder/rape.

CASE STUDY 3.1   MOVIE AND RAPE: REACTIVE VIOLENCE

A 15-year-old black female went on a date with an acquaintance she knew from the neighborhood. It was their first date, and they were going to a movie and a local fast-food restaurant. Blackboy was the offender's street name, and he was a 17-year-old drug dealer. After the movie, Blackboy invited the victim to his apartment where he lived with his family—his mother, stepfather, and three siblings—to watch television and talk.

The victim stated that once she entered Blackboy's bedroom, he locked the bedroom door for privacy. She said she was down for some kissing and fondling, but she said "no" when it came to sex. Blackboy asked repeatedly, and the victim refused. The victim stated that she could see that Blackboy was getting upset, so she got off the bed and said she was going home. Blackboy grabbed her by the arm and threw on her on the bed and tried to pry her legs open with his hands. The victim had scratch marks and bruises on both thighs. The more the victim resisted Blackboy's attempts, the more violent he became, striking the victim in the face and giving her a black eye, and punching her in the mouth and splitting her lip open. The victim continued to resist, and Blackboy punched the victim in the chest, resulting in bruises, bit her left breast, and punched the victim in the stomach repeatedly. During the examination at the hospital, each of these injuries was confirmed and supported by bruising.

When asked whether Blackboy said anything during the attack, the victim stated the following: "Bitch, you know what the deal is. I take you to a movie and dinner; I paid for that pussy, and it's mine. So you are going to give me what you owe me or I am going to beat it out of you." As the physical assault continued, Blackboy stated, "I like it this way because when I am done with you, you will be my bitch, and every time you see me, you will give me what I want and do what I say. I own you, bitch." After he beat the victim into submission, Blackboy forced the victim to perform fellatio and have intercourse. When he was done, Blackboy made the following statement: "You are my bitch now. I own you, and that where I bit you on your titty is my mark; every time you see it and touch it, you will think of only me."

The assault and rape took place in a small two-bedroom apartment. Blackboy's bedroom was next to the living room. During the sexual assault, his parents and siblings were in the living room watching television. When they were interviewed, they said they heard nothing and that victim was fine when she left the apartment.

An hour after the incident, I interviewed the victim. I located Blackboy on the street. We had a history because I had arrested him several times for sale and possession of crack cocaine. In every encounter from the time he was 14 years old, he had always been violent and combative, and he became more so with each encounter. Initially he denied that he touched the victim or that they had sex. I arrested him on charges of sexual battery and aggravated battery. Once at the jail, I read him Miranda, and he laughed and said that I would never make this stick. He then made the following statement: "I took the bitch to a movie and dinner; she knew the deal; she was going give up the pussy; that's the way it is. I paid for that ass and I was going to get it. When she said no, I beat her ass until she sucked my dick willingly, and then I fucked her. I told her then and I am telling you now, that's my bitch; I own her." Later that night I obtained a search warrant to search Blackboy's bedroom. During the search, we recovered a 9-mm Glock pistol loaded with seventeen rounds and two grams of crack cocaine, as well as evidence that the rape had taken place as the victim described.

I returned to the jail and charged Blackboy with two additional charges: possession of crack cocaine and possession of a firearm by a convicted felon. The sexual assault was also confirmed with the evidence obtained from a rape kit at the local hospital. I met with Blackboy to advise him of the additional charges, and my last words to him were these: "I am not sure what happened to you over the years. For me this is a game, and sooner or later I will put you away for good. But you have become so evil and you think the world owes you something. Hear me: The people on the street are going to get tired of your bullshit, and someone is going to kill you."

Blackboy was out on bond, awaiting trial on the rape case, when he was shot with a shotgun. The hospital X-rayed his body to confirm that they had removed all the pellets from his chest. Based on the results of the X-ray, all the pellets were accounted for. However, unbeknownst to hospital staff, one pellet entered his carotid artery on the right side of his neck and remained there undetected. Blackboy bled internally until he died (Thomas, 1994).

- *Predatory violence* is an act of violence where the offender has taken the time to reflect on the crime and the goals to be accomplished (Meloy, 2000). An offender committing predatory violence is no different from a lion hunting prey or a hunter hunting a deer. Whereas reactive violence is spontaneous, predatory violence is just the opposite: Every detail of the act is thought out. Here there are a number of goals, and it is only through the accomplishment of each goal does one become satisfied. The offender has a victim type and hunts in particular locations to find someone that meets the offender's psychological need. Unlike reactive violence, predatory violence is all about some psychological need being met, which may include the victim's looks, body type, or even social status. There are two groups or locations that offer a variety of potential victims: college campuses and prostitutes. Either group is great prey because college students are away from home and trying to break the bonds by not having a lot of contact with their parents, and prostitutes walking the streets have no one who publicly cares about them.

As I walk my campus during the day and at night, female students are distracted or look away when I try to make eye contact and say "Hello." Today many are preoccupied with their cell phones or MP3 players. In my classes,

I discuss these observations, and the following week, after making their own observations, students all agree that there is very little situational awareness. The danger is compounded at night because there are so many dark spaces on a campus, which makes it a great hunting ground. The beauty of hunting on a college campus is that it is open to anyone, so we have no idea who belongs and who does not. The next great location for hunting is the street corner of any city where prostitutes work. Prostitutes are easy prey because they will get into a car willingly, which is half the battle won. Although more situationally aware than students, prostitutes focus on money, and many abuse substances to get through the day, both of which inhibits their judgment.

CASE STUDY 3.2   THE PROWLER: PREDATORY VIOLENCE

The Jones family lived in Grand Rapids, Michigan. It was an unusually hot and humid August, so they were leaving the windows open to get a breeze in the house. During the day, the windows on the first floor were open; and at night, the windows on the second floor were open, with fans placed in the rooms to circulate the air.

At 2:00 A.M., the parents were awakened when Oscar Chrisman entered the bedroom and began beating the father into unconsciousness. The father was tied up, and later, after the assault, it was learned that the suspect, Chrisman, had tied up the children prior to entering the parents' bedroom. After beating the father, the suspect punched and beat Mrs. Jones, torturing her and threatening to kill her kids and husband if she did not cooperate. At knife point, the suspect made Mrs. Jones perform fellatio, threatening that if she bit him he would tie her up and force her to watch as he raped her kids and killed her husband. Mr. Jones became conscious during the sexual assault on his wife and was helpless. Chrisman taunted Mr. Jones while Mrs. Jones was performing fellatio, and then he raped Mrs. Jones vaginally and anally.

The only thing police had on the suspect was that he was a black male, about 5'11", and muscular—and that he was dressed in black and the crotch from his sweat pants was missing. The information was broadcast to the public with no leads. There were several sightings of a man fitting his description, but he was able to elude us until after his tenth sexual assault, where the father was able to break free and call police right after the incident. Officers working the detail were in the area and were able to catch the suspect as he was fleeing the scene.

During the interview, Chrisman stated that he loved the hunt. When asked how he picked the victims, he advised it was at random and that was exciting for him not knowing who might be in the house. Chrisman stated that he enjoyed breaking in the house and prowling without being discovered. He noted that if they had kids, it was even better because he could always use them as a bargaining chip to get what he wanted. Where he felt most powerful was beating the husband or boyfriend because he left them helpless and made them feel less than a man. Chrisman stated, "Just think, the poor bastard had to watch his girlfriend/wife suck my dick and then watch me fuck her. Man, that's power" (Thomas, 1982).

PSYCHOLOGICAL UNDERPINNINGS

Many thoughts and diagnoses could lead one to become a sexual serial killer or serial rapist, and therefore it is impossible to lump sexual serial killers and serial rapists into one category. When in class my students choose "antisocial personality disorder" for every suspect as a catchall, I remind them they are failing to observe the other personality disorders and the nuances that differentiate each. In addition, another common diagnosis is "psychopathy," and yet there is no such diagnosis in *The Diagnostic and Statistical Manual of Mental Disorders,* fourth edition (*DSM-IV-TR*; American Psychiatric Association, 2000).

Krafft-Ebing (1894/1965) was one of the first to describe human perversions in detail and provide specific diagnoses, such as those found in the DSM-IV-TR today. Krafft-Ebing noted that which is physiologically and psychologically disgusting by most accounts finds its way to being sexually pleasurable, and then the act becomes what is known as sexual perversions (p. 56). Krafft-Ebing is quick to differentiate between perversion as a sexual instinct and perversion as a sexual act, meaning that the perverse sexual instinct manifests itself through such acts as sadism and lust murder, whereas perversion in the sexual act leads to sexual preference; to understand the difference, one must investigate and diagnose.

Krafft-Ebing (1894/1965) classifies sadism in its many forms, and these variations are closely associated with diagnoses or paraphilias we acknowledge today:

- Lust murder cannibalism: the eating of the victims' flesh
- Mutilation of corpses and necrophilia
- Injury of women through picquerism, which is the cutting of the flesh or flagellation (e.g., whipping with a belt or whip)—an erection can only be accomplished after the victim has been bleeding

- Defilement of women by sprinkling victims' bodies with acid, urinating on victims, spreading feces on victims, or smearing the victims' bodies with ink
- Symbolic sadism/other attacks on women: There is a routine based on the way a woman dresses, an act such as touching the woman's face, and so on—in any case, the male ejaculates without ever having sex with the woman
- Sadism with living sensitive objects other than females, such as whipping boys or the observation of others being punished
- Sadistic acts with animals (pp. 62–87)

Not all the items on the list would necessarily be given a diagnosis today, but they do all fall into the category of paraphilias. As mentioned earlier, there is no way to provide a diagnosis for a subject who is involved in sexual crime. This is supported by Krafft-Ebing. Our nature, however, is to simplify things and place them in nice neat boxes. Also keep in mind that when you review patients' psychiatric histories and have them fill out surveys that are self-reports, you may never get honest answers, so we must become investigators with the understanding that the truth lies in the past history.

When I think of sexual serial killers or serial rapists, I begin by categorizing them as compulsive, and their behavior can best be described as obsessive-compulsive because it comes from a drive or need that has to be satisfied. This is supported by the DSM-IV's definition of a paraphilia as recurrent, intense, sexual urges or fantasies (American Psychiatric Association, 2000, p. 566).

Paraphilias can be listed on a continuum from least harmful to most harmful, which would be lust murder, described by Krafft–Ebing as a form of sadism. Contemporary thought places each of Krafft–Ebing's classifications under the umbrella of paraphilias where sexual sadism is but one of many, and the most dangerous. What you will find missing in the continuum is rape; its only mention is under pedophilia, which, like sexual sadism, describes acting on sexual urges. In the case of pedophilia, there is no such thing as consent, and with sexual sadism, the acts are committed against nonconsenting adults (American Psychiatric Association, 2000, pp. 573–574).

CLASSIFICATIONS OF RAPISTS AND SEXUAL SERIAL KILLERS

Theorists have developed many classification systems based on empirical data, much like that provided in Chapter 1 in the discussion of what causes crime. Classification systems are rarely used from a law enforcement perspective, since the goal of law enforcement is to detail the crime and the acts that happened in painstaking detail. From a clinical perspective, however, classification systems are important because they help in the development of a treatment plan as well designing treatment programs. From the clinical perspective, then, one size does not fit all. Here I provide some of the classification systems that theorists have developed for rapists and sexual serial killers to give you the opportunity to choose the ones you believe are best.

Classification Systems

As early theorists, Groth and Birnbaum (1979) created three classifications for rapists—anger, power, and sadistic—with each having its own set of psychodynamic characteristics:

- *Anger rapist:* one who uses sexuality as a means to discharge feelings of rage and anger and is almost always brutal
- *Power rapist:* one who must possess the victim's sexuality through conquest; most often associated with an offender who feels inadequate and has a need to be defined by power, authority, and strength
- *Sadistic rapist:* one who transforms anger and power into aggression so that the act of aggression is eroticized; sexual satisfaction is found in the acts of brutality (pp. 13–34)

Later, Douglas, Burgess, Burgess, and Ressler (2006) offered four categories of rapists that are similar to those provided by Groth and Birnbaum. The categories are power assurance rapist, exploitive rapist, anger rapist, and sadistic rapist. The only unique category here is exploitive rapist, whose behavior is described as impulsive and predatory, with the attack being controlled by situation rather than by fantasy (p. 194). In essence, this offender sees rape as a crime of opportunity.

More recently, Salters (2003) offered descriptions for three categories of rapists, noting that all rapists share two things: distorted thinking patterns and a willingness to use brutality to achieve their goals. Salters's three categories are: opportunistic rapists (similar to the Douglas et al. exploitive rapist), compulsive rapists, and sadistic rapists. Although titled differently, compulsive rapists are similar to anger rapists; however, Salters takes a slightly different slant in describing compulsive rapists as using their assaultive behavior to vent their anger but noting that their behavior is not associated with opportunity (pp. 84–85).

Hall and Hirschman (1991) also offered a set of categories in which they described motivational precursors that are rooted in the physiological, cognitive, affective, and personality components of one's personality. Hall and Hirschman's four categories are: physiological sexual arousal, which is similar to the anger or compulsive rapists described earlier; cognitive; episodic dyscontrol, which is similar to the opportunistic and exploitive rapists described earlier; and developmentally related personality problem. Unique in this discussion is the cognitive motivational model, which is described as offenders justifying their actions rationally. This type of rationality absolves the offender of responsibility and places blame on the victim (p. 666). A second type not mentioned in previous models is the developmentally related personality problem, which is described as offenders being emotionally shunted, suffering from intellectual impairment, history of delinquency, poor social skills, and poor adult adjustment.

When we reflect back on each typology, we can see that most, if not all, possess one or more of the same characteristics, which is not surprising given the role that the family plays in one's developmental process. Although the classification systems for rapists vary somewhat in terminology, in the end, they all address the same issues—and it becomes a choice for each clinician or researcher as to which one to use. A serial rapist could be classified in any category, based on the offender's behaviors during the incident. What is missing here, however, is a classification for sexual serial killers.

The sexual serial killer is a unique animal. This group needs its own category. Sexual serial killers would have to be classified as sexual sadists and, as described by Krafft-Ebing, are truly lust murderers. The motivational dynamics of sexual serial murder and serial rape are similar; however, one minor nuance or deviation in the attack may create a situation where a violent rape becomes a homicide (Canter, 1994; Clarke & Carter, 1999; Egger, 2002; West, 1987). With that said, no one knows why one chooses to rape but the other to rape and kill, when so little otherwise differentiates them.

When I reflect on this unknown, I go back to an interview with Leo Boatman, a murderer who stated that he had fantasized about committing murder and that's all he wanted to do. When he had the opportunity to do so, he killed; however, when it came time to dispose of the bodies in a pond, he could not do it. When asked why the bodies were only partially hidden in the pond, Boatman replied, "Touching the bodies was gross. It wasn't what I thought it would be" (Marion County Sheriff's Office, 2006). Here is where fantasy and reality collide.

Since sadism is an essential component of sexual serial murder, it is important to examine the key points as provided by the American Psychiatric Association (2000):

- The paraphilic focus of sexual sadism involves acts (real, not simulated) in which the individual derives sexual excitement from psychological or physical suffering (including humiliation) of the victim.
- In all cases, it is the suffering of the victim that is sexually arousing.

- Sadistic fantasies or acts may involve activities that indicate the dominance of the person over the victim (e.g., forcing to crawl or keeping the victim in a cage). They may also involve restraint, blindfolding, paddling, spanking, whipping, pinching, beating, burning, electrical shock, rape, cutting, stabbing, strangulation, torture, mutilation, or killing.

- When sexual sadism is practiced on nonconsenting partners, the activity is likely to be repeated until the person with sexual sadism is apprehended.

- When sexual sadism is severe, and especially when it is associated with antisocial personality disorder, individuals with sexual sadism may seriously injure or kill someone. (pp. 573–574)

THE ROLE OF FANTASIES IN SERIAL RAPE AND SERIAL MURDER

Central to every discussion regarding serial rape, pedophilia, and sexual serial homicide is the idea that fantasies fuel the crime, meaning the offender ruminates regarding the fantasy. In essence, offenders replay their fantasies over and over until they are compelled to act because (1) their behavioral inhibitions are overwhelmed, possibly (2) through substance use or abuse or (3) in response to an action—or any combination of these three factors occurs. To truly understand the role of fantasies and their relationship to healthy sex as well as to violent sexual acts, it is important to explore discussions associated with both.

> **Questions for Reflection:** How do fantasies play a role in activating or fueling a sex offender's obsession to offend? What role does pornography play?

Every human being fantasizes about sex with another person at some point in time, and it is the very essence of masturbation. Researchers support this observation, noting that in a survey, both men and women stated that they had fantasies; in fact, 71 percent of men and 72 percent of women fantasized while with their partners to enhance their sexual arousal, and fantasies were most common during masturbation (Masters, Johnson, & Kolodny, 1998; Reinisch & Beasley, 1991). Hariton and Singer (1974) completed a study of 141 suburban housewives, determining that it is common for women to fantasize during intercourse and that this cognitive process is not associated with interpersonal disturbances, adjustment problems, or psychological disorders. The use of fantasies is associated with enhancing arousal and excitement (p. 321). Reinisch and Beasley (1991) reported that the same is true for men (p. 92).

These descriptions address healthy individuals, but is there a difference between this group and sex offenders?

Although the literature is rich with arguments stating that fantasies and pornography are key elements in sex offending and that sex offenders have more fantasies than nonsex offenders, there are very little data to support these often-mentioned arguments. The nature and the extent to which fantasies play a role in sex offending varies based on the offender type and the extent of offending behavior. In other words, there is a distinct difference in the nature and frequency of fantasies with someone who commits one rape (a one-time offender) versus a serial offender (Terry, 2005).

To support the argument of differences in frequency and nature of fantasies, several researchers have noted a distinct difference between the fantasies of child molesters and those of rapists (Marshall, Barbaree, & Eccles, 1991; Pithers, Beal, Armstrong, & Petty, 1989). Specific to serial rape and sexual serial homicide, researchers describe a progression from fantasy to the commission of the act: Offenders experience recurring masturbatory fantasies based on violence and aggression; the offenders seek actors and outlets to act out their fantasies; and once the substitutes become insufficient and behavioral inhibitions are overcome, humans become the target of the aggression (Purcell & Arrigo, 2006; Schlesinger, 2008). Prentky et al. (1989) support these observations in their study of twenty-five convicted sexual serial killers; they found that 86 percent of them admitted that deviant sexual fantasies were a part of their motivation (p. 889).

In almost every description regarding fantasies, what needs to be considered is that fantasies and surrogate objects are temporary, while the offender has a need to fulfill all of his or her senses. The imagination has its limitations, and the offender needs to touch, smell, hear, taste, see, and sense the fear the prey feels as he or she is being hunted by the predator. Palmero and Farkas (2013) argued that sensory inputs drive erotic attraction, whether it is mutual or one-sided, in healthy relationships. When these same inputs are applied to a sexual aggressor, they only compound the aggressor's anger and frustration because of an inadequacy that drives the aggressor to attack (pp. 23–24).

TWO CASE STUDIES OF SERIAL OFFENDERS

You have had an opportunity to examine all the theories associated with serial rape and sexual serial murder. The two cases in this section were chosen not for their notoriety but because of what they offer in terms of insight into the distorted cognitive processes and justifications of offenders. It is important to note that each offender is unique in his motivations. As you preview these two case studies, examine the theories and typologies to determine which will best fit each of these offenders.

CASE STUDY 3.3   SERIAL RAPE: FROM PEEPING TOM TO SERIAL RAPIST

Offender Thomas Franklin was born on February 5, 1958, and began his criminal history at the age of 18. He had no juvenile history; however, based on my experience, I have to believe that his deviant behavior started long before the age of 18, even though he was not arrested until then. From June 1976 through January 1980, he was arrested for loitering and prowling in the state of Florida twelve times. Loitering and prowling in the state of Florida means that a subject is usually out at night, lurking in the shadows, often between houses and cars, and casing property or even stalking. The charge allows police to act in a preemptive capacity to prevent crime if the elements of loitering and prowling are met. In 1980, Franklin was arrested twice for burglary; both times the charge was reduced to trespass, and he was released after serving 75 days and paying a fine of $157.

The cycle started all over again from May 1980 to August 1982, during which time Franklin was arrested eight more times for loitering and prowling, all misdemeanors with minimal time served. There were several misdemeanor charges from 1986 to 1990, including two burglaries that were reduced to misdemeanors. In 1990, Franklin graduated to robbery, which he pleaded down to a lesser charge of grand theft and for which he served 163 days in the county jail and was then released.

It wasn't until 1996 that the skills Franklin had developed as a prowler and burglar were put to use with the following incidents and charges: August 17, 1996—burglary, battery, and sexual battery; March 10, 1997—burglary, battery, and sexual battery; July 28, 1997—burglary, battery, and sexual battery; August 5, 1997—burglary, assault, and sexual battery; and August 5, 1997—burglary, battery, and sexual battery. When asked why he raped the women, Franklin made the following statement: "I was convicted of robbery in 1990 and went to jail for a crime that I did not commit. While I was in jail I was mistreated by jail staff because they refused to allow me to have visitors and make phone calls."

Franklin's victims ranged in age from 67 to 90 years. The following statement regarding his first victim reveals his distorted thinking: "I was riding my bike [bicycle] at 3:00 A.M., and this dog was chasing me trying to bite. I parked my bike and went to catch the dog. The dog ran in a house and I followed him. I tried to grab the dog and fell on the lady. She *batterized* herself; that's how she got the bruises on her body." The victim stated that she was sleeping on the couch and was awakened by Franklin, who overpowered the victim by placing a pillow over her face and who penetrated her with his penis vaginally, then orally and vaginally, and then penetrated the victim's anus and vagina with his fingers. In addition to the sexual battery, Franklin stole the victim's purse (Thomas, 1998).

In assessing Franklin's criminal history in Case Study 3.3, it is interesting to note that he had an extensive history of loitering and prowling. As noted previously, these are precursors to other behavior. It is my belief that those arrests do not reflect all his habitual offending, but only the times he was caught by police, and that his behavioral pattern indicates he was habitual offender long before he committed the rapes. The problem is that loitering and prowling are considered misdemeanor crimes and are not tracked by police, as would be the case with felonies such as burglary. In addition, the courts had all but excused Franklin for all of his crimes, even the felonies, by dropping the charges or accepting pleas that lowered charges from felonies to misdemeanors.

Just think: Every time Franklin was caught, he was sentenced to serve one or two nights in jail, with no other penalty. I would argue that he developed a strong sense of entitlement that enhanced his distorted thinking, provided him with a sense of invincibility, and allowed him to move from the peeping Tom status and masturbation to rape. Franklin's mental health and medical records were not available due to Health Insurance Portability and Accountability Act (HIPPA) laws; however, I did assess him to determine if he was a psychopath. Based on the results obtained from *Hare Psychopathy Checklist—Revised (PCL-R)*, his score indicated that he was a psychopath. One interesting note concerning Franklin although he knew that he was guilty and admitted to each of the rapes he demanded that he be tried for each individually. What purpose would this serve?

CASE STUDY 3.4   SEXUAL SERIAL KILLER: FROM RAPE VICTIM TO SEXUAL SERIAL KILLER

Offender Glen Register was born on May 28, 1959, and described himself as a loner and one who was lost at the age of 6 after his father died. He said that he first began to run from place to place to get away from his sadness, and later continued to move from place to place because he was not accepted; he had HIV and stated that he was forced out of every town he tried to live in. He described that everyone he thought to be a friend just wanted him for one thing (sex), and once they got what they wanted, they disowned him. He says that he was brutally raped and provided the following in a written statement: "Do you know what it's like—be held down and having a dick jammed in your ass over and over and bleed for a week and try and hide it from everyone—or to have one [a dick] crammed down your throat, gagged out and choked unconscious?" (Register, 1999). As a result of the rape, he contracted HIV and became very angry, stating that he snapped at certain points.

Register's first homicide was committed in Ocala, Florida, on January 12, 1987. His modus operandi was to pick up males at local bars and go back to their place. He would get the victims drunk, and after he was done having sex, he would shower, take the top of the toilet tank from the toilet, and beat the victims in the head with the tank lid. His second attack was an attempted murder in Daytona Beach, Florida, on November 12, 1998, where he met the victim in a bar, went to a hotel room, had sex with the victim, took a shower, and beat the victim with the toilet tank lid. He admitted in a letter to detectives that he left the victim to die, but the victim was saved by the cleaning lady. Register stole the victim's pickup truck, credit cards, money, and a number of miscellaneous items.

On December 1, 1998, Register was in Pueblo, Colorado, hitchhiking, and was picked up by his next victim. They returned to the victim's home, had sex, and Register took a shower. Instead of using the toilet tank lid, Register used a short homemade night stick to beat the victim to death. In this incident, he stole the victim's car, credit cards, phone card, and money. This was the only victim to fight back.

On January 13, 1999, Register was back in Gainesville, Florida, where he picked up another victim at a bar. They stopped at a local liquor store, and then went to the victim's house and had sex. Register took a shower, and then he used both the toilet tank lid and a pool cue to beat the victim to death. Register stole the victim's car, credit cards, and checks.

After the offender in Case Study 3.4 was caught, Register admitted in his statement to several other murders, but none could be verified. He also stated: "If you want me to confess to any others, let me know, and I will on tape" (Register, 1999). Interestingly, he would not admit to the murder in Ocala; however, his signature (i.e., there was evidence of homosexual activity after which the suspect showered and used a toilet tank lid to commit the murder) was the only one ever submitted to the Violent Criminal Apprehension Program (ViCAP).

In examining Register's background, you can trace his road to becoming a killer and see how his response to his experiences was to victimize. He used alcohol to seduce his victims, each victim was homosexual, and he attacked each brutally. In this case, Register did not have an extensive criminal history: grand theft auto in 1979, aggravated assault in 1984, and possession of a firearm by a convicted felon in 1989. In each instance, he was sent to prison and served time; there were no plea deals. Register's mental health and medical records were not available because of HIPPA laws; however, I did assess him to determine if he was a psychopath. Based on the results of the *Hare Psychopathy Checklist—Revised (PCL-R)*, his score indicated that he was a psychopath.

CONCLUSION

The very idea of rape shocks the conscience of nearly all in a society. The question will always be: How someone can attack another human being and literally take the one thing that is so closely associated with his or her dignity—the right to refuse. If you review the reasons for the sexual assaults and the typologies of rapists and sexual serial killers, there is one thing missing: a sense of humanity. In addition, all the offenders lack empathy, just as the examples in this chapter did: Blackboy, who beat his victim into submission; the prowler who hunted his victims and forced the husbands to watch helplessly; Franklin, who claimed he raped because he was a victim of the criminal justice system; and Register, who was a victim of rape, had contracted HIV during the rape, and selected his victims out of anger and disgust—for him, it was pure revenge, with each victim acting as a surrogate.

When I reviewed each of these cases, it was like viewing the very essence of evil. Register was the only one that I understood. I often wonder if there is a way that we can identify these subjects before they become serial offenders. While in grad school, I examined ten sexual serial killers, ten serial rapists, and ten child molesters. I looked at their previous criminal histories to determine if there were indicators that could have predicted their future offending. I believed that if we could identify them through the use of psychological instruments, a preemptive strategy could be developed. What I found is that the instruments offer no insight into predicting future acts of sexual offending. With that in mind and understanding the impetuses for these crimes, I believe the only strategy is early intervention, since some the antisocial behaviors start appearing at an early age.

REFERENCES

Abel, G. G., & Rouleau, J. L. (1990). Male sex offenders. In M. E. Thase, B. A. Edelstein, & M. Hersen (Eds.), *Handbook of outpatient treatment of adults* (pp. 271–290). New York: Plenum.

American Psychiatric Association. (2000). *The diagnostic and statistical manual of mental disorders, IV-TR*, 4th ed. Arlington, VA: Author.

Beck, A. T. (1999). *Prisoners of hate: The cognitive basis of anger, hostility, and violence.* New York: HarperCollins.

Bert, V. K., & Stein, K. (2008). Treatment of women. In R. E. Hales, S. C. Yudofsky, & G. O. Gabbard (Eds.), *Textbook of psychiatry*, 5th ed. (pp. 1489–1528). Arlington, VA: American Psychiatry.

Blake, A. (2012, August 19). Todd Akin, GOP senate candidate: Legitimate rape rarely causes pregnancy. *Washington Post*, A1.

Canter, D. (1994). *Criminal shadows: Inside the mind of a serial killer.* London: HarperCollins.

Clarke, J., & Carter, A. (1999, September). *A typology of sexual murderers: Validation and application.* Paper presented at the Association for the Treatment of Sexual Abusers Conference, Orlando, FL.

Douglas, J. E., Burgess, A. W., Burgess, A. G., & Ressler, R. K. (2006). *Crime classification manual,* 2nd ed. San Francisco: Wiley.

Egger, S. A. (2002). *The killers among us: An examination of serial murder and its investigation.* Upper Saddle River, NJ: Prentice-Hall.

Federal Bureau of Investigation (FBI). (2011). *The uniform crime reports: National incident-based reporting system 2011.* Washington, D.C.: Author.

Frick, W. B. (1995). *Personality: Selected readings in theory.* Itasca, IL: F. E. Peacock.

Frijda, N. C., Manstead, A. S. R., & Bem, S. (2000). *Emotions and beliefs: How feelings influence thoughts.* New York: Cambridge University Press.

Freund, K. (1990). Courtship disorder. In W. L. Marshall, D. R. Laws, & H. E. Barberee (Eds.), *Handbook of sexual assault: Issues, theories and treatment of the offender* (pp. 195–207). New York: Plenum.

Gelles, R. J., & Straus, M. A. (1979). Violence in the American family. *Journal of Social Issues, 35*(2), pp. 15–39.

Gray, F. P. (1998). *At home with the Marquis De Sade.* New York: Penguin Books.

Groth, A. N., & Birnbaum, H. J. (1979). *Men who rape: The psychology of the offender.* New York: Plenum Press.

Hall, G. C. N., & Hisrchman, R. (1991). Toward a theory of sexual aggression: A quadripartite model. *Journal of Consulting and Clinical Psychology, 59*(5), pp. 662–669.

Hariton, E. B., & Singer, J. L. (1974). Women's fantasies during sexual intercourse: Normative and theoretical implications. *Journal of Consulting and Clinical Psychology, 42*(3), pp. 313–322.

Hobbs, T. (1886). *Leviathan or the matter, form and power of a commonwealth, ecclesiastical and civil,* 2nd ed. London: Routledge.

Keppel, R. D., & Birnes, W. J. (1997). *Signature killers: Interpreting the calling cards of the serial murderer.* New York: Pocket Books.

Krafft-Ebing, R. (1965). *Psychopathia sexualis: The classic study of deviant sex* (F. S. Klaff, Trans). New York: Arcade Publishing. (Original work 1894).

Lundin, R. W. (1989). *Alfred Adler's basic concepts and implications.* Levittown, PA: Accelerated Development.

Marion County Sheriff's Office. (2006). *Leo Boatman interview: Case number 06001267.* Ocala, FL: Author.

Marshall, W. L., Barbaree, H. E., & Eccles, A. (1991). Early onset and deviant sexuality in child molesters. *Journal of Interpersonal Violence, 6,* pp. 323–336.

Masters, W. H., Johnson, V. E., & Kolodny, R. C. (1998). *Masters and Johnson: Sex and human loving.* Mumbai, India: Jaico.

Meloy, R. (2000). *Violence risk and threat assessment.* San Diego: Specialized Training Services.

Milner, J. S., & Dopke, C. A. (1997). Paraphilia not otherwise specified: Psychopathology and theory. In D. R. Laws & W. O'Donohue (Eds.), *Sexual deviance: Theory, practice, and treatment* (pp. 424–434). New York: Guilford Press.

Palmero, G. B., & Farkas, M. A. (2013). *The dilemma of the sexual offender,* 2nd ed. Springfield, IL: Charles C. Thomas.

Parrish, K. (2012, January 20). *Panetta announces initiatives targeting sexual assault.* Retrieved August 28, 2013, from: http://www.army.mil/article/72243/

Pettinelli, M. (2008). *The psychology of emotions, feelings, and thoughts,* 3rd ed. Author.

Pithers, W., Beal, S., Armstrong, J., & Petty, J. (1989). Identification of risk factors through clinical interviews and analysis of records. In D. R. Laws (Ed.), *Relapse prevention with sex offenders* (pp. 77–87). New York: Guilford.

Prentky, R. A., Burgess, A. W., Rokous, F., Lee, A., Hartman, C., Ressler, R., & Douglas, J. (1989). The presumptive role of fantasy in serial sexual homicide. *American Journal of Psychiatry, 146*(7), pp. 887–891.

Purcell, C. E., & Arrigo, B. A. (2006). *The psychology of lust murder: Paraphilia, sexual killing and serial homicide.* New York: Academic Press.

Register, G. R. (1999). *Gainesville Police Department sex crimes files: Letter to detectives.* Gainesville, FL: Author.

Reinisch, J. M., & Beasley, R. (1991). *The Kinsey Institute new report on sex.* New York: St. Martin's Press.

Ressler, R. K., Burgess, A. W., & Douglas, J. E. (1995). *Sexual homicide: Patterns and motives.* New York: Lexington Books.

Roys, D. T. (2005). The emotional world of the sexual offender: Does it matter? In B. K. Schwartz (Ed.), *The sex offender: Issues in assessment, treatment, and supervision of adult and juvenile populations* (pp. 2-2 to 2-20). Kingston, NJ: Civic Research Press.

Salters, A. C. (2003). *Predators: Pedophiles, rapists, and other sex offenders: Who they are, how they operate, and how we can protect ourselves and our children.* New York: Basic Books.

Schlesinger, L. B. (2008). Compulsive repetitive offenders: Behavioral patterns, motivational dynamics. In R. N. Kocsis (Ed.), *Serial murder and the psychology of violent crime* (pp. 15–34). Totowa, NJ: Humana Press.

Terry, K. J. (2005). *Sexual offenses and offenders: Theory, practice, and policy.* Belmont, CA: Thomson Wadsworth.

Thomas, D. (1982). *Grand Rapids Police sex crimes files.* Grand Rapids, MI: Author.

Thomas, D. (1994). *Gainesville Police Department sex crimes files*. Gainesville, FL: Author.

Thomas, D. (1998). *Volusia County Sheriff's Department sex crimes files*. Daytona Beach, FL: Author.

West, D. J. (1987). *Sexual crimes and confrontations: A study of victims and offenders*. Brookfield, VT: Gower.

Widom, C. S. (1992). *The cycle of violence*. Washington, D.C.: U.S. Department of Justice, National Institute of Justice.

Wille, W. S. (1974). *Citizens who commit murder*. St. Louis, MO: Warren H. Green.

Yochelson, S., & Samenow, S. (1976). *The criminal personality: A profile of change*. Northvale, NJ: Jason Aronson.

Crimes Against Children

When I started this project, I was aware that children are victims of crimes far too many times and that those who are supposed to be their protectors are usually the violators. During my career as a law enforcement officer, I spent a great deal of time investigating crimes against children that were horrible. In the previous chapters, I outlined the impact of negative environments on personality development: The end result is the creation of monsters.

This chapter addresses sex crimes against children. I separated discussion of these crimes from that of adult sex crimes and predators because I want you, as a reader, to understand the nature of the problem. In addition, any discussion of serial rapists and sexual serial killers in the same context with sex crimes against children diminishes the importance of these crimes against children because of the sensational interest in serial crimes.

Much of this text so far has been focused on the long-term impact of family violence on the developmental features of a child's personality, so in this chapter we will not revisit the issue of family violence per se. We will, however, examine the theories associated with sex crimes against children, including the predators' justifications, the typologies of hunters, and their predatory behaviors.

ETIOLOGY OF SEXUAL OFFENSES AGAINST CHILDREN

In the previous chapters, I have argued that our personality deficits are directly related to three systems that intersect: environmental, psychological, and biological. This view is also known as a biopsychosocial model. Each of these systems interacts with the others; in many instances, we have no idea to what degree unless we have been diagnosed with a disorder such as schizophrenia, which is biologically based.

As you might guess, there are a number of theories about why some choose to victimize children. As I have done in previous chapters, I will provide you with a discussion of some of these theories and let you decide which ones work best for you. Again, case studies are provided as a reference for you to use in examining the various theories.

The Biopsychosocial Model

Ward and Beech (2005) offered an integrated theory of sexual offending that explains the biopsychosocial model in detail. These authors argued that human behavior and psychopathology requires four levels of analysis:

1. Influence of genetic and environmental factors
2. Brain development and function, which are influenced by genetics and may predispose a subject to psychopathology, and environmental factors, which may exacerbate any genetic condition
3. Neuropsychological systems, which are the brain-based systems responsible for human behavior
4. Symptomology, meaning that if the integrated systems are abnormally affected, the end result will be some form of psychopathology (p. 48)

Using the research of Pennington (2002) and Luria (1966), Ward and Beech also argued that the central nervous system is divided into three systems with distinct functions: motivation/emotional, perception/memory, and action selection and control (p. 48). When these systems function abnormally, some of the common issues discovered upon examination are lack of emotional regulation, cognitive distortions, social and relationship difficulties, and deviant sexual arousal. Each of these issues was discussed in Chapter 3.

The Conditioning or Modeling Process

Another theory is known as conditioning or modeling process. Theorists who hold this view have argued that the relationship between children and sexual excitement by adults is a learned condition response. The behavior is associated with an experience the offender may have had in childhood with an adult. The behavior is learned, and as a result, the child's fantasy is associated with other children. Since this is the model to which they were introduced, during masturbation, these people as adults become fixated on children and associate pleasure and orgasm with the image of a child (McGuire, Carlisle, & Young, 1965).

Laws and Marshall (1990) argued that deviant behavior is learned through the same mechanisms by which traditional sexual behavior is learned, which supports the theory presented by McGuire et al. (1965). The Laws and Marshall theory is closely associated with the concept of *operant conditioning,* which is a system of learning that is reinforced through reward and punishment. Skinner (1953) argued that the only way to determine if an event has been reinforced is to see whether there is a change in the frequency of the event. Skinner described two types of reinforcers:

- *Adding something,* which is *positive reinforcement* and is associated with food, water, and sexual contact
- *Removing something,* which is *negative reinforcement* and can be associated with that which makes us uncomfortable, such as loud noises, bright lights, extreme cold or heat, and electric shock

If a child is taught that another child is an object of desire by an adult and that behavior is positively reinforced through praise, fantasy, masturbation, and ultimately orgasm, then it is easy to see how this behavior could be viewed as normal by the individual, even though this belief system is contrary to social norms. It is through this process that deviant sexual preferences and cognitions are developed. It is similar to the process by which conventional thoughts regarding human sexuality are developed.

This argument is supported by Seligman (1971) and by Mineka and Ohman (2002), both of which argue that behavior is learned and theorize that when one is exposed to unprepared conditioning/fear as opposed to prepared conditioning/learning, the unprepared exposure has greater impact on one's psyche. In fact, the impact of unprepared learning is so great, the learning can be acquired in one trial when speaking of grooming or the sexual act; may well be reinforced with praise, encouragement, fantasy, and/or pleasure; is selective in nature, meaning that we chose to accept or reject it; is contingent on the nature of the reinforcements, either positive or negative; is resistant to extinction; and may be noncognitive, meaning that it is associated with our basic needs as described in Maslow's hierarchy of needs. When associated with the physiological needs, the learning becomes embedded in the amygdala, which is responsible for the basic instincts and needs of human beings.

When associated with sexual deviance, the process of conditioning is also associated with maintenance. Laws and Marshall (1990) asserted that reinforcement of sexual deviance can be found in acts of autoerotica; here, offenders condition themselves to be responsive to certain stimuli by combining fantasy and masturbation with focus on a potential or actual victim (p. 223).

Correlation Between Childhood Sexual Abuse and Sexual Offending Against Children

A third theory holds that there is a correlation between childhood sexual abuse and physical and sexual offending against children. Seto (2008) argued that there is evidence to suggest a strong link between childhood sexual abuse and pedophilia. Seto noted the following research findings: Sex offenders who were sexually abused were more likely to admit to being aroused by children; adolescent sex offenders who were sexually abused showed greater arousal toward children when assessed photometrically; sexual abuse histories are correlated among adult and juvenile sex offenders as having boy victims; and sexual abuse history is associated with having multiple child victims (p. 104).

Widom (1992) argued that a childhood history of physical child abuse predisposes the survivor to violence in later years, and the victims are more likely to engage in violent behavior. After examining and following 908 cases, Widom noted that childhood victims of sexual abuse were not at greater risk of being arrested for rape or sodomy; however, those who were physically abused showed a greater tendency toward the crimes of rape and/or sodomy (p. 6). It is important to note the limitation of Widom's study in that it was based on official arrest records, and therefore addressed only cases in which an arrest had been made.

One long-standing argument is that those who sexually abuse children were victims in their youth. Salters (2003), however, argued that the numbers are so varied, there is no consistency, and no correlation has been found; depending on the study, the numbers range from as low as 22 percent to as high as 82 percent. You might wonder why such a disparity exists. It is because in most instances, the data sets were collected from those who were incarcerated and self-reporting (p. 73). As discussed throughout this book, offenders look for a way to justify their behavior and not take responsibility for their actions; in this case, they are often trying to obtain empathy from treating clinicians. Of all the criminals I have encountered over the years as a police officer, this group is the best at manipulation (an issue that will be discussed in detail later).

From society's point of view, we want to understand how child sexual abuse can occur, and we are willing to accept that which is logical. It seems logical that there would be a correlation between being a sexual abuse victim as a child and becoming an adult predator. Evidence for this correlation, however, is not clear-cut.

TYPOLOGIES OF CHILD SEXUAL PREDATORS

Groth and Birnbaum (1978) completed a study of 175 males convicted of sexual assault against children. Upon completion of the study, they were able to create two classifications of those who offend against children: fixated and regressed. A fixated offender is defined as someone who since adolescence has a maintained a sexual preference for prepubescent children and for whom peer-appropriate sexual relationships have been unsuccessful because of the offender's attraction to those who are underage. A regressed offender is one who looks to a child because his or her intimate relationships with mature age-appropriate peers have failed. The regressed offender has not developed a preference for children, and his or her primary interest is in age-appropriate or mature relationships.

Lanning (2010) has argued that criminal behavior is too fluid to be pinned down in two or three categories. This author believes that the motivations of child sexual offenders are better placed on a continuum. At the far left of the continuum, offenders are motivated at the base level of human existence: biological or physiological needs, and the gratification of those needs is primarily related to power or anger and is nonsexual in nature. On the far right of the continuum, the behavior is driven by a psychosexual/deviant need, and the gratification is sexual in nature.

Lanning described two classifications of offenders, situational and preferential, with the understanding that each can cross over to become the other type at any given point in time. The situational offender is seen as an opportunist, with the act being reactive, while the acts of the preferential sex offender are seen as being predatory in nature, with the aggression being both planned and purposeful (Lanning, 2010, p. 33). Lanning's descriptions are very similar to the reactive and predatory behavior patterns described in Chapter 3 that were associated with serial rapists and sexual serial killers.

Knight, Carter, and Prentky (1989) developed another system that is used to classify child molesters in a clinical setting; it is known as the Massachusetts Treatment Center: Child Molester Typology, version 3 (MTC:CMT3). This system has been validated by other researchers. The MTC:CMT3 evaluates the offender with information that is applied to categories called Axis I and Axis II. It should be noted that these are not the same clinical axes used in diagnosing patients with the *Diagnostic and Statistical Manual of Mental Disorders, IV-TR* (*DSM-IV-TR;* American Psychiatric Association, 2000). Rather, these axes are used to classify subjects based on their predatory crimes against children and to assist in treatment protocols and prediction of recidivism once released.

Axis I has two components: degree of fixation on a child and level of social competence. There are four typologies in this axis: *Type 0* is high fixation/

low social competence, *Type 1* is high fixation/high social competence, *Type 2* is low fixation/low social competence, and *Type 3* is low fixation/high social competence. Axis II describes a series of decisions associated with offender types: *Type I* is the interpersonal offender, who attempts to establish a relationship with a child that is not sexually exclusive; *Type II* is the narcissistic offender, who seeks contact with children for the purpose of sexual gratification. In addition, offenders are judged based on the amount of contact, either high or low, and the nature of injury, which also is classified as high or low. A final consideration is whether there is evidence of sexual sadism (Knight et al., 1989, pp. 14–15).

Among the classification systems offered, I keep coming back to a comment by Salters (2003), who noted that, regardless of how we classify them, this is what we know about child sexual predators: Some are sexually attracted to children; others molest because they are antisocial or psychotic and feel entitled; others use children to fill a void due to a lack of competence or social skills; and others molest for an unknown reason (p. 75). Although the information given in this text offers insight into the offender, there is no clear-cut path by which one becomes a predator of children.

VICTIMIZATION OF CHILDREN

The numbers concerning the rate at which children are victims of sexual assault are sketchy at best, and the behaviors vary, as we will discuss later. The data from the Federal Bureau of Investigation (FBI) in its *Uniform Crime Reports 2011* (FBI, 2011) detail all sexual assaults, providing both general and specific information regarding the children and the offenders. As you move from general to specific, it is important to note that our children are under attack from every possible source, with the Internet becoming the most powerful tool for those who prey on children.

In 2011, there were 64,382 reported incidents that were classified as forcible sex crimes committed in the United States; of those incidents, there were 69,356 offenses, 69,356 victims, and 67,550 of the offenders known (FBI, 2011). There are four categories of forcible sex crimes: rape, sodomy, sexual assault with an object, and fondling. In addition to the forcible sex offenses, there were a number of nonforcible sex offenses, which have two categories: incest and statutory rape. In 2011, under the category of incest, there were 1,034 reported incidents; of those incidents, there were 1,152 offenses committed, and 1,071 known offenders. In the category of statutory rape, there were 5,343 reported incidents, with 5,613 incidents, 5,613 victims, and 5,662 known offenders (FBI, 2011). One cautionary note:

As you view the FBI data, keep in mind that these are only the incidents reported to the police.

The most common victim profile is a white female, age 15 or under; the rate of incidents in many categories is on average two times greater for white than for black females. In the areas of forcible rape and forcible fondling, white female adolescents aged 15 and under were victimized at a rate four times of that of black females in the same age group (FBI, 2011). One factor not revealed in the statistics is cultural differences between whites and blacks. Members of the black community do not report acts of rape and violence as often as whites for a number of reasons: shame and embarrassment, a lack of trust in the police, and a belief that the matter is personal.

In 2011, the most common offender for each category was in the following age bracket: forcible rape, between the ages of 16 and 30; forcible sodomy, age 15 and under and 16 to 20 years of age; rape with an object, age 15 and under and 16 to 20 years of age; forcible fondling, age 15 and under and 16 to 20 years of age; statutory rape, ages 16 to 25; and incest, age 15 and under, 16 to 20 years of age, and 31 to 40 years of age (FBI, 2011).

Snyder (2000) examined data sets from the National Incident-Based Reporting System (NIBRS) from twelve states for the years 1991 through 1996 and offered observations regarding the age and sex of the victims, the nature of the offenses, and the offender profile based on age. Snyder noted that juveniles accounted for 66 percent of all the victims of all the sexual assaults utilized in the study. The breakdown of percentages of victims by age in each category is as follows:

- *Forcible rape:* Between the ages of 12 and 17, 33 percent; between the ages of 6 and 11, 8 percent; and between 0 and 5 years of age, 4 percent
- *Forcible sodomy:* Between the ages of 12 and 17, 24 percent; between the ages of 6 and 11, 31 percent; and between the ages of 0 and 5, 24 percent
- *Sexual assault with an object:* Between the ages of 12 and 17, 25 percent; between the ages of 6 and 11, 30 percent; and between the ages of 0 and 5, 26 percent
- *Forcible fondling:* Between the ages of 12 and 17, 34 percent; between the ages of 6 and 12, 29 percent; and between the ages of 0 and 5, 20 percent (p. 2)

In contrast to the number of juvenile victims in this study, juveniles accounted for a small percentage of the offenders in the sexual assault categories listed earlier. For all the sexual assaults committed between 1991 and 1996, juvenile offenders were responsible for only 23.2 percent of them, whereas adults were responsible for 76.8 percent (Snyder, 2000, p. 8).

The largest study to date on nonincarcerated paraphiliacs was completed in 1987 by Abel and colleagues. That study provided great insight into the nature of offenders who are diagnosed with a range of paraphilias, which are not limited to sex crimes against children. The data sets collected enabled the researchers to develop a classification system for sex offenders that has been validated and supported by other researchers. As noted earlier, the Abel study was the first of its kind to collect data from nonincarcerated paraphiliacs; there were 561 participants. There are limitations to studies based on self-reports; however, in this case, none of the participants were under court order or awaiting trial. To avoid the possibility of having to report for violations of the law, the offenders were not allowed to offer details regarding any specific crime or crimes and were limited to answering questions regarding frequency, age, victim preference, and gender.

In the Abel study (Abel et al., 1987), the 561 offenders were responsible for a staggering 291,737 paraphilic acts against 195,407 victims (p. 19). There were five major categories in regard to victims and the nature of paraphilias:

a. *Pedophilia nonincestuous*

  1. *Female victims:* 224 of the offenders committed 5,197 acts against 4,435 victims. The data indicate that some victims were victimized more than one time.

  2. *Male victims:* 153 of the offenders committed 43,100 acts against 22,981 victims. The data indicate that the victims were victimized more than once.

b. *Pedophilia incest*

  1. *Female victims:* 159 of the offenders committed 12,927 acts against 286 victims. The data indicate that some victims were victimized more than one time.

  2. *Male victims:* 44 of the offenders committed 2,741 acts against 75 victims. The data indicate that the victims were victimized more than once.

c. *Rape* was reported as nongender-specific: 126 offenders committed 907 rapes against 882 victims. The data indicate that some victims were victimized more than one time.

Note that researchers have reported that rapists have three or more paraphilias besides rape (Abel & Rouleau, 1990; Freund, 1990). Abel and colleagues reported similar findings in this study, with each offender reporting at least two paraphilias. In addition, in this Abel study, many of the offenders reported more than one paraphilic offense, and each was recorded separately.

CASE STUDY 4.1   BIRTHDAY PARTY AND RAPE

Eunice Thomas was celebrating her 35th birthday and invited a number of friends over to celebrate. Ms. Thomas had two daughters, Tiffany age 6 and Samantha age 3. The last guest left at 2:00 A.M. It was then that Tiffany came out and pulled on Eunice's skirt. Eunice thought Tiffany wanted one of three things: something to drink, some comfort because she'd had a bad dream, or to go to the bathroom. Getting a drink was a ploy Tiffany used when she was excited and did not want to sleep. Eunice gave Tiffany a cup of water and ordered her back to bed. On this night, however, Tiffany's behavior was not usual; she hugged Eunice's leg and started crying, which Tiffany rarely did even when she had experienced a bad dream.

When Eunice asked Tiffany if she'd had a bad dream or was afraid of a monster again, Tiffany said, "No, mommy." Eunice asked her again, and Tiffany began pulling Eunice by the hand to the bedroom. Finally, when Eunice insisted on an answer, Tiffany said, "Marvin is in the bed with Samantha." Eunice was puzzled at first because Marvin had left the house at 11:00 P.M., long before the last guest left, but then became enraged, grabbed a baseball bat, went into the girl's bedroom, and found Marvin having anal intercourse with Samantha.

The police responded to a call at 2:30 that morning and found a woman beating a man with a baseball bat in the middle of the street. The responding officers arrested Marvin Turner for *sexual battery* and several other charges. Samantha was transported to the hospital where she underwent surgery to repair internal injuries and recovered.

In the interview at the station, Marvin stated that he had known Eunice since high school and they had been friends forever. In fact, he stated that they had dated for a while, and then Eunice left him. He also stated that when Eunice left him, she started dating another guy and got pregnant—not once, but twice—and that those little girls should have been his. So, on this night, he set out to hurt Eunice like she had hurt him and that is why he raped the little girl. His final comment was: "Both will be scarred for life, just like I am. Eunice, because she will never look at her daughter the same, and the little girl because I will have been her first. I am happy now" (Thomas, 1984).

CASE STUDY 4.2   BOYFRIEND SEXUALLY ASSAULTS GIRLFRIEND'S CHILD

Damon McGee had been dating the victim's mother for approximately one year. The child was a 4-year-old boy, and the mother would leave him with McGee when she went to work. Police responded to a call from hospital personnel, who reported what they believed to be child abuse. Their patient was a 4-year-old victim who was bleeding from the rectum, and there were other injuries consistent with child abuse.

When police interviewed the victim, he stated that every time his mom would leave the house to run short errands or go to work, McGee would beat him, slamming him against the bed and the floor, as well as choking him until he could not breathe. In addition to the beatings, McGee would sexually assault the victim anally by inserting his penis or foreign objects into the victim's rectum.

During the interview with the mother, she stated that the victim always had some bruising, but she thought it was because he fell. She noted that he was rough and played rough. When asked if the victim ever acted withdrawn, she said no, but she commented that there were days when he was lethargic; she had thought that he did not feel good or was moody. She also stated that she never noticed any injuries on the victim other than the bruises for which there was always a logical explanation. It was not until the victim complained when he went to the bathroom that she discovered blood in the victim's stool and underwear.

The 4-year-old victim made the following statement concerning the suspect: "My dreams were for Damon to go to jail; that was my only dream" (Swirko, 2013).

CYBERSPACE

The two greatest inventions in the last fifty years have been the personal computer and the Internet. With all their advantages, these two inventions have provided an outlet for child sexual predators and paraphiliacs by giving them the ability to target, hunt, and engage unsuspecting juveniles.

Questions for Reflection: What skill set might an Internet child molester use to initiate a relationship with a child? Do these molesters use similar techniques and follow the same patterns, or are they all different in their approach?

We are constantly reminded that cyberspace predators are out there hunting our children, but do we really know what we are up against? Wolak, Finkelhor, and Mitchell (2004) argued that whatever stereotype you might have about cyberspace child molesters, it is probably a misconception. This is especially true if you believe that these offenders use trickery and/or violence to sexually assault children. They are wilier than that. The one thing I have learned about this group from my experience in law enforcement is that these offenders are cunning, conniving, and convincing.

How prevalent is the problem? Fortunately, there has been a decline over the years. In 2000, online solicitations were approximately 19 percent of offenses, but in 2006, they were 13 percent (Finkelhor, Mitchell, & Wolak, 2000; Wolak et al., 2004). Of course, even one is too many. Also in 2006, approximately 81 percent of the recipients of such solicitations were between the ages of 14 and 17.

Researchers have provided some interesting insights into the problem of sexual solicitation of youth on the Internet. The perpetrators of Internet sex crimes are typically adult men who meet their victims online and seduce them through the spoken (or, in this case, typed) word. What this means is that the offender finds a way to meet a need—something that the child is missing. Most often this is attention or affection. If we recall Bowlby's (1940) discussion on attachment, we are reminded that relationship is something that all humans yearn for. Offenders foster the relationship in chat rooms and through e-mail and instant messaging.

Anyone who has thought that the main ploy of Internet predators is trickery—and that therefore their kids would never fall for such solicitations—should note that Wolak and colleagues (2004) found that only 5 percent of the offenders pretended to be teens. It is not trickery, but the attention that the teen receives, which is associated with romantic notions and the expectation that there will be some form of sexual encounter, that sways the children. To support the concept of willingness, Malesky (2005) noted than one half of the girls in his study described being in love or having a close relationship with an adult. Thus, these relationships are based not on trickery, but on consent, although a teen cannot give consent to an adult, and therefore they do fall under the statutory rape laws.

Online Child Pornography

One area in which all researchers agree is the fact that there is a correlation between child pornography and pedophilia. However, little research has been done in this area. Seto, Cantor, and Blanchard (2006) examined some 685 forensic patients utilizing a "penile plethysmograph," which is essentially a lie detector for sex offenders measuring the blood flow to the penis and sexual arousal based on the presentation of still pictures. The patients were separated into nine groups, and each group was presented with child pornography. The following were the most interesting groups:

- Offenders with no history of child sexual abuse
- Offenders who had been convicted of one sexual offense against one child
- Offenders who had been convicted of two sexual offenses against children
- Offenders who had been convicted of three sexual offenses against children

Oddly both groups—those who had never committed a crime against children and those who had done so—responded to the pictures of children. The authors argued that child pornography offending is a valid indicator of pedophilia. They also argued that child pornography offenders were more likely to show pedophilic arousal than groups of offenders who have actually committed sexual offenses against children (p. 613).

In reviewing other literature, the numbers are inconclusive regarding the use of child pornography as a precursor to the commission of a sex crime against a child. However, it is clear that child pornography is ever available and ever abundant, and that there are different categories of pictures. This is an issue for the police when reviewing child pornography, since identifying the nature or intent of the photographs can determine what they do with the material.

Taylor, Holland, and Quayle (2001) argued that pictures of children should be placed on a continuum, noting that some parents take pictures of their children in swimsuits, underwear, or even naked with no suggestion of erotica, while other pictures are clearly designed to evoke adult sexual interests. Taylor and colleagues noted that the Combating Paedophile Information Networks in Europe (COPINE) Project examined more than 80,000 photographs and classified them in the following ten categories to indicate whether or not they were considered erotic:

- Nudist pictures taken in legitimate situations, such as a taking a bath or leaving the swimming pool
- Erotic surreptitiously taken photos of kids in play areas in underwear or varying degrees of nakedness
- Deliberate posing in varying degrees of clothing or naked suggesting sexual interest
- Erotic deliberate posing where a child is provocative or sexualized
- Explicit erotic emphasis is placed on genitals
- Explicit involving touching or some sexual activity (masturbation, oral sex, intercourse) not involving an adult
- Assault: children being subjected to a sexual assault, digital touching involving an adult

- Gross assault or obscenity

- Sexual assault, involving penetration, masturbation, and/or oral sex with an adult

- Sadistic: child tied, bound, bestiality, and/or beaten (Taylor et al., 2001, p. 101)

Reading some of the Internet porn case files that I have received from investigators, along with the confessions, has been enough to make me feel sick. Here are some titles of short video clips of child porn that have been passed from one offender to the next:

- 2 cute 12yo Preteen Gay Boys Strip to Naked Nude Close Up View Playing with Cute Boners and Balls Pedo Young Child Sex

- 12 yo boy fucks 12 yo girl kiddie pedo boy Lolita

- 2 cute little boys having fun child porn pre-teen

As you review these titles, think about what victimization means, and what it took to get these kids to perform such sex acts.

CHILD SEX OFFENDERS: TECHNIQUES AND CHARACTERISTICS

Seto (2008) stated that there is distinct difference between pedophiles and nonpedophilic offenders. Pedophiles are likely to have boy victims, multiple victims, prepubescent victims, and unrelated victims. These findings are supported by Abel and colleagues. In contrast, nonpedophilic offenders are more likely to have girl victims, single victims, pubescent victims, and related victims (p. 63). Finally sex offenders of children use different techniques that include grooming, gifts, threats, attention, or force/coercion.

The Grooming Process

Grooming is undoubtedly one of the best-known skill sets that offenders use. This tactic can be used online as well as in face-to-face encounters. The process of grooming involves several stages:

- *Selecting the target:* Here the offender obtains an understanding of the child and the dynamics necessary to gain access to the child. If the grooming is taking place face-to-face, then the offender—whether a boyfriend, relative, or acquaintance—will need to gain the confidence of the family or family members. If it is done online, then the offender has access to the child.

The offender also determines the child's needs. Most often the child suffers from low self-esteem, has not received attention from his or her parents, is lonely, or has been a victim of child/sexual abuse.

- *Developing a strategy to interact and break down the barriers that family members and the child may have:* Often this is easier than one would think because the caregiver's attention is diverted due to work or relationship problems. Earlier in the text I described the process of fantasy that offenders use. I argue that children who feel neglected also use this process, which makes them vulnerable to outsiders who offer attention or some sort of enticement.

- *Initiating the strategy:* This includes addressing any needs or questions caregivers may have. Here trust is gained, and the caregiver and child are lured into the offender's trap. A number of techniques are used to gain the confidence of a child. One technique is to assume a role that people in society normally view as trustworthy, for example, teacher, coach, minister, martial arts instructor, scout master, and the like. We can no longer assume these people are safe; everyone is suspect. Coach Sandusky is an example; because he was a football coach with Penn State University's football program and had a youth foundation, parents and children alike trusted him, which allowed him to target, strategize, and victimize a number of young boys (Freeh, Sporkin, & Sullivan, 2012).

- *Isolating the child once trust is gained:* This involves convincing the child that the offender is the only one who cares. Behavior is reinforced through gifts, praise, violence, threats, and/or intimidation.

- *Moving into the courtship period:* In the courtship stage, the offender gradually moves the relationship from friendship to sex, which may begin with fondling and kissing, with a sexual relationship being the ultimate goal. The offender may introduce the victim to alcohol or other drugs to lower the victim's inhibitions.

- *Initiating a sexual relationship:* Once the target is comfortable, the offender moves from touching to a sexual relationship. The offender gains control of the child and the relationship by doing this, and gains confidence that he or she can control the sexual component without being discovered.

- *Maintaining the relationship:* There are two primary goals at this stage—to maintain the relationship and to avoid detection. Maintenance is accomplished by reinforcing the behavior with gifts, praise, threats, and the use or abuse of substances such as alcohol. In some instances, these relationships have lasted for years, especially in cases of incest. In addition, there have been a number of incest cases where a father has moved from one daughter to the next as each reaches a certain age.

Use of Deception

The greatest tool that a child sex offender has is deception. In fact, these offenders are some of the most convincing liars I have ever seen. If an offender has been released from prison, the conditions of probation/parole are therapy once weekly, meetings with the probation/parole officer as required, and random polygraphs. Group therapy is great because the group forces individuals to admit to their offender history. The great equalizer, however, is the threat of random polygraphs, which keeps offenders on the straight and narrow.

Although there are great benefits to the polygraph, be aware that the polygraph is only as good as the polygrapher. In addition, because the offender's crimes are based on distorted cognitive patterns and belief systems, an offender may well be able to deceive the polygrapher and the instrument through denial and minimization. Some of the statements that I have heard over the years from offenders include:

- It wasn't that bad.
- She wanted it; all I did was follow her lead.
- It's not my fault.
- I was just loving her like any grandfather would.
- It was the alcohol.
- I'm bipolar, and that is what caused this.

Because of these belief systems, sex offenders are able to manipulate the results of the polygraph. This is compounded when the polygrapher does not ask specific questions concerning a specific incident. If generalized questions are used—such as "In the last three months, have you had sexual contact with any juveniles?"—an offender may answer with a statement similar to those listed earlier; if he or she really believes it, the response will likely not show deception.

Currently, two polygraph methods are in use: the Post-Conviction Sex Offender Polygraph Test (PCSOT), which verifies sex offender self-reporting, and the Comparison Question Technique or Control Question Test (CQT), which is used by law enforcement and focuses on a specific incident or crime. Meijer, Verschuere, Merckelbach, & Crombez (2008) noted that each of these methods, when used as a sole source, is not effective, and the CQT cannot be effective because it is designed to address specific incidents, meaning that the polygrapher must already have an idea of the infraction or incident. Without this knowledge, CQT is on a fishing expedition, asking generalized questions.

In contrast, Abrams and Abrams (2003) argued that there are three points when sex offenders can self-disclose prior to taking a polygraph: when advised that they will be taking a polygraph at some time in the future; during the pretest interview with the polygrapher, which gives the offender every opportunity to disclose so the admissions can be accounted for in the examination;

and after the test, when reviewing the results. Grubin, Madsen, Parsons, Sosnowski, and Warberg (2004) determined that in most cases, the information was disclosed during the preinterview, which means that it is not the polygraph that prompts disclosure, but rather fear of the instrument and the potential consequences if the offender is found to be deceptive during the examination.

Salters (2003) noted that sex offenders are great liars because they have been living a lie all their lives. Their distorted thoughts and their ability to minimize are forms of self-protection because they realize that they have to protect themselves from society and how society views them. Even in a prison setting, sex offenders are quick to point out that their charges cannot be discussed in front of other inmates, meaning that they have constructed a lie to survive. Salters stated that there are two instances when one can detect a deception: (1) when the liar contradicts himself or herself and (2) when the liar says things that the listener discovers from outside sources are not true (p. 196). Another method of detection is the reading of the offender's body language, which is described as emotional leakage.

Lack of Empathy

The worst personality deficit of offenders is their lack of empathy. While doing therapy with inmates, it became clear to me that they could lie about their offending at the drop of hat. When they did discuss their crimes, they displayed little or no empathy toward their victims and would strive to make me believe that everything that happened was not their fault.

In interviews I conducted with sixty-seven child sex offenders, they all stated that the reason they turned to the child in their households was because their relationships with their significant other had failed. In almost every interview, the offenders stated that the child gave them unconditional love whereas the women no longer communicated with them. In addition, when the offenders were asked to write a letter to their victims and apologize, none expressed empathy for their victims; the letters were all about the offenders and their needs. What I learned is that these offenders felt a strong sense of entitlement and felt that they had a right to use the victim as a surrogate because their spouse or significant other created the problem.

The fact that the offenders lacked empathy is not unusual, because those who are diagnosed with a personality disorder usually demonstrate a lack of empathy. However, what I did notice is that when the offenders complained about issues at work or about a probation officer or a prison guard, each of the group participants had the ability to show and express empathy. Covell and Scalora (2002) support my observations and offer a model that consists of four constructs that are interrelated and responsive to each other, yet markedly different:

- Perspective taking, which allows offenders to put themselves in the place of another
- Fantasy, or the ability to recognize and place themselves in fictitious situations in the media and entertainment
- Empathetic concern, including the experience of sympathy for others in distressing situations
- Personal distress, which does not allow personal experiences of distress and anxiety to interfere when experiencing another's emotional state (p.254)

CASE STUDY 4.3 ROOMMATE

Frank Smith was a 40-year-old white male who was on disability. He was homosexual. In interviews, he stated that he had been homosexual since the age of 10 or 11 and that his sexual preference had been young boys since the age of 12. It is interesting to note that he was sexually assaulted weekly by his priest for approximately three years between the ages 11 and 13. The priest would have Frank perform fellatio in the beginning, and later it evolved to the priest having anal sex with Frank. Frank stated that he was sworn to secrecy; the priest would seal the deal by stating, "This is your godly duty, and if you tell anyone, God will punish you and your family." Frank was afraid, and ultimately that is why he stopped being an altar boy.

Frank stated that he had his first consensual sexual experience with another boy at the age of 13. He described it as magical. When he described his first sexual experience, his face became flushed and he looked like a school boy in love reliving the experience. His passion for young boys did not change even as an adult. However, he was aware that he could go to prison for sexual activity with a minor, so to avoid jail, Frank's target group was 18-year-old boys who looked 12, with very little facial and body hair.

Frank described his past relationships as being failures. He wanted love, and he believed that his relationships should be similar to his first sexual experience. To keep his partners happy, Frank bought them anything and everything they wanted, thinking material things would make them stay. He realized that, in each instance, his lovers had used him and then left. Frank became frustrated and had the idea that if he could find a family with a young boy of 12 or 13, he could groom the boy and get the boy to love him; then Frank would have a lover for life.

Frank knew a couple who were having financial and marital problems; they also had an 11-year-old boy. Frank offered a solution to the couple: Let him move in and he would cook, take care of the boy, and pay half of the rent. The couple agreed, believing that if Frank moved in, it would eliminate their financial problems. And since he was willing to take care of their son, they also could work on their marriage. How could they get a better deal than that?

By the time Frank moved in, the boy had turned 12. Frank began to groom both parents and child. He cooked and cleaned and bought the child everything he wanted. Frank convinced the parents to allow him to sleep in the same bed with the child; and he described a series of touching and fondling, which progressed to oral sex and finally anal sex. Frank stated that he took about six months for the grooming and that the relationship lasted until the child was 16 years old. He also stated that as the child got older, he started losing interest; Frank then had to buy the child expensive gifts. Finally, at 16, the child said no more; he was becoming interested in girls. Frank advised that at that point, he was devastated and had lost control. However, he did not stop there. Frank admitted that he stalked the child to see what he was doing and to determine the child's sexual preference. It was clearly girls, so Frank moved out.

Once out of the house, Frank moved in with another single male friend, and their relationship was plutonic. The friend came home from work one day, saw some videos that Frank had next to the VCR, and popped one into the VCR, thinking that he was going to watch an episode of *Law and Order*. What he saw was Frank having sex with the child from the previous home. The roommate called the police, turned the evidence over to them, and Frank was arrested.

ANALYSIS OF FRANK SMITH IN CASE STUDY 4.3

Frank Smith was a homosexual man, and he stated that boys had been his preference since he was an adolescent. When asked if he was attracted to boys before or after he was sexually assaulted by his priest, he stated that his preference began before the sexual assault by his priest. Frank was incapable of maintaining a relationship with adults, and age had little to do with it. By his own admission, Frank was so fixated on sex, demanding loyalty, and even trying to purchase his partners' loyalty that he would physically assault his partners when they left him. He felt that every partner had used him for what he could get, and that no one loved him. Socially, Frank was withdrawn and lacked social skills; again, he admitted that the only way he knew to have an intimate relationship was to give the person gifts and money. Frank had no concept of love and relationship building; in fact, he believed that sex and love were one and the same.

Rather than change his thought processes and work on his understanding of relationships and love, his thinking became more distorted. Instead of working on himself, Frank chose a family that he knew and used money and the fact that the couple had relationship problems to his advantage. The plan was to groom his victim to become a lifetime partner—at least until the victim no longer fit Frank's paraphilic design. If you review the stages of grooming that were outlined earlier in this chapter, you will find that he engaged in every one of them.

In fact, Frank found that the grooming of the victim only worked for so long; when the victim became 16 and the social isolation the victim had experienced was broken, the victim's interests became more diverse. The victim wanted his peers, friends from school, and girls more than Frank, who admitted to stalking the victim until finding out that he was dating girls and had a girlfriend. Frank stated that he was confused and wondered what she could offer the victim that he could not. Interestingly, while in prison, Frank became involved in a relationship with another inmate who was 20 years old. When I asked Frank about the relationship, there had been no grooming, but in order to maintain it, Frank had to buy him things.

When I last met with Frank, he showed me a letter that he had received from the Catholic Archdiocese requesting a meeting about a monetary settlement for his victimization by the priest. In that interview, I asked Frank whether he saw any difference between his actions and those of the priest, and he stated: "The priest forced me to have sex with him and threatened me, using God as the ultimate threat. In my case, I gave the kid love, bought him everything that he wanted, taught him how to make love; I was his first sexual experience. My actions were about love, and that's the difference." When I asked him if he felt sorry for his victim, he replied: "No, I gave him everything. What should I be sorry about? The only thing I am sorry for is that he betrayed me, and turned his back on me for some bitch who could give him nothing" (Thomas, 2001).

Questions for Reflection: In what ways do you think Frank's thought processes and behaviors were influenced by his sexual abuse experience with the priest? If Frank had the skills to prey on an unsuspecting family and groom a young boy, then why didn't he have the skill set necessary to develop and maintain a healthy adult relationship? Or did he have it, and choose not to use it?

CASE STUDY 4.4   IT BEGAN IN A CHAT ROOM

At the time of the offense, James Nelson was 72 years old. He had used the Internet to watch child pornography online and to groom a young teenager for the purposes of a sexual relationship. Nelson entered a chat room used by sex offenders and began to chat with a man named Andy, who was a 35-year-old single father with custody of his 13-year-old daughter. Nelson wanted to know if Andy had ever shared his daughter with anyone and, if not, whether he would like to do so. Nelson stated he was looking for a long-term relationship and was serious.

When Andy asked what he wanted to do, Nelson responded: "I love to eat pussy and, if she is into it, have her suck and fuck." Nelson admitted that he had done this on one other occasion by moving in with a family and paying part of the rent while they allowed him to be a grandfather and teach their daughter about sex. He was the girl's first sexual encounter from the age of 14, and that relationship lasted until she was 17. Nelson stated that he had been looking for another situation like that one for years but had been unable to find one. Noting that most people online just teased and shared pictures, Nelson tried to demonstrate how serious he was by sending two photographs, one of his face and another of his penis. Andy expressed concern that his daughter would get pregnant and/or contract a sexually transmitted disease. Nelson then shared the following: "I have ED and use a pump, I have a cock ring that is so tight no cum will get out, and I will use a condom."

Nelson, who lived in Pensacola, Florida, drove to Orlando, Florida, one week after meeting Andy and his daughter Brooke in the chat room and speaking to them on the phone. During one phone conversation, Nelson told Brooke that what he wanted was a full-time relationship between Nelson, Brooke, and her dad and that he wanted to be Brooke's lover. Upon Nelson's arrival in Orlando, he was arrested and charged with *solicitation of a minor for sex via the computer, traveling to meet a minor for sex,* and *transmitting harmful material to a minor.*

In the interview, Nelson stated that he had met Andy online, that they had been chatting online for a week, and that Andy was looking for someone to move in and watch his daughter Brooke while he (Andy) got back into the dating scene. Nelson also stated that Andy was looking for someone dependable. During the interview, Nelson stated that when he made sexual innuendos regarding Andy's daughter, he was just joking. Nelson's posture made it clear that he was being defensive. Nelson stated that nothing else had taken place, and he minimized his behavior. He was confronted with the chats and admitted to his involvement.

Nelson stated that Andy wanted Nelson to move to Orlando and move in with him. He also stated that Andy was looking to have an older gentleman be a grandfather figure, make his daughter into a woman, and be gentle with her. Investigators asked Nelson if he had done this in the past, and he denied the previous relationship that he had mentioned earlier. Investigators asked for consent to examine Nelson's computer, and it was granted. Investigators asked if Nelson had any remorse and he stated "yes." When advised that Brooke had a mother, Nelson appeared shocked, noting that the mother was never mentioned. They asked Nelson to write Brooke's mother a letter of apology, and Nelson replied, "Do I have to?" and then stated "no." He denied that he had pornography or used it (Child Predator Cyber Crime Unit, 2010).

ANALYSIS OF JAMES NELSON IN CASE STUDY 4.4

James Nelson was a divorced father of three; he and his wife had divorced when his children were young. He would not disclose the reason for the divorce, but he did say that it was not due to his preference for young girls. He also denied ever abusing his children. Nelson stated that he enjoyed having a relationship with young teenaged girls because they were virgins and he would be the first. In addition, they would take what he taught them to please their future lovers. Nelson refused to discuss the first girl he had done this with; even when confronted with the evidence, he refused to discuss it.

When asked whether he felt remorse, Nelson said yes; however, when asked to write a letter to the victim's mother, he refused, stating that he was not one to put together words and apologize. Yet, he could spend days and hours on the Internet in a chat room describing his relationship with the victim and what he wanted. When arrested, Nelson was found to be in possession of two handguns, which were fully loaded, a toy dog that he had purchased for the victim, $5,900 in cash, a Garmin GPS, a penis enlargement device, several cock rings, and a box of condoms. Nelson stated that he did not want to leave the guns in Pensacola and that the money was his "get out of Dodge" fund because he was once caught in a hurricane and left with nothing.

The only time during this process that Nelson showed any remorse was when he was told that his truck was being seized, that law enforcement was seeking forfeiture of the vehicle, and that his computer in Pensacola was also going to be seized. Nothing else mattered; it was at that point that Nelson made the statement: "Man, I screwed up. What will I do without my truck and my computer? I have no way to get around. I am 72 years old, and I am lost without my truck" (Child Predator Cyber Crime Unit, 2010).

Questions for Reflection: Why do you believe James was so fixated on young girls? Do you think he learned this behavior from someone else, and adopted it as his own? Or do you believe that he used the younger girls because he was incapable of having a sexual relationship with adults? Was there any difference between the emotional needs of James and those of Frank in Case Study 4.2, or were the two men driven by the same needs?

COMPARING THE SUSPECTS FROM CASE STUDIES 4.3 AND 4.4

Smith and Nelson had interest in the same age group of adolescents, with the difference being that Smith preferred boys and Nelson girls. Both used a similar style in that they addressed the parents first and attempted to appeal to the parents in order to reach the children. In each case, the parents had flaws, with money and relationship problems being common themes.

A difference between Smith and Nelson is that Smith did everything face-to-face and was an excellent manipulator, whereas Nelson used the computer. Nelson feared that he was undesirable because of his age, so his lure was playing the role of a grandfather. From a practical standpoint, Smith had superior people skills; he could read people like a book. Nelson had poor communication skills and used the computer as his voice.

Both Smith and Nelson described their roles as teachers by teaching children how to become lovers, and loving the children unconditionally. Both saw nothing wrong with their relationships with children. The reality is that both were very self-centered; everything centered on their needs, and not on the needs of their victims.

Questions for Reflection: Based on the research and data supplied in this chapter, how would you classify the suspects? Here are some possible answers: (1) Both are pedophiles. (2) Smith is a pedophile, and Nelson is a rapist. (3) Smith is a rapist, and Nelson is a pedophile. (4) Both should be classified as rapists. (5) Both are rapists and pedophiles. Do you think an adult having sexual contact with a child should always be classified as rape, as it is in statutory rape laws?

CONCLUSION

The idea of becoming a victim of violent crime is something that many Americans fear. The reality is that our children have a much better chance at being victimized than we do as adults. Children are easy prey and naïve, especially when they are being preyed upon by adults. When I examine the final two cases studies, I think of how each offender sought out the parents and used their weaknesses against them. This is what sometimes happens when a single mom is looking for a mate to share her life with and someone who will make her life easier by babysitting, working, and filling the mother's void of adult companionship. In fact, the same theme runs through all the case studies in this chapter. In each case, the predator found the weakness and exploited it to his benefit.

From the front lines, having served in law enforcement, I can say that we need to be very careful not to make our children someone else's responsibility. Our focus has to be on protecting our greatest resource. There will never be enough cops to stop the predators; we as parents are the last line of defense.

REFERENCES

Abel, G. G., Becker, J. V., Mittelman, M., Cunningham-Rathner, J., Rouleau, J. L., & Murphy, W. D. (1987). Self-reported sex crimes of nonincarcerated paraphiliacs. *Journal of Interpersonal Violence, 2*(1), pp. 3–25.

Abel, G. G., & Rouleau, J. L. (1990). Male sex offenders. In M. E. Thase, B. A. Edelstein, & M. Hersen (Eds.), *Handbook of outpatient treatment of adults* (pp. 271–290). New York: Plenum.

Abrams, S., & Abrams, J. B. (2003). *Polygraph testing of the pedophile.* Portland, OR: Ryan Gwinner Press.

American Psychiatric Association. (2000). *The diagnostic and statistical manual of mental disorders, IV-TR*, 4th ed. Arlington, VA: Author.

Bowlby, J. (1940). The influence of early environment in the development of neurosis and neurotic character. *International Journal of Psychoanalysis, 25,* pp. 154–178.

Child Predator Cyber Crime Unit. (2010). *Solicit a minor for sex via computer: Case Number 10-10-0249.* Tallahassee, FL: Florida Office of the Attorney General.

Covell, C. N., & Scalora, M. J. (2002). Empathetic deficits in sexual offenders: An integration of affective, social, and cognitive constructs. *Aggression and Violent Behavior, 7*, pp. 251–270.

Federal Bureau of Investigation (FBI). (2011). *The uniform crime reports: National incident-based reporting system 2011.* Washington, D.C.: Author.

Finkelhor, D., Mitchell, K. J., & Wolak, J. (2000). *Online victimization: A report on the nation's youth.* Alexandria, VA: National Center for Missing and Exploited Children.

Freeh, L. J., Sporkin, S., & Sullivan, E. R. (2012). *Report of the special investigative counsel regarding the actions of the Pennsylvania State University related to the child sexual abuse committed by Gerald A. Sandusky.* Washington, D.C.: Author.

Freund, K. (1990). Courtship disorder. In W. L. Marshall, D. R. Laws, & H. E. Barbaree (Eds.), *Handbook of sexual assault: Issues, theories and treatment of the offender* (pp. 195–207). New York: Plenum.

Groth, A. N., & Birnbaum, H. J. (1978). Adult sexual orientation and attraction to underage persons. *Archives of Sexual Behavior, 7*(3), pp. 175–181.

Grubin, D., Madsen, L., Parsons, S., Sosnowski, D., & Warberg, B. (2004). A prospective study of the impact of polygraphy on high-risk behaviors in adult sex offenders. *Sex Abuse: A Journal of Research and Treatment, 16,* pp. 209–222.

Knight, R. A., Carter, D. L., & Prentky, R. A. (1989). A system for classification of child molesters: Reliability and application. *Journal of Interpersonal Violence 4*(3), pp. 3–23.

Lanning, K. (2010). *A child molester: A behavioral analysis,* 5th ed. Washington, D.C.: Center for Missing and Exploited Children.

Laws, D. R., & Marshall, W. L. (1990). A conditioning theory of the etiology and maintenance of deviant sexual preference and behavior. In W. L. Marshall, D. R. Laws, & H. E. Barbaree (Eds.), *Handbook of sexual assault: Issues, theories, and treatment of the offender* (pp. 209–230). New York: Plenum Books.

Luria, A. (1966). *Higher cortical functions in man.* New York: Basic Books.

Malesky, L. A. (2005). The use of the Internet for child exploitation. In S. W. Cooper, R. J. Estes, A. P. Giardino, N. D. Kellogg, & V. I. Veith (Eds.), *Medical, legal, and social scientific aspects of child exploitation: A comprehensive review of pornography, prostitution, and Internet crimes* (pp. 469–487). St. Louis, MO: G. W. Medical.

McGuire, R. J., Carlisle, J. M., & Young, B. G. (1965). Sexual deviation as a conditioned behavior: A hypothesis. *Behavioral Research and Therapy, 2,* pp. 185–190.

Meijer, E. H., Verschuere, B., Merckelbach, H. L. G. J., & Crombez, G. (2008). Sex offender management using the polygraph: A critical review. *International Journal of Law and Psychiatry, 31*(5), pp. 423–429.

Mineka, S., & Ohman, A. (2002). Learning and unlearning fears: Preparedness, neural pathways, and patients. *Biological Psychiatry, 52,* pp. 927–937.

Pennington, B. F. (2002). *The development of psychopathology: Nature and nurture.* New York: Guilford.

Salters, A. C. (2003). *Predators, pedophiles, and other sex offenders: Who are they, how they operate, and how we can protect ourselves and our children.* New York: Basic Books.

Seligman, M. E. P. (1971). Phobias and preparedness. *Behavior Therapy, 2*, pp. 307–320.

Seto, M. C. (2008). *Pedophilia and sexual offending against children: Theory, assessment, and intervention.* Washington, D.C.: American Psychological Association.

Seto, M. C., Cantor, J. M., & Blanchard, R. (2006). Child pornography offenses are a valid diagnostic indicator of pedophilia. *Journal of Abnormal Psychology, 115*, pp. 610–615.

Skinner, B. F. (1953). *Science and human behavior.* New York: Free Press.

Snyder, H. N. (2000). *Sexual assault of young children as reported to law enforcement: Victim, incident, and offender characteristics.* Washington, D.C.: National Center for Juvenile Justice.

Swirko, C. (2013, August 18). Man caught in standoff now held for sexual battery. *The Gainesville Sun*, B1.

Taylor, M., Holland, G., & Quayle, E. (2001). Typology of peadophile picture taking. *Police Journal, 74*, pp. 97–107.

Thomas, D. (1984). *Grand Rapids Police Department sex crimes files.* Grand Rapids, MI: Author.

Thomas, D. (2001). *Florida Department of Corrections Interview with Sex Offender Frank Smith.* Gainesville, FL: Author.

Ward, T., & Beech, A. (2005). An integrated theory of sexual offending. *Aggression and Behavior, 11*, pp. 44–63.

Widom, C. S. (1992). *The cycle of violence.* Washington, D.C.: U.S. Department of Justice, National Institute of Justice.

Wolak, J., Finkelhor, D., & Mitchell, K. J. (2004). Internet-initiated sex crimes against minors: Implications for prevention based on findings from a national study. *Journal of Adolescent Health, 35*(5), pp. 424.e11–424.e20.

Human Trafficking

As Americans, we know that slavery no longer exists. We are reminded almost daily that this country was founded on principles of freedom and has been about change and moving forward since the Civil War and the signing of the Emancipation Proclamation. Supreme Court cases like *Brown v. Board of Education of Topeka* (1954), the civil rights movement of the 1960s, voting rights legislation, and finally the election of Barack Obama as the first African American president of the United States are all symbols that slavery no longer exists, right?

If you answer yes, you would be incorrect. Human trafficking is modern-day slavery. It comes in many forms, from the homeless child snatched off the street and sold into the sex trade, to a family selling a daughter into domestic slavery or the sex trade to end their poverty, to the promise of freedom for domestic services, and finally to the indentured servant working in the field. The only common theme in human trafficking is that the victims in most instances have had no say regarding the terms of how they are used. Human trafficking is a transnational problem; it consists of crimes against persons who have no borders.

TRANSNATIONAL CRIME

The United Nations (2005) has defined *transnational crime* as people in more than one country maintaining a system of operation and communication that is effective enough to perform criminal transactions, sometimes repeatedly (p. 14). Mueller (2001) noted that transnational crime is an enterprise that has many tentacles, including business, white-collar crime and corruption, works of art and other cultural property, narcotics, and violence (p. 14). Reuter and Petrie (1999) provided categories of transnational crime that they deemed to be significant, and which correspond to Mueller's description:

- Smuggling—commodities, drugs, and protected species
- Contraband (goods subject to tariffs or quotas)—stolen cars and tobacco products
- Services—prostitution, immigrants, money laundering, indentured servitude, and fraud (pp. 11–12)

These crimes may fluctuate based on the successful level of enforcement. In addition, although these acts are viewed from a global perspective, it is difficult for local law enforcement to look beyond their jurisdictional boundaries. A good example of such a crime is the sale and abuse of narcotics.

Beare (2003) argued that transnational organized crime can be seen as a chain of local criminal transactions that have a direct impact on communities (p. xxxvi). Passas (2001) made an interesting point that not all criminal activity has reached the point of being transnational; some may occur only at the local level but is best understood in a global perspective as the local market becoming the retail end of large transnational markets. Commodities that have a direct impact on the United States are narcotics, child porn, and human trafficking (Liddick, 2004; Miko, 2007). Thachuk (2007) made a clear distinction between the quality of the local citizens' lives and actual transnational threats with the understanding that one may well impact the other.

HUMAN TRAFFICKING

Human trafficking is defined by the U.S. State Department (2008) as "sex trafficking in which a commercial sex act is induced by force, fraud, or coercion, or in which the person induced to perform such an act has not attained 18 years of age; or the recruitment, harboring, transportation, provision, or obtaining of a person for labor or services, through the use of force, fraud, or coercion for the purpose of subjection to involuntary servitude, peonage, debt bondage, or slavery" (p. 6). There are three components to human trafficking as noted in the definition: *action,* which can be defined as recruitment, transportation, transfer, harboring, or receipt of persons; *means,* which can be defined as force, coercion, deception, or abuse of power; and *purpose,* which is defined as exploitation for purposes of sex, labor, slavery, servitude, or removal of organs. These are three primary services that those who fall victim to human trafficking are expected to perform: cheap labor in the form of construction, manufacturing, agricultural, and domestic work; sexual exploitation; and organ donation.

The number of people who fall victim to human trafficking is unknown, according to a U.S. State Department *Trafficking in Persons (TIP) Report* (2008), but it is estimated that annually between 600,000 and 800,000 men, women, and children are trafficked across international borders; approximately 80 percent of them are women and girls, and up to 50 percent of them are minors (p. 51). Although I would like to stop discussing sexual abuse, the U.S. State Department report articulated that the majority of the victims are trafficked into sexual exploitation. In addition, most, if not all, reports on victims of human trafficking do not focus on those who are trafficked within the borders of the country in which the report was produced.

Think about all the complaints regarding illegal immigrants you hear in discussions of labor in the United States, including what hardship they pose on the country. In fact, there is a constant clamoring to send them back to their home countries. However, very little is said in these discourses about human trafficking, or about how many of these illegals are forced into some form of servitude. They are kept in that position with constant threats of being turned over to immigration authorities, or threats against the victim's family, and/or threats of death and serious injury. Yet, as a country, the United States takes advantage of the cheap labor that illegals and trafficked individuals provide because it allows business owners to forego all the rules associated with hiring U.S. citizens, such as unemployment insurance, workers' compensation insurance, and filing and maintaining tax records, as well as paying into Social Security.

Thomas (2013) has argued that, beginning in the 1970s, the United States abandoned its role as the great industrial nation, providing large numbers of unskilled labor and manufacturing jobs to the poor and disenfranchised. At that point, the United States moved from being the great industrial giant to what is now considered a prison-industrial economy. Historically, the country was heralded as the great industrial giant because of Henry Ford's introduction of mass production in making the Model T. However, the industry that built the country and supported U.S. efforts during World War II began to crumble in the early 1970s with the oil embargo, gas shortages, soaring gas prices, poorly made automobiles, and the American passion for foreign automobiles with excellent gas mileage. As factories began to close, the United States moved away from industry and manufacturing and began to invest in what we now call the prison-industrial economy (Kirchhoff, 2010; Wildeman & Western, 2010).

The elements of the prison-industrial complex are as follows: Unskilled laborers lost their jobs, factories closed, and the economy crashed in communities where businesses collapsed. Some communities, cities, and states have never recovered. Detroit, Michigan, is one such city; it has never recovered from the decline of the automobile industry. To offset the loss of jobs in the prison-industrial complex, communities have replaced factories with prisons and jobs related to the prison industry (Thomas, 2013).

Along with this change in the U.S. economic base came the moving of jobs overseas. As the economic base changed, cheaper labor markets were discovered overseas; the end result was a demand for unskilled labor in foreign markets. The International Labor Organization (ILO) and the United Nations (UN), which are charged with addressing labor standards, employment, and social protection issues, estimate that in 2006, approximately 12.3 million people had been trafficked and forced into labor, child labor, and indentured servitude, as well as sexual exploitation; other estimates are between 4 and 7 million at any given time (U.S. State Department, 2006, p. 9). How did we move from the State Department numbers of 600,000 to 800,000 given at the beginning of this section to the ILO and UN estimate of 12.3 million? The discrepancy is explained by how human trafficking is defined.

Kravitz (2009) wrote an article titled "'Nanny' Issue Still Vexes Candidates" regarding the many political figures who have used illegal or undocumented aliens and immigrants in the United States to avoid paying taxes. This author stated that such practices have halted a number of presidential nominees and other politicians aspiring to coveted offices. Some of the candidates listed in the article are:

- Zoe E. Baird—selected by Bill Clinton in 1993 to be attorney general; she withdrew her name during her confirmation hearing, admitting that she had hired an illegal alien as a nanny.
- Kimba Wood—Bill Clinton's pick after Baird was forced to step down; she withdrew her name after admitting that she, too, hired an illegal alien as a nanny.
- Charles Ruff—an ex–Justice Department official and candidate for deputy attorney general; he had to be removed from Bill Clinton's short list of candidates because it was discovered he did not pay Social Security taxes for a woman who worked for him for more than eight years.
- Linda Chavez—former president George W. Bush's original choice to be labor secretary; she was forced out after she admitted to giving an undocumented Guatemalan woman free housing and $1,500 over two years in the 1990s.

These examples are all associated with domestic work, but that does not automatically eliminate them from the category of human trafficking. The Polaris

Project (2010) specified that such cases are considered trafficking, regardless of the nature of the trade, if the trafficker or employer uses force, fraud, and/ or coercion to maintain control over the worker and to cause the worker to believe that he or she has no other choice but to continue to work.

Exploitation of Children

There is clearly a world market for children who are missing and exploited. Many of the countries from which children go missing or are exploited are third world countries, and the children are homeless, begging, and on the street, which makes them an easy prey (Montgomery, 2001; U.S. State Department, 2008). In the United States and in most modern societies, an additional variable that is not present in the third world is the Internet, which also makes children an easy prey. Children are being recruited and coerced into the world of prostitution in our own cities. Child predators often use the Internet to identify, and then coerce, their victims to engage in illegal sex acts. The use of the Internet for preying on children has become such a problem that law enforcement agencies have developed cybercrime units to deal specifically with that and other computer-related crimes; in doing so, these agencies have at times joined forces with others around the world to successfully prosecute individuals. Akdeniz (2008) noted that these crimes are often transnational in nature because the Internet is global and has no borders; because of this, we need to harmonize child pornography laws as well policies and procedural laws (pp. 275–276).

Independent of the Internet, the exploitation of children has become a serious problem in the United States. Crimes against children have been brought to the forefront because of their brutality and the loss of innocence that the victims suffer. Because of the publicity, state and federal legislation has been passed in an attempt to protect children from sexual predators; however, some laws have been more effective than others. Zogba, Witt, Dalesaandro, and Veysey (2008) noted that Megan's law, which requires the registration of sex offenders, has had no impact or deterrence effect on sex offenses and sexual offenders (p. 2).

To understand the magnitude of the problem in the United States, we can examine data from the National Center for Missing and Exploited Children (2006), which offers insight into the problem. According to that organization, an estimated total of 58,200 children were abducted by a nonfamily perpetrator in 1999; of that number, an estimated 115 children were victims of stereotypical kidnappings; in stereotypical kidnappings, 40 percent of the children were killed; in only 21 percent (12,100) of these cases was the child reported missing and law enforcement became involved while the child was still missing; youths aged 15 to 17 were the most frequent victims of these nonfamily abductions (59 percent); girls were more frequent victims than boys in this study, making up about two-thirds all victims; and nearly half of these victims (46 percent) were sexually assaulted by the perpetrator (p. 53).

The U.S. Department of Justice (2010) made the following statement concerning the victimization of children: "Sexual abuse and exploitation of children rob the victims of their childhood, irrevocably interfering with their emotional and psychological development" (p. 8). Children are trafficked in a number of ways: online enticement of children; commercial sexual exploitation of children; and child sex tourism, which refers to Americans or U.S. resident aliens traveling abroad for the purpose of sexually abusing foreign children (usually in economically disadvantaged countries) (U.S. Department of Justice, 2010).

A British study made the following observation regarding the sexual exploitation of children in Britain: "Child sexual exploitation and abuse takes place in both online and offline environments and . . . the distinction is in many ways artificial to children and young people in 2012" (Child Exploitation and Online Protection Centre, 2012, p. 6). This study provided several themes regarding the sexual exploitation and trafficking of children:

- Indecency generated by the victim through still photographs, live one-to-one video chats via instant messaging, files uploaded to video hosting websites, and profile images posted on social networking websites
- Group sexual exploitation of children, which is defined as offending and takes place within loose networks, connected through formal and informal associations
- Gang sexual exploitation of children, which is very organized and described as complex—with the causes, behaviors, and motivations often very difficult to untangle

The difference in the function of a gang and group is that the gang will use coercion while the group will use traditional grooming methods. Victims of a gang's sexual exploitation describe themselves as being vulnerable, and under social as well as economic pressures. Some of the victims were classified as runaways, some were from foster care, and some others needed income. There are additional victims who refuse to be classified as victims: Those within gangs endure sexual exploitation for the inclusion and perceived protection afforded by their gang.

Regarding the number of groups and gangs in Britain, they are, just like in the United States, primarily underground, so the exact number of such associations, whether loosely affiliated or criminal enterprise, is not known. In both instances, these groups have the anonymity of the Internet and can hide much like domestic terrorist organizations that participate in what they call a "leaderless resistance." The goal of a leaderless resistance is to use their anonymity to fly under the radar, with the understanding if law enforcement can identify a leader, then both the leader and the organization will become targets.

PSYCHOLOGY ASSOCIATED WITH SEX
CRIMES AGAINST CHILDREN

In Chapter 4, I described the many reasons why predators prey on children. There is a certain psychology associated with predation on children, although I would argue that it is not so much a psychology as a way to justify the actions of those who prefer intimate relationships with children to such relationships with adults.

For years, the North American Man/Boy Love Association (NAMBLA) has espoused that such relationships are healthy and a normal part of life. NAMBLA argues that the criminal justice system is nothing more than a system of injustice, beginning with the establishment of laws and categories that create what we now know as juvenile sex offenders. The organization describes violent sexual acts that juveniles commit as nothing more than playing doctor and nurse (NAMBLA, 2013a). NAMBLA (2013b) also argues that the criminal justice system is especially unfair to adult offenders, calling the actions of the system authoritarian and its punishment of men who love boys draconian. Some of the injustices NAMBLA lists include "forced 'therapies,' long prison sentences, impossible terms for parole, lifetime registration and community notification, and for some, indefinite confinement *after* their sentence has been served" (NAMBLA, 2013b).

To support the notion that there is no harm to children who engage in sexual relationships with adults, NAMBLA cites several researchers. Rind and Tromovitch (1997) argued that all of the past research that addresses child sexual abuse has had an inherent bias, namely, the fact that the researchers have assumed that such relationships are abusive, which has impacted the outcome of the findings (p. 249). They stated that the purpose of their study was to determine if child sexual abuse was psychologically harmful to both genders by completing a meta-analysis of previous studies. First, they noted that all previous studies were based on clinical or criminal justice samples, which were not representative of the general population and was a limitation of those studies. For a different perspective, they examined studies that used national probability samples to determine the perceptions of the general population. These researchers refuted previous studies, claiming that child sexual abuse and adjustment issues later in life are not related, and that the long-term effects of trauma are minimal at best. These findings, however, applied only to boys; with girls, such experiences were found to be traumatizing (Rind & Tromovitch, 1997, p. 253).

Finally, in an article titled "Pedophiles Want the Same Rights as Homosexuals," Jack Minor (2011) noted that pedophiles have started using the same tactics as gay rights activists by arguing that their sexuality or sexual orientation is no different from that of homosexuals and heterosexuals. Minor pointed out that pedophilia is a sexual orientation that is protected by the hate crimes statutes. This author also noted that two Canadian psychologists, Dr. Vernon Quinsey and Dr. Hubert Van Gijseghem, have asserted that pedophilia is a sexual orientation and that there is little evidence that it can be changed through treatment.

> **Questions for Reflection:** Considering the findings of Rind and Tromovitch, as well as the article from Minor, ask yourself whether a relationship between an adult and a child can be legitimate? Are there situations where a child could give consent while understanding the consequences? Under what circumstances does a child give consent? Might a child give consent in a case of grooming as opposed to a situation of coercion or force?

SEXUAL TRAFFICKING

Sexual trafficking in its simplest form is coercing a person to perform sexual acts against his or her will. Many have argued that this situation is a long way from what is commonly known as prostitution and that prostitution is a victimless crime. However, as noted earlier, coercion can take different forms, including threats, physical abuse, promises, deception, and abuse of power. The goal of the trafficker is simple: to make money at the expense of the victim. The customers who participate in the market have just one goal also: their sexual satisfaction, with the idea that they will be free from prosecution and can offend with a certain degree of anonymity.

Kara (2009) stated that all sex trafficking crimes have two components—slave trading and the act of slavery; that these two components have three stages or steps—acquisition, movement, and exploitation; and that each of these steps is interrelated (p. 5). Kara believed that understanding the core—acquisition, movement, and exploitation—is the only way to destroy this criminal enterprise.

In assessing Kara's model and reviewing the research, I have come to the conclusion that a more appropriate model for sex trafficking involves four stages or steps: acquisition, transportation, indoctrination, and facilitation. Each of these is discussed in the sections that follow.

Acquisition

Acquisition refers to how victims are lured into sex trafficking. Deception is one such method, for example, luring those from other countries with false promises of lucrative opportunities in the United States or on the false promise of marriage. The most vulnerable group to date has been refugees in refugee camps, who often have been lured into trafficking with the promise of escaping the horror and violence of war and genocide. Estimates identify 32 million refugees worldwide, 72 percent of which are women and children (Decker, Oram, Gupta, & Silverman, 2009; Kara, 2009). Other forms of acquisition include sale by family, abduction, seduction/romance, and recruitment by former slaves.

Transportation

Transportation refers to the moving of slaves from their country of origin to top transit points and then to a final destination. This is very similar to the pattern used in sanctioned slavery in the United States in the 1800s. Unlike the U.S. slave trade, though, trafficking victims are moved by any means available. Traffickers use bribes and false passports to move victims from country to country. Note that slaves are nearly always moved from poor countries and areas to more affluent countries and areas.

Indoctrination

Indoctrination is a continuation of what begins in the transportation stage. It must be understood that the only way one will buy into a system, culture, or subculture is by being indoctrinated into it so that they can identify with it. This process happens by creating a system in which one comes to understand and believe that compliance is best for the individual and the group as a whole. This is the belief system employed by the military and police in recruit training and by large corporations in their onboarding processes. The goal is compliance, group cohesion, and unity.

Group think also plays into the picture. Group think is a concept that describes how a group thinks as a unit; there are no individuals, and all ideas support the mission or goal of the organization. Again, this concept is used in military and police recruit training and onboarding in large corporations. For organizations, the tactics used to produce group think include isolation, providing images of role models, discussing accomplishments, defining expectations and rules, and providing training that reinforces the ideas and goals of the group. One executive described the process to me as "drinking the Kool-Aid": As an individual goes through the process, he or she buys into the organization's philosophy, so that the organization defines the individual, as well as his or her role, and learns whether or not the individual can be trusted.

The indoctrination of sex slaves and organizational onboarding share only one tactic of indoctrination: isolation. At that point, the two processes depart because the indoctrination of a slave requires an additional element: violence. To truly master and own a sex slave requires total destruction of his or her sense of well-being, and the most common tactics by which that is accomplished are rape, torture, substance abuse, humiliation, and threats (Raymond, Hughes, & Gomez, 2001).

Facilitation

Facilitation is the process of placing the slave in a business and serving the customers. Unfortunately, in order to maintain control over slaves, the same tactics that were used to break the slaves down now become the maintenance tactics used to keep them working and loyal. Raymond and colleagues (2001), who conducted interviews with a small sample of international and U.S.-born women in the sex industry, provided a snapshot of their entry into the sex industry:

- 80 percent of the international women entered the sex trade before age 25, and most as children.
- 83 percent of the U.S. women entered the sex trade before age 25, and most as children.
- 60 percent of the international women were in the sex trade before entering the United States.
- 73 percent of the international women had little or no understanding of the English language.
- 53 percent of the international women entered the United States through some form of legal visa while the others were trafficked in using fraudulent documents.
- 60 percent of the international women were recruited and trafficked through organized businesses and criminal enterprises such as biker gangs and the mafia.
- 40 percent of the U.S. women were recruited and trafficked through organized businesses and criminal enterprises such as biker gangs and the Mafia.
- The majority of the women reported that they were recruited or trafficked by a pimp or trafficker associated with the sex industry. (pp. 7–8)

These researchers also noted that the majority of the U.S. women were held in captivity with guards posted to keep them from escaping. The number of women who were guarded was considerably less with the international women, but they were at a disadvantage because they had no English-language skills and had never experienced life in the United States with total freedom.

SEXUAL TOURISM

Sexual tourism is the final piece of the human trafficking puzzle. Traditionally sexual tourism has been defined as a traveling to another country for the primary purpose of having sex. What many travelers are looking for is to act out their fantasies or to have sex with juveniles in countries where it is legal, unlike the United States. Mullings (2000) has argued that this definition needs to be expanded because it is too limited now that the Internet allows people to live their fantasies without ever leaving their homes.

In addition, there is another aspect to sexual tourism besides the fulfillment of fantasies that is rarely examined: the economic benefit to the country that supports the sexual tourism activity. Davidson (2005) noted that prostitution in a foreign land can appear magical because it is devoid of all the legal constraints mandated by most societies and is protected by many foreign governments because of its economic impact. Davidson explained that age is something different where children grow like exotic plants and age means nothing (p. 137). To help us better understand the problem, Nagle (1999) estimated that, in Thailand alone, some 250,000 people from industrialized countries such as the United States, Britain, Germany, and Japan visited Thailand in order to have sex with minors (p. 125).

CASE STUDY 5.1   DISCOVERING HUMAN TRAFFICKING FOR THE FIRST TIME

October 1985 at 3:00 A.M. the SWAT Team of the Grand Rapids Police Department executed a high-risk search warrant on a local heroin dealer. After securing the drug dealer the officers began an exhaustive search of the residence. During the search a half-pound of marijuana and 10 grams of heroin, along with several guns and $5,000, were seized.

The investigating officers stumbled upon a series of uncashed American Express Travelers Checks in excess of $10,000. In addition to the uncashed travelers' checks, officers discovered travelers' check receipts in excess of $50,000, all of the transactions had been made in Las Vegas.

At the time it was believed that the travelers' checks had been obtained through theft or some sort of scam where American Express was the victim. When American Express was contacted, it was found that each of the travelers' checks was associated with a legal transaction. During questioning the suspect refused to answer any questions and refused to discuss travelers' checks.

One officer contacted a prostitute who had been his informant in the Ronnie Crawford case (Case Study 2.4) and inquired about the checks. The informant advised that as she had in the past that there was a whole underground culture that police knew nothing about and that drugs and prostitution were even more intertwined than the police could ever imagine. The informant advised that the big money was not in local prostitution but in prostitution in cities like Las Vegas and New York because of their appeal to tourists and conventions. The informant noted that at least four times a year the girls would travel to Vegas or New York and cities that hosted large sporting events such as the Super Bowl, the NBA All-Star Game, and World Championship Boxing events. She advised that this was the best kept secret until police stumbled upon the receipts and travelers' checks during the search.

The girls would travel as a group (without their pimp) from Grand Rapids to the aforementioned cities or events to sell their wares. Nightly the most respected and lead prostitute collected the money, purchased the travelers' checks, and sent them by mail to Grand Rapids. The "lead bitch" as the informant described her was responsible for keeping the other girls in line and for disciplining them when the pimp was not around. The girls understood their place and the hierarchy within the group.

The officer had worked the streets for years investigating a number of cases where the local prostitutes had been brutality assaulted, beaten, and raped with hangers yet they stayed and refused to press charges. After everything the girls had been through and witnessed, the officer wondered why the girls stayed.

The informant advised that the girls stayed for several reasons: most, if not all, of them had babies by the age of 15 and had been abused by one or both parents. A few had been raped by their mother's boyfriends so the girls ran away. The pimp offered security, shelter, food, clothing, and money. For someone who had nothing, this is great and for the abused it is often equated with love. After the girls were in love the pimp would turn them out onto the street. Sometimes it took beating the girls to get them on the street, the introduction of drugs, while others went willingly because they understood in order to maintain the lifestyle they had to work. The informant reminded the investigator of the cases he had investigated noting that the bond between pimp and prostitute went beyond any personal feelings. She used words such as fear, the need for praise, disappointment, the need to belong and feel loved, and safety, which meant that the girls had a loyalty much like that of a domestic violence victim. The informant made one final statement regarding the girls:

> As bad as you see the life that we live and you believe that a man is abusing us we find this life fun. Just think we travel, have sex, live out our fantasies and are desired by men and women. With that said we are loyal bitches because this world turned its back on us and we have found a way to make it preying on the very ones that turned their backs on us. (Thomas, 1985)

Questions for Reflection

After reading this case study would you call it human trafficking?

1. Are the girls there by choice, or have they been coerced into this life?
2. What psychology is associated with creating such a bond?
3. If the girls were given a choice, do you believe that they would leave the life or has it become so appealing that nothing else could compare?
4. After reading the chapter do you believe that there is a similarity between victims of trafficking and the enslavement of blacks in the 1800s?
5. What enforcement efforts do you believe should be initiated to stop human trafficking?

CONCLUSION

Worldwide, the issue of human trafficking touches every possible category of criminal activity. The United States has become a source, a point of transit, and a final destination point for men, women, and children in the human trafficking trade. As noted throughout the chapter, the types of slavery to which these victims are subjected vary: forced labor, debt bondage, document servitude, human organ harvesting, and sex. The industries in which slaves work may be as simple as farming or as complex as manufacturing, and include everything in between. The U.S. State Department noted that the weakness in the system is in the visa programs where legally documented temporary workers and students gain entry into the country and get lost through the cracks (U.S. State Department, 2011, p. 373).

If we examine the data provided by the U.S. Department of Justice in regard to the number of arrests and prosecutions for human trafficking in the United

States in 2007, we find a clear discrepancy between those figures and the numbers of people estimated to be victims of human trafficking. This may be due to a lack of effort on the part of law enforcement, or to the difficulty law enforcement has in identifying those who profit from trafficking. Either way, the numbers are deplorable. In 2007, the U.S. Department of Justice initiated 182 investigations, charged 89 individuals, and obtained 103 convictions for human trafficking (p. 51). In contrast, between 2000 and 2007, the Department of Health and Human Services certified 1,379 victims of human trafficking to be granted protection in the United States (U.S. State Department, 2008, p. 51).

As I researched the topic, I was hoping to see a significant change in the 2010 data, but I was disappointed. For the fiscal year 2010, federal law enforcement charged 181 individuals, and obtained 141 convictions in 103 human trafficking prosecutions (32 labor trafficking and 71 sex trafficking) (U.S. State Department, 2011, p. 373). When we compare these numbers to the estimates of human trafficking victims provided earlier, the effort to stop human trafficking appears to be less than stellar. As noted in Chapter 2, the fact that we protected animals legally long before we established laws to protect children and later women does not speak well of our values as a society.

Questions for Reflection: If we have identified a problem, then why can't we fix it? Even though politics plays a major role, shouldn't we have values as a society that lead us to put an end to human trafficking? Or do the benefits of human trafficking outweigh the negatives to the point that, as long as it stays underground in the United States, we need not put forth any more effort to end it?

Finally, it is important to note that the United States has long had a posture of differentiating between its citizens and those who are not citizens. In fact, the United States was founded on the principle of protecting the civil rights of its citizenry. The key words here are civil rights *of its citizens*—without that citizenship status, one has no protection under the Constitution. The first ten amendments of the U.S. Constitution guarantee U.S. citizens their rights; more specifically, the First, Second, Fourth, Fifth, Sixth, Tenth, and the Fourteenth Amendments spell out the limitations of the government and the rights of U.S. citizens. I would argue, however, that these guarantees are dependent on race, gender, sexual orientation, ethnicity, and/or religious affiliation. From a practical position, it could be argued that the concept of civil rights is in the eye of the beholder and that here, as in other discussions in other chapters, "one's perception is one's reality."

The law on civil rights is dependent on society's view of what is right and wrong. In America, the foundation of our society and culture is the Judeo-Christian ethic. The U.S. Constitution and the Declaration of Independence are each founded on and strengthened by the same ethic. These documents espouse that all men are created equal and profess to protect the rights of citizens. Interestingly, though, even today we argue and debate the issue of whether noncitizens should have the same civil rights.

Though the case is old and outdated, the U.S. Supreme Court determined in *Dred Scott v. Sandford* (1857) that slaves were not citizens but property and that their descendants were not and could not be citizens because they were inferior (pp. 10–12). The term *citizenship* describes something that most Americans covet because they recognize it has a particular meaning, and that despite its faults, the United States is one of the best places in the world in which to live.

So, as we consider human trafficking, we need to acknowledge that the argument of civil rights for U.S. citizens was built upon documents and an ethic that supported men owning other men. Today many would claim that this is irrelevant because slavery has been abolished; the days of Dred Scott are over, and this country is now truly a country of equality. Yet, when we look at the issue of human trafficking, we can see this is not true: When it comes to slavery, there have been some changes, but it still exists. It has just become more sophisticated and harder to detect and prosecute.

Questions for Reflection: Are those who are subjects of human trafficking to be considered as less than full human beings, as Dred Scott and his descendants were in the Supreme Court's 1857 decision? Or should they be granted the same rights as full U.S. citizens in terms of enforcement and protection? Review and reflect on the numbers of victims in human trafficking and the numbers of prosecutions for the crime. If the number of victims is in the thousands and possibly millions, why is so little being done to halt the trade?

REFERENCES

Akdeniz, Y. (2008). *Internet child pornography and the law: National and international responses.* Burlington, VT: Ashgate.

Beare, M. E. (2003). *Critical reflections on transnational organized crime, money laundering and corruption.* Toronto, ON: University of Toronto Press.

Brown v. Board of Education of Topeka, 347 U.S. 483 (1954).

Child Exploitation and Online Protection Centre. (2012). *Threat assessment of child sexual exploitation and abuse.* London: Author.

Davidson, J. O. (2005). *Children in the global sex trade.* Malden, MA: Polity Press.

Decker, M. R., Oram, S., Gupta, J., & Silverman, J. G. (2009). Forced prostitution and trafficking for sexual exploitation of women and girls in situations of migration and conflict: Review and recommendations for reproductive health care personnel. In S. F. Martin & J. Tirman (Eds.), *Women, migration, and conflict: Breaking the deadly cycle* (pp. 63–86). New York: Springer.

Dred Scott v. Sandford, 60 U.S. 393 (1857).

Kara, S. (2009). *Sex trafficking: Inside the business of modern slavery.* New York: Columbia University Press.

Kirchhoff, S. M. (2010). *Economic impacts of prison growth.* Washington, D.C.: Congressional Research Service.

Kravitz, D. (2009, January 23). "Nanny" issue still vexes candidates. *Washington Post.* Retrieved September 25, 2013, from http://voices.washingtonpost .com/washingtonpostinvestigations/2009/01/nanny_issues_a_common_ problem.html

Liddick, D. R. (2004). *The global underworld.* Westport, CT: Greenwood.

Miko, F. T. (2007). International human trafficking. In K. L. Thachuk (Ed.), *Transnational threats: Smuggling and trafficking in arms, drugs, and human life* (pp. 36–52). Westport, CT: Praeger Security.

Minor, J. (2011, July 3). *Pedophiles want the same rights as homosexuals.* Retrieved October 1, 2013, from http://www.greeleygazette.com/press/?p=11517

Montgomery, H. K. (2001). *Modern Babylon? Prostituting children in Thailand.* New York: Berghahn Books.

Mueller, G. O. W. (2001). Transnational crime: Definitions and concepts. In P. Williams & W. Vlassis (Eds.), *Combating transnational crime: Concepts, activities, and responses* (pp. 13–21). New York: Routledge.

Mullings, B. (2000). Fantasy tourism: Exploring global consumption of Caribbean sex tours. In M. Golldeiner (Ed.), *New forms of consumption* (pp. 227–251). Lanham, MD: Rowman & Littlefield.

Nagle, G. (1999). *Tourism, leisure and recreation.* Cheltenham, UK: Nelson Thornes.

National Center for Missing and Exploited Children. (2006). *Missing and abducted children: A law enforcement guide to case investigation and program management.* Alexandria, VA: Author.

North American Man/Boy Love Association (NAMBLA). (2013a). *The criminalization of youth.* Retrieved on October 1, 2013, from http://www.nambla.org/ crimyout.html

North American Man/Boy Love Association (NAMBLA). (2013b). *The criminal injustice system.* Retrieved October 10, 2013, from http://www.nambla.org/ crimjust.html

Passas, N. (2001). Globalization and transnational crime: Effects of criminogenic asymmetries. In P. Williams & W. Vlassis (Eds.), *Combating transnational crime: Concepts, activities, and responses* (pp. 24–56). New York: Routledge.

Polaris Project. (2010). *Identifying victims of human trafficking.* Washington, D.C.: Author.

Raymond, J. G., Hughes, D. M., & Gomez, C. J. (2001). Sex trafficking of women in the United States. In L. Territo & G. Kirkham (Eds.), *International sex trafficking of women & children: Understanding the global epidemic* (pp. 3–14). Flushing, NY: Looseleaf Law Publications.

Reuter, P., & Petrie, C. (1999). *Transnational organized crime: Summary of a workshop.* Washington, D.C.: National Academy Press.

Rind, B., & Tromovitch, P. (1997). A meta-analytic review of findings from national samples on psychological correlates of child sexual abuse. *Journal of Sex Research, 34*(3), pp. 237–255).

Thachuk, K. (2007). *Transnational threats: Smuggling and trafficking in arms, drugs and human life.* Westport, CT: Praeger.

Thomas, D. J. (2013). Dissecting the perfect storm: Law, policy, and violent African American juveniles. *Journal of Forensic Investigation, 1*(1), pp. 1–9.

Thomas, D. J. (1985). Execution of search warrant, Grand Rapids Police Department. Grand Rapids, MI. Author.

United Nations Office on Drugs and Crime. (2005). *Transnational organized crime in the West African Region.* New York: Author.

U.S. Department of Justice. (2010). *The national strategy for child exploitation prevention and interdiction report: A report to congress.* Washington, D.C: Author.

U.S. State Department. (2006). *Trafficking in persons report 2006.* Washington, D.C.: Author.

U.S. State Department. (2008). *Trafficking in persons report 2008.* Washington, D.C.: Author.

U.S. State Department. (2011). *Trafficking in persons report 2011.* Washington, D.C.: Author.

Wildeman, C., & Western, B. (2010). Incarceration in fragile families. *Future of Our Children, 20*, pp. 157–177.

Zogba, K., Witt, P., Dalesaandro, M., & Veysey, B. (2008). *Megan's law: Assessing the practical and monetary efficacy.* Washington, D.C.: National Institute of Justice.

Arson

Arson is a mysterious crime that few people can understand, and a crime that is rarely talked about in police circles. In fact, it is the one crime that most officers do not understand because it is not "traditional" in the way that robbery, rape, murder, burglary, and theft are—in the sense that they are more common and therefore more familiar. In addition, investigating an arson requires the participation of other agencies and the expertise of fire marshals or the local fire department, and often police and fire departments do not play well together.

From a practical standpoint, fire or arson is rarely discussed unless the loss of property and/or life is so devastating that it requires a multiagency response and the case makes the national news. The reality, however, is that arson is more common than one might think. The U.S. Fire Administration (2001, p. 1) estimated that arson was the leading cause of fire in the United States and offered the following data: Arson is responsible for 475 deaths, 2,000 injuries, and $1.4 billion in property loss each year with a total of 267,000 arsons annually.

Arson is defined in statute as intentional in nature where the act of creating a fire or explosion is willful, unlawful, and/or done while in the commission of any felony (Colorado General Assembly, 2013; Florida State Legislature, 2013; Texas State Legislature, 2013). The definitions are clear in most instances. Arson is considered a property crime. However, the legislative bodies recognize that many different motives are associated with arson besides property destruction. Fire has been used to mask crimes of violence, and also as the sole source of acts of violence and/or injury. Arsonists are known to have an impulse control disorder similar to those with reactive and predatory violence, as outlined in Chapter 3.

Since arson is such an unusual crime and rarely discussed in mainstream circles, this chapter will attempt to dissect arson, both its etiology and the psychology behind it. As you examine the etiology, classification systems, motives, and case studies, compare and contrast the behaviors of an arsonist to those of murderers, rapists, and child abusers.

Questions for Reflection: Is the etiology of all criminal behavior the same? Or are the logic and motivations behind crimes unique to the specific criminal? Is an arsonist different from other criminals? If so, how and why?

ETIOLOGY OF ARSONISTS

To understand arson, it is important to understand the etiology of arson. In the previous chapters, I have argued that the deficits in our personalities are directly related to three systems that intersect: environmental, psychological, and biological. This is also known as a biopsychosocial model. Each of these systems interacts with the others; in many instances, we have no idea to what degree unless an individual is diagnosed with a disorder such as schizophrenia, which is biologically based. As you have seen from the discussion in the previous chapters, there are a number of theories about why people commit violent crimes, and yet the literature provides few theories about the etiology of arson. There are, however, a number of theories regarding the typology or classification of arsonists. Therefore, as in the previous chapters, I will provide you with a sampling of the theories on this subject, and let you apply them singularly or in tandem to your understanding of arsonists and their acts. Again, case studies are provided for you to use as a reference.

If the prevailing belief is that who we are is based on what happens to us early in life, as discussed in the previous chapters, then it is important to examine the background of juvenile fire-setters. Schwartzman, Stambaugh, and Kimball (1998) found that juvenile fire-setters had been exposed to a number of family problems, including abuse, neglect, poor parental judgment, poor or no parenting skills, substance abuse in the home, and poverty; also, as with some cases we examined in earlier chapters, there was a disconnect between the parents and children that directly correlated to Bowlby and the attachment theory (p. 7).

Social learning theorizes that one's environment is responsible for how humans learn to respond to adversity or in challenging or stressful situations. A healthy environment provides one with the building blocks for a healthy personality along with sound emotional support and attachment. However, as noted in the previous chapters, if the environment is negative, then the result can be the development of poor coping mechanisms, poor social and communication skills, and academic failure. In humans, this sense of failure will manifest itself in some form of maladjusted behavior (Bandura, 1977; McKerracher & Dacre, 1966; Vreeland & Levin, 1980).

The concept of child abuse is closely associated with fire-setting behavior in juveniles; however, most of the studies have been of children who were institutionalized and came from homes where they were abused. This is a true limitation of the research. Root, MacKay, Henderson, Del Bove, and Warling (2008) recognized this limitation and conducted a comparative study of 205 juvenile fire-setters between the ages of 4 and 17. These authors compared those who came from abusive homes with those who did not and determined the following in regard to the children who were abused:

- The abused children were conditioned not express feelings of anger and frustration for fear of retaliation by their caregivers. They learned to repress their feelings as a means of survival.
- The children sought alternative passive outlets to express the repressed feelings of anger, anxiety, etc.—and one of them was fire-setting.
- The trigger was associated with a family stressor.
- The children used fire as an emotional expression or outlet, and thus set fires more frequently than children who had not been abused.
- These children used different types of ignition sources than those children who had not been abused.
- The abused children were prone to higher rates of fire-setting recidivism.

In examining the study by Root and colleagues as well as the other studies that have addressed the issue of child abuse in relationship to crime and future acts of violence, the conclusions are generally the same. McCarty and McMahon (2005) noted that the set of risk factors for youth who choose fire-setting behavior as an emotional expression is at best generalized and can be associated with child psychopathology or juvenile delinquency.

Gaynor (2002) described fire behavior as learned and as part of our developmental process, which is sequential like all other forms of human development; through proper guidance in school and home, and proper social interaction, a child learns the appropriate responses, rather than distorted ones like fire-setting (p. 1). However, negative social influences, family dysfunction, and stressors can lead to repeated intentional acts of fire-setting. Gaynor identified four distinct levels in the development of fire-setting behavior:

- *Fire interest*—between ages 3 and 5: Questions focus on the physical properties of fire.

- *Fire-starting*—between ages 3 and 9: The child experiments at least once with fire-starting material under the supervision of a parent or caregiver. It should be noted that the majority of children will engage in at least one unsupervised incident motivated by curiosity.

- *Fire-setting intentional, no psychological problems*—between the ages of 7 and 10: Children have learned the rules of fire. Although intentional, fire-setting in this stage may not represent a psychological problem, and the behavior can be stopped with parental involvement and intervention.

- *Fire-setting intentional, with psychological or social problems*—between the ages of 7 and 10: Some in this age group are motivated by psychological or social problems, and the fires have been planned for weeks or months. Motives for this fire-setter may be anger, revenge, attention seeking, criminal mischief, crime concealment, or an intent to destroy property or people.

Quinsey, Harris, Rice, and Cormier (1998) determined in their studies that fire-setters exhibited significant personality deficits in assertiveness and that their most common motive for arson was revenge. Based on the examination of 243 fire-setters, they developed four motivational categories of arsonists:

- 33 percent were psychotics and their motives were delusional
- 28 percent were unassertive, with little or no prior criminal history
- 23 percent were multifire-setters
- 16 percent were criminals (pp. 100–111)

The second group had the best family, employment, and educational histories of all the groups. The third group had the worst childhoods, poor adjustment history, started fires in their youth, and had a history of aggression; their motivations were anger, revenge, and, for a few, excitement. The fourth group had similar backgrounds to the multifire-setters in the third group; they were the most assertive, most likely to have been diagnosed with a personality disorder, and set another fire upon release.

Although dealing with a much smaller group than the Quinsey study, researchers Labree, Nijman, van Marle, and Rassin (2010) examined the backgrounds and characteristics of arsonists, and their research supported the findings of Quinsey and colleagues. The Labree group examined twenty-five adult male arsonists sentenced to treatment in a maximum security treatment facility and compared the arsonists' characteristics to fifty inmates sentenced for committing violent crimes who were receiving treatment at the same facility. These researchers compared and examined the following items: Axis I and Axis II disorders, family backgrounds, level of education, treatment history, intelligence, and scores on the Hare Psychopathy Checklist. The Labree authors identified several differences between the male arson offenders and the control group of violent offenders. They found that the arsonists received more psychiatric treatment than the control group, had a higher level of alcohol abuse than the control group, and were less likely to be diagnosed as suffering from a psychotic disorder. In regard to the Hare Psychopathy Checklist, the arsonists received a high score in the area of impulsivity, and lower scores for superficial charm and juvenile delinquency. In addition, the majority of the arsonists' motives were driven by delusional thinking (52 percent), revenge (36 percent), and excitement (12 percent) (Labree et al., 2010, p. 152).

CASE STUDY 6.1   ABUSED CHILD AS ARSONIST

Jason Wright was a 7-year-old second grader. While at recess he injured his leg, and the school nurse called his mother to advise her of the injury and request that she come get Jason and take him to the doctor. Ms. Wright refused, stating that Jason could take the school bus home and she would attend to his leg once he arrived.

When Jason arrived home, Ms. Wright was in a hurry to get to work so she took Jason and his 10-year-old sister, Anne, to the babysitter's house. The sitter was Ms. Wright's sister Patricia. When the kids arrived, Patricia gave Anne a hug and kiss, but when she reached to kiss Jason, he pulled back, yelling in pain. Patricia pulled up Jason's T-shirt and discovered that he had welts all over his back, stomach, buttocks, and legs. She took both children to the local hospital, and hospital personnel called the police regarding child abuse.

The responding officers interviewed both children. Jason stated that he had injured his leg at school and the nurse had called his mom, who refused to pick him up. Jason and Anne rode the school bus home, and Ms. Wright met them at the school bus. Once they were in the house, Ms. Wright began yelling at Jason for having the nurse call her. She then took a belt and beat Jason until he could not stand. While she was beating him, Jason continued to complain about his leg, and also fell to the ground and asked for forgiveness.

Jason's sister Anne provided a similar account and added that this was not the first time that Ms. Wright had beaten Jason like this. Anne stated that every time Ms. Wright became angry with Jason's dad, she would beat Jason, blaming Jason for his father's actions.

When the children's aunt, Patricia, was interviewed, she explained how she had discovered the injuries to Jason when she reached out to give him a hug and immediately brought him to the hospital. Besides injuries from the beating, X-rays of his leg revealed that Jason had fractured his femur in the accident at school. Supervisors advised the officers that very little would be done if Ms. Wright was arrested. Officers failed to heed their supervisor's advice and arrested Ms. Wright at her place of employment, which was a nursing home. Jason and Anne were removed from their mother's home, and custody was given to Ms. Wright's sister Patricia.

During the transport of Ms. Wright to the police station, she denied any wrongdoing, stating that she did not know how Jason was injured. The officers advised Ms. Wright of the evidence, and she immediately changed her story, moving from crying to threatening. Ms. Wright told one officer, "I will get your black ass when this is all over." Ms. Wright filed a formal complaint against the officers, stating that the officers had handcuffed her too tightly as punishment for abusing Jason, she hired an attorney, and Internal Affairs investigated the complaint. When investigators asked Ms. Wright to wash her hands, however, so the pictures would be clear, the makeup she had applied to look like bruises washed off, and the complaint was dropped.

Six months later, both Jason and Anne were returned to their mother. A week after returning home, Jason began acting out. The first fire he set was a trash fire, and a month later he set a second fire by igniting the curtains in the living room. Investigators discovered that Jason had been victimized again. Ms. Wright was charged and convicted; and she lost her parental rights. Jason received mental health treatment and never started another fire (Thomas, 2008).

In reviewing the literature, we find that there is very little that differentiates the etiology of arson and the arsonist from that of other criminals. One similarity between arsonists and other criminals who have committed violent crime is that they have chosen to retaliate through their crimes. In this sense, arsonists are exhibiting the same behavior as students who have been bullied and retaliate in the form of a school shooting; workers who feel they have been wronged through job termination and retaliate through mass murder, killing their supervisors and coworkers; and students or workers who use arson as a form of retaliation by burning down their school or place of employment, or the principal's or CEO's home. I argue that in each of these cases, the perpetrator has become so angry about perceived wrongs, a system's failure to protect him or her, or actual wrongs that he or she feels like there is no recourse but to retaliate violently. Such acts do not happen in a vacuum, but through a series of events. As those events are processed, there is a failure of the offender's coping mechanisms, coupled with distorted or delusional thinking. The offender finds, through his or her cognitive process, that the only recourse is retaliation through an act of violence or property destruction.

If we reexamine the research of the Quinsey and Labree groups, although there were subtle differences in the findings of the two studies, both groups had certain characteristics in common. The arsonists in both research groups had personality deficits: They were shy and not assertive, lacked superficial charm, and had distorted or delusional cognitive processes. Based on the research, it is my belief that arsonists are similar to rapists. Like the rapist Thomas Franklin, examined in Case Study 3.3 in Chapter 3, arsonists, when finally caught, often have been setting fires since they were juveniles and yet have no criminal history of arson. In many instances, previous charges were reduced or ignored, or the behavior was seen as a developmental issue— something the child would grow out of. Lack of attention and lack of intervention has allowed many juvenile fire-setters to grow into adult multifire-setters.

Dickens and colleagues (2009) argued that when we try to classify arsonists based on dangerousness, the natural tendency is to believe that the multifire-setter is far more dangerous than the single-event arsonist. These authors noted, however, that there is no correlation between dangerousness and recidivism when examining arson. They pointed out that when examining dangerousness, the determining factor is the subject's intent to harm another by setting fire to an occupied building. Therefore, these researchers believed that arsonists should be classified in one of two categories: expressiveness or instrumentality. These categories are specific to the arsonist's orientation, whether it is property or people. *Expressiveness* is associated with the offender's propensity to damage property, while *instrumentality* is defined as the offender's propensity to harm. From a mental health standpoint, such a distinction can assist in deciding on the appropriate course of treatment; from an investigative standpoint, it may well assist in determining motive and narrowing the suspect pool in arson investigations.

The goals and/or motivations of arsonists are many and are based on a complex series of maladaptive behaviors. In order to better understand these offenders, it is important to examine the different classification systems associated with arson, which are directly related to motives.

CLASSIFICATION SYSTEMS OF ARSONISTS AND MULTIFIRE-SETTERS

Theorists have developed many classification systems for arsonists based on empirical data, much like that provided in Chapter 1 in the discussion of what causes crime. Classification systems are rarely used from a law enforcement perspective, since the goal of law enforcement is to articulate the facts of the crime in painstaking detail. From a clinical perspective, however, classification systems are important because they help in the development of a treatment plan as well designing treatment programs. From the clinical perspective, then, one size does not fit all. Here I provide some of the classification systems that theorists have developed for arsonists and multifire-setters to provide you with insight regarding motive.

Rider (1980) argued that very little is known concerning the psychopathology of fire-starters because what we have learned is from those who are incarcerated or receiving psychological treatment. As I have noted in the past with each population discussed, there are limitations to such a sample for two reasons: first, these individuals are self-reporting, meaning that they provide the background information they want the listener to know, which may or may not be substantiated; and second, in many instances, the data are not compared to that of groups that are not institutionalized, which can be almost impossible to do. As long as we acknowledge these limitations, however, we can still discover important and helpful information in the research.

Lewis and Yarnell (1951) provided a comprehensive examination of 1,145 adult male arsonists and noted that no normal person sets fires habitually; psychotic fire-setters set fires because of delusional or distorted cognitive processes (p. vii). These researchers provided the following classification system based on mental health status: *accidental,* associated with mental retardation; *delusional,* where the offender is psychotic and experiences command auditory hallucinations directing him or her to set fires; *erotic,* which is associated with pyromania, sex, and excitement; *revenge,* where the offender seeks to right a wrong, whether perceived or real; and *children,* who seek to set fires out of excitement or mischief. What Lewis and Yarnell failed to address with children was the developmental stages, as well as those who act in response to abuse and anger (pp. vii–viii).

Prins (1994) cautioned that it is important to distinguish between the offender's behavioral characteristics, the various types of fire-setters, and their motives. I agree with Prins here because if investigators or mental health professionals attempt to assign one typology or classification system to an offender, then they miss the possibility that the offender may have committed the crime with more than one motive in place. With this in mind, Prins offers the following classification system:

- Arson committed for financial reward
- Arson committed to cover up another crime
- Arson committed for political purposes
- Self-immolation, which is defined as putting oneself on fire as a form of protest or political statement
- Arson committed for mixed motives (a cry for help, depressed, or under the influence of alcohol)
- Arson due to the presence of a severe mental or associated disorder
- Arson for motives of revenge
- Arson to get attention or sexual gratification
- Arson by young adults, vandalism (16 and over)
- Arson by children 15 and under (p. 41)

In addition to the classification system for adult fire-starters, Prins provided four specific typologies of juvenile fire-starters: curiosity leading to fire; younger fire-starters who are motivated by anger; older juveniles who engage in arson as a pattern of juvenile delinquency; and the pathological juvenile who starts fires ritualistically and is the equivalent of an adult pyromaniac (pp. 81–82). Although Prins differentiates between younger and older juveniles, he refuses to place a specific age to the crime.

Douglas, Burgess, Burgess, and Ressler (2006) classified arson into eight major categories that are similar to those Prins offered, and each is related to a motive:

- *Vandalism-motivated arson* is defined as the destruction of property with no other motive. From a police perspective, property destruction or vandalism is a crime that is common in juvenile circles. In regard to arson, it may be that a child is experimenting or made a mistake, not understanding the true destructive power of fire. As Gaynor (2002) noted, this behavior is not unusual; it is part of a child's developmental stages. Yet the behavior needs to be addressed.

- *Excitement-motivated arson* is defined as setting fires for excitement and where there is no intent to injure anyone. This type of fire-setter is classified by the American Psychiatric Association (APA, 2000) as exhibiting symptoms of pyromania. *Pyromania* is an impulse control disorder where the offender has a history of fire-setting, fire-setting is in response to tension or affective arousal (the act is not planned), and there is a fascination with fire and its paraphernalia. Pyromaniacs are described as watchers, may set off false alarms, and find pleasure in the mobilization of resources needed to tend to the fire (fire department, police, media, etc.). They find release of tension or pleasure in these activities. Such an offender may even become a firefighter. The behavior is not for monetary gain, revenge, or other psychopathology or ideology; it is strictly for pleasure or a release of tension (Douglas et al., 2006, p. 669).

- *Revenge-motivated arson,* as detailed earlier in the chapter, is similar to the actions of school shooters who seek revenge for being bullied and workers who retaliate through mass murder when they believe they have been wronged. In each of these cases, the perpetrator has become so angry through perceived wrongs, a system's failure to protect them, or actual wrongs that he or she feels there is no recourse but to retaliate violently. Through the processing of a series of events, the offender's coping mechanisms fail and the offender engages in distorted or delusional thinking. The distorted cognitive processes of these offenders lead them to believe that the only recourse is retaliation through an act of violence or property destruction.

- *Crime concealment arson* is defined as using arson to conceal or hide another crime. Murder-suicide, burglary, theft, and destruction of records are a few examples of crimes the arsonist may be trying to hide. The goal of the offender is to destroy or contaminate evidence of the primary crime.

- *Profit-motivated arson* is defined as fire-setting for material gain. The gain can be in the form of insurance fraud, property liquidation, employment, or destroying the competition.

- *Extremist-motivated arson* is defined as arson or bombing that has been committed by a group that espouses an ideology different from the individuals, group, or government it is attacking. Such tactics have been used by white supremacist organizations who have attacked African American families and churches in the South and by Timothy McVeigh in the Oklahoma City bombing.

- *Serial-motivated arson* describes the actions of an arsonist who sets three or more fires and selects his or her victims randomly. Douglas and colleagues (2006) noted that serial arson is not a distinct motive, but a pattern. These types of arsons are categorized as mass, spree, or serial.

- *Serial-motivated bombing* describes the actions of a bomber who attacks three or more targets. The targets are usually public, government buildings, or installations. The targets may be individuals or institutions, such as the targets chosen by Ted Kaczynski, the Unabomber.

FIREFIGHTERS WHO ARE ARSONISTS

Occasionally there is a breaking story that details the criminal exploits of a firefighter who has been arrested for arson, and in some cases, murder. If we were to classify such individuals, they would more than likely be classified as arsonists who set fires for excitement, which is a category in each of the previously discussed classification systems.

Excitement arson is associated with pyromania and impulsivity disorder, as described in the *Diagnostic and Statistical Manual of Mental Disorders, IV-TR* (*DSM-IV-TR;* APA, 2000). Central to the disorder are stressors and an immediate release of tension. The motivations of someone in this category may be sexual, but the satisfaction received from property destruction may also involve a cluster of other personality deficits, such as low self-esteem, sensitivity to criticism, impulsive behavior, a lack of empathy, and a disregard for others. These deficits, which were taken from the *DSM-IV-TR,* are a combination of diagnostic criteria associated with *antisocial personality disorder* and *narcissistic personality disorder.*

I offer these personality deficits here because they appear to be what is described as central in most, if not all, arsonists. Yet, the category of excitement becomes even more pronounced for the firefighter arsonist in that the offender may set the fire, contact public safety personnel, and then become actively involved in putting out the fire or saving lives. This individual is described in the literature as the "would-be hero" and uses arson as the tool to address his or her own personality deficits in order to gain the recognition and admiration of peers or the community, or both, for his or her actions.

Many enter the profession of firefighting and policing because they crave the excitement. When it comes to policing, I will argue that the job is 90 percent boredom and 10 percent sheer terror (Thomas, 2011). I do not see the fire service as being much different in that firefighters spend a large amount of time waiting to receive a call. Unlike law enforcement, however, the majority of firefighters in the United States are volunteers. Karter and Stein (2012), in their analysis of the U.S. fire service in 2011, stated that of the more than one million firefighters in the United States, 69 percent were volunteer firefighters and 31 percent were career firefighters (p. iii).

An examination of firefighter standards reveals that there is a distinct difference between the requirements of career firefighters and volunteer firefighters. In most instances, a career firefighter's selection process is the same as that of a law enforcement officer, which requires an investigation of the candidate's background, a polygraph test, and a psychological evaluation. However, in a sampling of volunteer firefighter candidate selection processes, missing were the requirements of successfully passing a background investigation, polygraph, and psychological examination. Many fire departments have limited funding, and it would be cost-prohibitive for volunteer departments with limited resources and personnel to participate in candidate selection, that is very extensive.

Although the Federal Bureau of Investigation (FBI) and the U.S. Fire Administration collect and keep data on the number of arsons annually, the data do not include information on the number of firefighters who become arsonists. Stambaugh and Styron (2003), while acknowledging that the data sets are limited, have claimed that the firefighter who is most likely to commit arson is a volunteer firefighter, for two reasons: the standards for hiring are not as strict, and there are far more volunteer firefighters than there are career firefighters.

Although excitement is seen as one of the primary motives, many firefighters who commit arson will also fit into one or more of the classifications systems discussed. Stambaugh and Styron (2003) have also argued that additional motives are unique to firefighters, such as the need to be seen as a hero, to practice extinguishing fires, and/or to earn extra money (p. 6). This supports Prins's argument that we must be careful not to focus on one classification or category when looking at an arsonist. Like the other criminals discussed throughout this text, firefighters who commit arson defend and justify their actions through a distorted cognitive process. The process is described as rationalizing the crime, projecting blame on another (failure to take responsibility), and minimizing the potential consequences—a process known as rationalizing, projecting, and minimizing (RPM).

TWO CASE STUDIES: WHY ARSON?

As a student of crime, I have found classification systems to be useful in helping me understand the process and attempt to get some insight into offenders and their actions. Yet, my years on the street have taught me to be cautious, as Prins instructed, and let the evidence dictate the course of investigation, which may well be devoid of the use of any classification system. In fact, I do not classify an individual until I understand all the elements of the crime and have examined the evidence because, from an investigative standpoint, the motive may never be known. With that in mind, Williams (2005) asked the question: Why arson? In dealing with those who exhibited what Williams classified as disordered coping mechanisms, two glaring facts were revealed: (1) The offenders were rarely influenced by their peers when compared to other types of fire-setters, and (2) most had no idea how or why fire-setting became their behavior of choice (p. 129). The two case studies in this section illustrate how elusive motive can be.

CASE STUDY 6.2   PSYCHOTIC MURDERER OR ARSONIST?

The local fire department responded to a house fire. Firefighters fought the fire for an hour, and upon entering the house, they discovered a body. Police were notified, and upon further investigation, the fire was determined to be a clear case of arson. The arsonist had made it appear that the victim was smoking in bed and fell asleep, dropping the lit cigarette on the mattress; but the investigation revealed that gasoline had been used as an accelerant at three points in the home: the victim's bedroom, the interior front door, and the back door. A lack of oxygen in the bedroom caused the bedroom fire to extinguish itself, leaving minimal damage to the body. It was the fire at the front and rear doors that firefighters had a difficult time controlling because the fire had spread to the kitchen and the living room.

An examination of the body revealed that the victim had been stabbed multiple times; there were wounds in the neck, chest, and groin area. Candles had been used as the ignition source, which gave the suspect an opportunity to leave and the fire to go undetected for approximately twenty minutes.

Officers canvassed the neighborhood and spoke to neighbors on either side of the victim's house. The neighbor directly to the north stated that the victim's girlfriend Monique came to their house and asked to use the phone to call a taxicab. Monique stated that she and the victim had an argument and that she was going to her mother's house for the night and would return the next day. The neighbors stated that there was nothing unusual about Monique, noting that she was calm and relaxed. Approximately a half hour after Monique left in the cab, the neighbors smelled smoke and went to investigate, discovered that the victim's house was on fire, and immediately called the fire department. They knocked on the victim's front door and got no answer, so they assumed that the victim had left.

Police contacted the cab company and discovered that Monique had the cab take her to the local mental health facility where she admitted herself. The cab driver offered nothing new, reiterating what the neighbors had said regarding Monique being calm and relaxed. The cab driver thought that her behavior was unusual, since she was going to the "nuthouse."

Investigators contacted the mental health facility, which refused to supply them with any information. A second call to the doctor in charge of the unit obtained the information that Monique had been admitted as a patient and that she was protected from arrest because of her mental health status. Investigators confirmed that Monique was voluntarily admitted, which meant that she could voluntarily leave. The doctor was reminded that the county jail provided mental health services and that if Monique left his facility, he would be charged as an accessory after the fact. Monique was released into police custody.

Once at the jail, Monique was assessed by the jail's mental health professionals and was cleared for questioning. During questioning, Monique admitted to killing the victim. She stated that the victim had cheated on her for the last time. Monique stated that she had planned the murder and that the victim had gotten what he deserved. What she could not understand was how investigators were able to catch her, since she used an accelerant in the bedroom.

Questions for Reflection

1. Based on the typologies discussed in this chapter, would you classify Monique as an arsonist?
2. Do her actions qualify as falling under more than one classification?
3. Which theorist classification system fits Monique best, and why?

CASE STUDY 6.3   MURDER OR REVENGE?

It was Sunday night at 9:00 P.M. when police received a call of an explosion at a local Latino bar on the southwest side of town. Upon arrival at the bar, there was smoke coming from inside the bar. When officers entered the bar, there were ten patrons still sitting in their chairs drinking, and no one was injured. The smell of gunpowder was strong, and there were remnants of the pipe bomb located throughout the bar. Pieces of shrapnel had ripped holes in the wall and the bar. The bartender stated that a piece of shrapnel just missed his head and lodged in the wall behind him. He also stated that he was pouring a drink when the front door opened, someone threw a piece of metal into the bar, and then the explosion occurred. The bartender and the witnesses both advised that they did not see who threw the bomb and that it happened so fast they could not react. After taking statements, the crime scene department was called, and the scene was turned over to arson investigators. The responding officers had worked for the department for more than ten years, and this was the first bomb call they had ever received.

Approximately an hour later, there was a second call of a bombing on the southeast side of town. The same two officers responded to this call; when they arrived at the address, a house was fully engulfed in flames. Three adults had made it outside, although they were burned on their lower extremities. When asked if anyone else was in the house, all three yelled that the children were inside, in a second-floor bedroom on the west side of the house. The officers, screaming into their radios to send the fire department as quickly as possible, tried to enter the house from the ground floor, but it was fully engulfed in flames at each exit point. Neighbors did not have a ladder. The officers had to stand there helpless, listening to the children scream as they burned to death.

At the scene, it appeared that the suspect(s) had thrown a Molotov cocktail through windows on the first floor, at each of the three outside doors, and targeted one into the children's bedroom. Three children died in the fire: Tommy, 4; Ricky, 3; and Michelle, 2. Police determined that the victim was a drug dealer and the bombing was payback because he had robbed another dealer.

Police used a number of tactics to identify the suspect and confirm the alleged story that this was payback. Eventually witnesses came forward because of a $50,000 reward, and after six months, police arrested and charged a drug dealer named Ed Sanchez. In the interview, Sanchez stated that he was responsible for both bombs and that the one at the southwest bar was designed to be a distractor. He failed there because no one was injured when he bombed the bar, and thus his goal of tying up police and fire resources while he bombed the second residence was not accomplished.

Sanchez stated that the victim, Darnell Smith, was a drug dealer and that Smith had robbed Sanchez of $10,000 worth of powdered cocaine. During the robbery, Smith had threatened to kill Sanchez and his family. Sanchez stated that he had no choice; it was to kill or to be killed. He further stated that he had learned to make bombs by reading *The Anarchist Cookbook*, a book that describes how to make bombs and other weapons. Sanchez had made some trial runs, trying different recipes until he created the perfect mix.

After hearing the police and fire sirens speeding to the southwest location, Sanchez drove to Smith's house but had to wait because there were a number of people on the street. In fact, Sanchez stated that he had to come back three times before he had the prime opportunity. He threw the Molotov cocktails in the following order: living room window, front door, side door, back door, and finally the children's bedroom window. Sanchez stated that he wanted Smith to suffer, so even if the adults survived, he wanted the kids to die. Sanchez watched as the Smith house burned. He did not expect the police to respond as quickly as they did, and that is why he did not shoot the three adults as they ran from the house. Sanchez stated that he did not see the kids, but he saw the police trying everything to get to them. He also stated that he was satisfied. When asked if he felt any remorse, Sanchez replied, "I have a clean conscience; Smith is responsible for this" (Thomas, 1986).

Questions for Reflection

1. What insights does this case offer in regard to the distorted cognitive processes and justifications used by offenders?

2. What theories and typologies best fit this case and offender?

3. How does Ed Sanchez compare with Monique in Case Study 6.2? In what ways are they similar as arsonists, and in what ways are they different?

Analysis of Ed Sanchez in Case Study 6.3

In examining Ed Sanchez's actions in Case Study 6.3, it is quite simple to determine his motive: His was a case of revenge. One might be inclined to identify him as an excitement-motivated arsonist because after he threw the Molotov cocktails, he watched from his car as the victims ran out of the house, and he stated that he was satisfied as he watched the house burn. The reality, however, is that he stood by because if the victims escaped, he intended to shoot them on the porch or force them back into the house to burn—either way, to make sure they died. What Sanchez did not count on was the police response.

Even though he could not kill Smith and the adult family members, Sanchez had the satisfaction of knowing that Smith's children had died in the fire. He later stated that Smith would live the rest of his life knowing that he (Smith) was responsible for their deaths. Sanchez stated that had Smith not robbed him, there would have been no arson and the kids would still be alive. Sanchez refused to take responsibility for the fire and the deaths for that very reason. Investigators asked Sanchez how he knew the location of the children's bedroom, and he stated, "You would be surprised how far a little cocaine goes." When asked why he chose fire, Sanchez replied, "Because I wanted it to be horror-filled and painful. If others saw what I did, then everyone would fear me. I would become king of the street" (Thomas, 1986). Sanchez was classified as a *revenge-motivated arsonist* and diagnosed with *narcissistic personality disorder*.

To better understand Sanchez, we need to revisit Wille, who was discussed in Chapter 2. Wille (1974) studied forty subjects in four groups—ten murderers with psychosis, ten murderers without psychosis, ten nonmurderers with psychosis, and ten nonmurderers without psychosis—and noted distinct differences between murderers and nonmurderers in their patterns of handling anger, fear, and overt aggression (p. 28). In Wille's analysis of the data, he determined that psychologically the murderers overall spent less time thinking about anger, fear, and aggressive behavior, meaning that a great deal of their energy was spent on repressing those thought and feelings. However, if provoked, there was an expectation that the response would be sudden, violent, and destructive. Finally, Wille described two syndromes in every murderer:

- *Syndrome of repression and intense thought,* which allows the subject to function normally in his or her world, with one exception—the syndrome of expectancy
- *Syndrome of expectancy,* which can be described as the subject being always on edge and ready (pp. 33–34)

I interpret the syndrome of expectancy to mean that the person's body is always in a state of "fight of flight," ready to respond with aggression to the slightest provocation. In such a constant state of hypervigilence, the body is never able to relax.

An examination of the actions of Sanchez shows that he exhibited both syndromes; and in fact, to be effective in his trade, he had to be that way in order to survive. Without action and retribution, Sanchez would be considered a target to everyone on the street. However, by attacking Smith, he ensured that everyone would fear him. Much like Lee Iacocca, who placed his reputation on the line to bring Chrysler back from bankruptcy in 1978, Sanchez felt his reputation on the street was on the line. Reputation means everything on the street, much like it does in any other business.

CONCLUSION

Similar to murder, arson has many motivations, and there are a number of classification systems for arsonists. Research indicates that we learn acts of violence as we develop from infants to adulthood and experience a number of disappointments. Often what happens is that in our development, we acquire coping skills and learn how to manage disappointment, anger, rage, jealousy, and resentment. Void of those coping skills, our behavior will be inappropriate and will begin to be revealed in social settings such as school.

I wish I could say that every arsonist fits a certain category and that everyone fits neatly into Wille's analysis; however, when dealing with human behavior, that would be impossible. To really understand the act of arson, it is important to understand the psychology associated with the incident, breaking down every aspect of the crime and the suspect's behavior prior to the incident. It is especially important to understand the stressors, substance abuse, failure, disappointments, losses, and psychosis, if one exists.

REFERENCES

American Psychiatric Association (APA). (2000). *The diagnostic and statistical manual of mental disorders, IV-TR*, 4th ed. Arlington, VA: Author.

Bandura, A. (1977). *Social learning theory.* Englewood Cliffs, NJ: Prentice-Hall.

Colorado General Assembly. (2013). *Arson, Colorado State Statute 4-1.* Denver, CO: Author.

Dickens, G., Sugarman, P., Edgar, S., Hofberg, K., Tewari, S., & Ahmad, F. (2009). Recidivism and dangerousness in arsonists. *Journal of Forensic Psychiatry and Psychology, 20*(5), pp. 621–639.

Douglas, J. E., Burgess, A. W., Burgess, A. G., & Ressler, R. K. (2006). *Crime classification manual*, 2nd ed. San Francisco: Jossey-Bass.

Florida State Legislature. (2013). *Arson and criminal mischief, Florida State Statute 806.01.* Tallahassee, FL: Author.

Gaynor, J. (2002). *Juvenile firesetter intervention handbook.* Emmitsburg, MD: U.S. Fire Administration.

Karter, M. J., & Stein, G. P. (2012). *U.S. fire department profile through 2011.* Quincy, MA: National Fire Protection Association.

Labree, W., Nijman, H., van Marle, H., & Rassin, E. (2010). Backgrounds and characteristics of arsonists. *International Journal of Law and Psychiatry, 33,* pp. 149–153.

Lewis, N. D.C., & Yarnell, H. (1951). *Pathological firesetting (pyromania).* New York: Nervous and Mental Disease.

McCarty, C. A., & McMahon, R. J. (2005). Domains of risk in the developmental continuity of fire setting. *Behavior Therapy, 36,* pp.185–195.

McKerracher, D. W., & Dacre, A. J. (1966). A study of arsonists in a special security hospital. *British Journal of Psychiatry, 112*(492), pp. 1151–1154.

Prins, H. (1994). *Fire-raising: Its motivation and management.* New York: Routledge.

Quinsey, V. L., Harris, G. T., Rice, M. E., & Cormier, C. A. (1998). *Violent offenders: Appraising and managing risk.* Washington, D.C.: American Psychological Association.

Rider, A. (1980). The firesetter: A psychological profile (Part 1). *FBI Law Enforcement Bulletin, 49,* pp. 7–17.

Root, C., MacKay, S., Henderson, J., Del Bove, G., & Warling, D. (2008). The link between maltreatment and juvenile firesetting: Correlates and underlying mechanisms. *Child Abuse and Neglect, 32,* pp. 161–176.

Schwartzman, P., Stambaugh, H., & Kimball, J. (1998). *Special report: Juveniles and arson: Responding to the violence: A review of teen firesetting and interventions.* Emmitsburg, MD: U.S. Fire Administration.

Stambaugh, H., & Styron, H. (2003). *Special report: Firefighter arson.* Emmitsburg, MD: U.S. Fire Administration.

Texas State Legislature. (2013). *Arson, criminal mischief, and other property damage or destruction, Texas State Statute 28.01.* Austin, TX: Author.

Thomas, D. J. (1986). *Case files of David Thomas, Grand Rapids Police Department.* Grand Rapids, MI: Author.

Thomas, D. J. (2008). *Case files of David Thomas, Gainesville Police Department.* Gainesville, FL: Author.

Thomas, D. J. (2011). *Professionalism in policing: An introduction.* Clifton Park. NY: Cengage Learning.

U.S. Fire Administration. (2001). *Arson in the United States, 1*(8). Washington, D.C.: Department of Homeland Security.

Vreeland, R., & Levin, B. (1980). Fires and human and behavior. In D. Canter (Ed.), *Psychological aspects of firesetting* (pp. 31–46). Chichester, England: Wiley.

Wille, W. S. (1974). *Citizens who commit murder.* St. Louis, MO: Warren H. Green.

Williams, D. L. (2005). *Understanding the arsonist: From assessment to confession.* Tucson, AZ: Lawyers & Judges.

Gangs

Gangs have been around since the beginning of time. They are not limited to humans. All animals are territorial, hunt in packs, and protect themselves from predators in large groups. If you examine the behavior of animals, we as humans are not so different. Society as a whole is based on the concept of a social contract where we give up our free will for protection by government. Giving up free will means that we agree to not violate the law and, if we choose to do so, accept that we will be punished. Yet, the term *gang* does not make us think of the civility of society based on a social contract; instead, it conjures up pictures of Al Capone and famous movies such as *The Godfather* and *Scarface*.

Some gangs are known regionally, while others are known nationally as well as internationally. An example of regional gang activity is that which took place in cities like Detroit in the 1970s, when violence was rampant due to the "heroin wars" that marked the beginning of the destruction of the traditional African American family and the creation of the prison economy. Today, street gangs such as the Crips, Bloods, and MS13 have international reputations. This chapter will provide you with a historical context of modern street gangs, beginning with the question of how to define a gang.

WHAT IS A GANG?

Before you read further, take a moment and define the term gang. When I think of the word gang, I define it as a group of three or more who are involved in criminal activity. In examining a number of state statutes, I found that each used similar language to define a gang as follows: a formal or informal ongoing organization, association, or group of three or more persons with a common name or identifying signs or colors whose primary activities are the commission of criminal or delinquent acts (California State Legislature, 2013; Florida State Legislature, 2013; New York State Legislature, 2013; Texas State Legislature, 2013).

Researchers in the Ministry of Justice (2011) in the United Kingdom interviewed forty-four incarcerated gang members and found that a percentage of the participants refused to participate in the research if they were going to be labeled as gang members. The Ministry of Justice researchers noted that the term gang has many meanings and can be defined by: cohesive friendships where there is no recruitment of members; or a cohesive unit that is competitive, with a defined hierarchy; or affiliations based on geography or territory.

Bouchard and Spindler (2010) offered a similar analysis of gangs, arguing that rather than using membership or structure to identify a gang, we would be better served if we defined a gang based on its level of organization. These authors argued that organizational sophistication defines organizational behavior in gangs, much as it does in business. In essence, the organization creates a culture that supports criminal activity, and in so doing, the acts of criminal activity become more violent over time. As we will discuss later in the chapter, organizational culture and behavior are an extension of the organization's leadership and are supported by the value system that the leaders espouse.

Klein and Maxson (2001) included the following gang types in their study of street gangs: prison gangs, organized adult crime groups, motorcycle gangs, terrorist groups, stoners, and satanic cults. After completing a series of surveys, these researchers determined that what we think of as the traditional gang is actually not the most common kind. Today, the ethnic differences are not as well defined as they were in the past; drug gangs make up a smaller percentage of the gangs today; and police reports that detail gang activity and relationships are not valid in representing patterns of gang crime (p. 15).

An examination of the work of the researchers makes it apparent that defining the term gang is difficult, as is knowing which types of organizations to include in the definition. Regardless of how we define or organize them, however, street gangs have been a real urban phenomenon for years. Beginning in the 1990s, they evolved into an even greater problem with which both urban and rural law enforcement has been grappling ever since. Let's turn to some of the risk factors, theories, and concepts associated with the attraction to gangs to try to better understand what makes one choose to join a gang.

Questions for Reflection: When it comes to gangs, do you believe that family violence is the cause of gang membership? What would make someone want to join a gang? For those in poverty, are gangs the only choice?

RISK FACTORS

In the previous chapters, in attempting to explain why people commit their chosen crimes, we have continuously been brought back to the beginning: the early years of a child's life. Since entrance into a street gang begins early for some—for example, by 10 years of age—it is important to revisit the risk factors. In regard to murder, rape, and arson, in many instances, family violence has been present; offenders were either victimized, witnessed violence in the home, or both, which often became the catalyst that led the offenders to commit the acts of violence.

Researchers have determined that there are a host of risk factors that can lead one to select gang membership over all else. Most are attached to developmental domains that influence our behavioral patterns. As discussed in previous chapters, central to the core of an individual is the interaction between the psychological, biological, and environmental influences; one, two, or all three can predispose an individual to be susceptible to a life of delinquency and crime. Environment seems to have the greatest influence regarding the decisions and needs of an individual. On a daily basis, a child is bombarded with influences, both positive and negative, from a number of sources. The family is the first source, and the environment that it provides is hugely influential—whether it is loving, supportive, and nurturing; or cold, distant, and fraught with acts of violence.

In Chapter 1, in connection with the role of the environment, we examined three theories that explain developmental outcomes: Maslow's (1943) hierarchy of needs, Bowlby's (1940) attachment theory, and Rothbart's (2007) temperament model. These theories, which are interrelated, detail the importance of a safe secure environment in the development of personality and temperament from birth. Safety and security provide a platform for a child to explore and learn through support and nurturing. Human beings are social creatures, and failure to provide such an environment has a direct impact on their overall well-being. Bandura (1973) argued that aggression is a learned behavior, either through modeling or practice, and that if not addressed through some form of control, then it will be reinforced (p. 68). The concept of development is directly related to each of the aforementioned theories.

Daycare centers and schools are where children step out for the first time to experience an environment that is different from that of their home. It is the place where they have to apply the social skills they developed in the home and where their actions and behavior will be judged independent of the family, and will be deemed socially acceptable or not. In addition, this environment is where the selection of peers and peer involvement begins independent of the family. Often, family members will have something to say, either positive or negative, regarding peer selection—although sometimes family members can misread peers. Just think about the mother who tells her son, "I wish you were more like Johnny; he's doing something positive with his life," while the son thinks, "Yeah, Mom, right, if you only knew the truth." Likewise, family members have been known to perceive a peer as a negative influence when he or she really is not.

Parents would like to think that they have done a great job with their children and that when they send them to school, the children will adjust and perform well. Lacourse, Nagin, Tremblay, Vitaro, and Claes (2003) determined that there are three different developmental stages at which a juvenile may become involved with deviant peers:

- *Childhood affiliation:* The juvenile becomes affiliated with deviant peers before or during preadolescence.
- *Adolescent affiliation:* This type of association begins during adolescence.
- *No affiliation:* The juvenile never or only sporadically chooses to associate with deviant peers (p. 194).

In examining the developmental stages provided by Lacourse et al., it seems that this would be the logical sequence of events.

However, Battin, Hill, Abbot, Catalano, and Hawkins (1998) found that gang involvement is unique and different from affiliations and, as noted by Bouchard and Spindler (2010), that membership and the organizational structure of the group are more important in determining actual ties and level of activity. The Battin group found that even after controlling for prior criminal histories and the number of criminal acquaintances/friends, it was the culture of the gang that had the greatest influence (p. 107). When comparing gangs to delinquent groups who were just friends, the Battin study found that gang members reported more violent crime, sold more drugs, and drank more alcohol than delinquent groups who were friends (p. 107).

Finally, Fuller (2009) stated that juveniles seek out gangs because they are highly structured and offer a strong sense of belonging and worth through symbols, signs, and rules that replace other institutions such as family, school, and community (p. 370). The gang provides a juvenile with a sense of identity, value, and self-worth, as well as a feeling of love and purpose.

Questions for Reflection: Does deviant behavior and affiliation with other deviant juveniles predispose one to become a gang member? Does it make any difference what the home life is like? Who has more influence over juveniles, parents or peers?

ORGANIZATIONAL AND LEADERSHIP THEORIES

Every aspect of the research on gangs states that gang involvement is based on the organization and the leadership of that organization. Central to every organization are the values and the culture, which make or break an organization. From a practical standpoint, I think there is no difference between a traditional organization, such as a police department, and a gang. My belief is that organizational culture, values, and leadership are the same in both types of organizations; the difference is in their goals.

Traditional Organizational Theory

Alvesson (2002) noted that organizational culture should not always be seen as something that has consensus and harmony, but rather should be viewed as dynamic and containing contradiction, hidden agendas, and conflict (p. 121). Schein (2004) argued that we cannot see the forces that cause certain types of organizational behavior and offered three types of culture inherent in every organization:

- *Artifacts:* These consist of everything one sees, hears, and feels when one encounters a new group or an unfamiliar culture (pp. 25–26). When applying this concept to new members, it is important that the current members support the leadership; this is easy if the leader is charismatic. This type of culture is the glue that holds the group together.
- *Espoused beliefs and values:* These are developed in response to a problem or a series of problems that requires a solution. Often the solution is based on someone's belief of what is right or wrong; the belief of group members in that person's position is what creates leaders (p. 28). In response to the issue of gang member misconduct or dissension in the ranks, for example, the leader must employ punishment. The answer to many problems is found in the history and past practices of an organization. Failure to address problems or to punish members who are out of line can destroy the very culture of an organization.
- *Basic underlying assumptions:* These are associated with solutions to a problem, and when applied they repeatedly work, and yet they are only supported by a hunch or one's belief system (p. 30).

Within one organization, there are multiple organizational cultures that are defined by rank, specialization, and even division or bureau. Each of these will have an impact on an individual's performance because each defines an organizational and operational standard. Organizational culture affects how members think and feel, but more importantly, it defines identification, loyalty, and commitment, and the concepts of value and self-worth within an organization (Cameron & Quinn, 2006; Druckman, Singer, & Van Cott, 1997; Schein, 2004).

The success or failure of an organization hinges on both the leadership and the organization's members having their needs met, or at least finding a healthy compromise (Gilley, Quatro, Hoekstra, Whittle, & Maycunich, 2001; Kurke, 1995). Gilley and colleagues (2001) described a successful leader as a servant leader (p. 210). Kurke (1995) outlined the needs of the leadership and the members:

- *Leadership:* operations, administrative, performance, political pressures, and successes
- *Members:* self-esteem, personal performance record, compensations, security, opportunities for advancement, and the intangible benefit of membership in the organization of choice (p. 395)

A good leader builds an organizational culture that meets the needs of both leadership and organizational members.

Leadership Styles

There are many leadership styles discussed in the literature, but those most commonly discussed are authoritarian/autocratic, laissez-faire, and democratic (Bennett & Hess, 2007; Dantzker, 1998; Panzarella, 2003; Schroeder & Lombardo, 2004). However, Whitfield, Alison, and Crego (2008) contend that it should be impossible to pigeonhole a leader because the dynamics of an organization are ever-changing and fluid (p. 81). Although their discussion focuses on critical incidents, they offer a description of how a member feels valued within an organization with the following observation: "Individuals remain productive and positive when their expertise is acknowledged, and officers need to be supported and monitored by leaders that are adaptive, participative, and empathetic" (p. 91).

The discussion by Whitfield and colleagues was supported by Hersey, Blanchard, and Johnson (2001), who described the situational leader. These authors offered three components of the leadership process: the leader, the follower, and the situation (p. 108). They noted that a leader who offers only one style of leadership for every circumstance puts the accomplishment of his or her stated objectives in jeopardy by failing to recognize the needs of the employees (p. 231).

Organizational Gang Theory

Jankowski (1991), who studied thirty-seven gangs, argued that the most important organizational features of a gang are structure, leadership, recruitment, initiation rites, role expectations, sanctions, and migration patterns. Jankowski described three types of structure adopted by gang leadership:

- *Vertical/horizontal:* a traditional command structure where power and authority are delegated through rank and hierarchy, much like they are in the military or a police department
- *Horizontal/commission:* where several officeholders share power and authority, as well as duties, equally
- *Influential:* in which no written duties or titles are assigned to any leadership position, but instead two to four members are recognized informally as leaders because of their charisma

The vertical and horizontal structures have the ability to plan and complete successful business transactions, successfully build coalitions, and mobilize political resource (p. 91). In the influential structure, there are no titles as described by Kurke, so in order to stay in power, leaders must meet the needs of their members, be flexible, and be fair (pp. 95–96).

One type of leader rarely mentioned in any discussion on gang leadership is the informal leader. Informal leaders have clout and are respected by their peers; therefore, they can be seen as a threat to any leader. They obtain their status because of their knowledge, their survival of violent encounters on the street, their refusal to back down from the police, and their ability to avoid jail and/or beat charges (Thomas, 2010).

Grossman (1996) argued that with leadership comes authority and power. In an organization such as a gang, when the group is tasked with an act of violence, the success of the task will be dependent on the legitimacy of the leader's authority. Grossman describes the elements of leadership authority as: proximity of the leader to the individual or group when committing a criminal act, respect for the leader, intensity of the leader's demands, and a belief that the leader's demands are valid (pp. 144–145).

A gang is a group in which members share the same value and belief system. Closely associated with this belief system is what is known as "groupthink," which means that the group thinks collectively, using distorted beliefs to logically support their actions. It is because of groupthink that violent acts can be generalized and the gang members find absolution in their acts. As noted in every chapter, violent offenders use a distorted cognitive process to justify their actions; when that thought process is applied to a group, it is a very powerful antidote to guilt. Self-preservation is not the key; rather, it is the bond and the sense of accountability that an individual has to the group (Decker, Melde, & Pyrooz, 2013; Grossman, 1996).

RISE OF THE GANG CULTURE IN THE UNITED STATES

Long before there was the Crips and Bloods, Detroit had a number of street gangs that were notorious. First were the *Errol Flynns,* named after the actor Errol Flynn, and in the 1980s the *Young Boys Incorporated* rose. Many people have asked how and why gangs became a staple in large urban areas such as Detroit, and some have wondered why they are so often associated with African American or Latino communities. Why these groups above all others? Thomas (2013) describes the proliferation of violence in the African American community as the result of a perfect storm brought on historically by a series of social events that came together and created this problem.

First in the equation is the African American family. For many years, the African American family unit has been described as a one-parent family void of the father. Many researchers have claimed that this family structure dates back to the time of slavery, when African American men were sold and traded, and often forced to leave their families. This long-held belief was also the assumption in a paper generated by New York senator Daniel Patrick Moynihan (1965) and released by the Department of Labor titled *The Negro Family: The Case for National Action.*

Herbert Gutman (1977), however, determined that although slaves were property for the most part, they were able to maintain two-parent families, and that after slavery, the family unit was still the two-parent family. Gutman supported his claim through a survey of 13,000 African American families in Harlem, New York, in 1925. The data obtained from the survey revealed the following: 85 percent of the households contained two parents; only 32 of the 13,000 families were headed by a single mother under the age of 30 with three or more children; 7–8 percent of the females between ages 25 and 44 were one-parent households (twenty years earlier, it had been 10 percent); three of four African American males over the age of 44 were unskilled laborers and were heads of two-parent households; and five in six children lived with both parents (p. xix).

Some African Americans have argued that the federal government and Senator Moynihan released such propaganda and misrepresentations of the facts to keep the African American population in a subservient role and perpetuate stereotypes and racism. Moynihan would argue that the purpose of the document was to detail injustice and provide a framework by which the United States could move forward and correct the mistakes of the past, even though his data distorted the truth.

Based on the findings of Gutman (1977), despite slavery, the African American family was stable for a long time. In the past fifty years, however, there has been significant change. The African American family has been deeply affected by a number of events: unskilled labor moving from the United States to underdeveloped countries with low wages, the influx of illegal drugs in the African American community, the drug wars and the war on drugs, and the incarceration of one or both African American parents. These events are discussed in more detail in the following paragraphs.

Item 1: The loss of jobs by unskilled laborers. As discussed in Chapter 5, the United States was heralded as the great industrial giant because of Henry Ford's introduction of mass production in making the Model T. However, the industry that built this country and supported U.S. efforts during World War II began to crumble in the early 1970s with the oil embargo, gas shortages, soaring gas prices, poorly made automobiles, and the American passion for foreign automobiles with excellent gas mileage. As factories began to close, the United States moved away from industry and manufacturing and began to invest in what we now call the prison-industrial economy (Howden & Meyer, 2010; Wildeman & Western, 2010).

The elements of a prison-industrial complex are as follows: Unskilled laborers lost their jobs, factories closed, and the economy crashed in communities where businesses collapsed. Some communities, cities, and states have never recovered. Detroit, Michigan, is one such city; it has never recovered from the decline of the automobile industry. To offset the loss of jobs in the prison-industrial complex, communities have replaced factories with prisons and jobs related to the prison industry (Howden & Meyer, 2010; Wildeman & Western, 2010). The end result was the loss of unskilled laborer positions, many of which were held by African American men.

Item 2: The influx of heroin in the black community. The entry of heroin into the black community had a negative impact on the African American family because one or both parents in many black families were attracted to the drug trade in some fashion. Detroit is the perfect example of how the two events referred to here as items 1 and 2 collided. *Time* magazine (1971) reported the following: Detroit was in the midst of an all-out heroin war for control of the $350 million heroin market; during that time, there was an estimated 20,000 addicts in the city, most of them black; and there was one homicide every four days associated with the heroin wars of Detroit (p. 20). In response to the heroin wars and rising crime rate at the same time that Detroit suffered a loss of unskilled laborer positions, the prison-industrial economy was introduced.

Item 3: Crack cocaine entered the picture. In the late 1970s, heroin began to die out and powder cocaine became the drug of choice, but it was unavailable to the poor because of the price. Cooper (2002) noted that for this reason, drug cartels and chemists began to experiment with various forms of cocaine, eventually creating "crack cocaine," in order to make the drug available to the masses; it quickly became the drug of choice in the African American community (pp. 27–28). Crack was small, easy to conceal, and cheap, meaning that one could buy a "piece" or a "rock" for as little as $5.00; and because it was a solid as opposed to powder, it was smoked, creating an instant feeling of euphoria. It was also very addictive. The African American community transitioned from heroin to crack without missing a beat.

Item 4: The "war on drugs." With the introduction of heroin and later crack, President Nixon declared a "war on drugs." Both Presidents Nixon and Reagan argued that since it would be impossible to interdict or eradicate the drugs, the most effective way to deal with the problem is to remove the customer and establish a zero-tolerance policy, with incarceration as the ultimate penalty for substance abuse (Rosenberger, 1996). This policy negatively impacted the African American family because the majority of crack abusers were black.

Item 5: Incarceration of parents. Incarcerating fathers, and often mothers as well, has destabilized a family foundation that was shaky at best. The victims of parents' incarceration have been the children. The children's response to one or both parents being incarcerated has included behavior-related difficulties described as acting out, withdrawal, anxiousness, depression, anger, frustration, failure in school, and an increased likelihood of incarceration as a juvenile and adult (Gibson, 2008; Wildeman & Western, 2010).

The cause-and-effect connections of these five items in the African American family and community are further highlighted by Kirchhoff (2010), who noted that in the last few decades, there has been a 400 percent jump in incarceration rates in the United States, and at the end of 2008, 2.3 million adults were incarcerated in state, local, or federal facilities, with another 5.1 million on probation or parole (p. i). Prison growth has been fueled by the war on drugs, lengthy prison sentences, minimum mandatory sentencing, and recidivism. Finally, data from the Bureau of Labor Statistics (2012) supported the claim that the United States has moved from an industrial society to a prison-industrial economy: Approximately 770,000 people were employed in the field of corrections in 2008, and that number is expected to increase by 5 percent by 2020. The growth of corrections as an industry is slowing down because the crime rates have been falling consistently over the past few years;

however, probation and parole are expected to increase by 18 percent by 2020 (Bureau of Labor Statistics, 2012).

CRACK COCAINE AND GANG VIOLENCE

For many years, there has been a debate regarding the causes and perpetrators of violence in the African American community. The African American community is one that does not willingly open its doors to outsiders or openly discuss its problems. Nor is it a community that has taken a stand to stop the violence, and often its members have criticized those who have attempted to bring the issue to the forefront (Unnever & Gabbidon, 2011).

To illustrate the seriousness of the problem, Harms and Snyder (2004) completed a meta-analysis of data and concluded that between the years 1980 and 1993, the juvenile homicide rate among African Americans aged 12 to 17 increased 163 percent (p. 1). This change in the homicide rate can best be described as sudden; the only new factor introduced into the African American community at that time was crack cocaine (Blumstein, 1995; Grogger & Willis, 1998). Cork (1999) determined that this rise in violence was dependent on two variables: crack cocaine and firearms. Independent of each other, there may have been some rise in homicides, but when placed together, those factors became the driving force for the meteoric rise of homicides involving African American juvenile males.

There are several reasons why juveniles became the foot soldiers during the crack cocaine epidemic. In interviews conducted with suppliers, many repeatedly stated that juveniles make the perfect dealers because if they are arrested, they will be released to their parents within 24 to 48 hours. If a juvenile is adjudicated (found guilty) and sent to a program, the juvenile's sentence will be less than a year as long as the crime did not involve violence, whereas adults can get up to twenty years or more, depending on the type and amount of narcotics in their possession at the time of their arrest. The incentives for juveniles to become involved in the drug trade are many: money, power, guns, girls, and the ability to help their families, who often are on welfare. If we look at all of the perceived rewards, we can understand why a juvenile drug dealer and gang member might not want to work in a fast-food restaurant or at the local grocery store.

During my career as a law enforcement officer, I arrested and interviewed hundreds of juveniles for the sale and possession of crack cocaine from 1992 to 1994. The activity on the streets was so intense that at one point I made 300 arrests for the sale and possession of crack cocaine in a six-month period. Ninety percent or 270 of those arrested were African American males under the age of 18. Many had been arrested multiple times on similar drug charges and, as predicted by the suppliers, had been detained, adjudicated guilty, and released within forty-eight hours. The profile of each juvenile offender was similar:

- A gang member
- Living in a single-parent home with the mother as the sole provider
- Family receiving welfare and living at or below the poverty line
- No contact with father, or he was incarcerated
- On average, two other siblings living with the offender
- Poor performance in school (Most had been labeled in school as *severely emotionally disturbed* (SED), which is a classification used as a designator for students with learning disabilities or behavior problems; SED students are assigned to special classes or an alternative school.)
- Multiple contacts with police in and out of school
- More aggressive and a growing sense of invincibility with each arrest, with the juvenile justice system being considered merely an inconvenience
- Continuance of behavior until either getting murdered, committing murder, or being arrested and receiving long prison terms as adults (Thomas, 2013)

I offer this profile along with the historical information in this section so that you will understand that this problem did not happen in a vacuum; rather, it is tied to a number of social issues. Now that we know the history, where do we stand today in regard to gang membership in the United States?

> **Questions for Reflection:** Why join a gang and participate in criminal activity? Why not work at McDonald's and go to school? Is America a land of opportunity in which anyone can succeed? Do people live in poverty only because they choose to?

GANG MEMBERSHIP IN THE UNITED STATES

Egley and Howell (2013) estimated that there are 29,900 gangs currently operating in the United States with 782,500 gang members (p. 1). These researchers revealed that in 2011, 56 percent of the gangs and 75 percent of the gang members were in urban areas, and 87 percent of the gang-related homicides occurred in the same areas (Egley & Howell, 2013, p. 2). The two primary reasons for gang violence were drugs and intragang conflict (members fighting among themselves), especially when members returned from incarceration and there had been change that led to challenges between the new leadership and the original members.

Many have claimed over the years that America is the land of opportunity. Some claim that those who live in poverty in the United States do so because they choose to. Opportunity Nation (2013), however, provided some alarming data that contradict the notion that everyone in America has an equal chance. This organization stated that success in the United States is determined by a person's zip code or where that person was born. In addition, 15 percent or 6 million youth between the ages of 16 and 24 are neither in school nor working (Opportunity Nation, 2013). This number of idle youth is staggering and does nothing but add to the potential for gang membership involvement, because these young people have become disconnected from mainstream society and view themselves as less than desirable. If these traits started early in life, then the problem is further exacerbated; the cognitive distortions and belief systems that these young people have about society are validated by their current situation, which makes gang emersion even easier.

GANG TYPOLOGY

Although some argue that leadership is more important than the type of gang in predicting member involvement and gang activity, I will argue, as I have in the past, that typologies are important in providing insight and understanding about gangs, and in battling these offenders. Nothing about gangs, however, is absolute; a number of variables may determine the typology of a gang. For example, is it for protection? Is it for participation in a criminal enterprise such as drugs? Does it limit itself in terms of location, race and ethnicity, or gender? As we look at research on typologies, keep in mind that all of these factors may help to define a gang; hence, it is difficult to pigeonhole such groups.

The National Gang Intelligence Center (2011) provided seven typologies of gangs, with each being involved in some form of criminal enterprise:

- *Street gangs* are gangs that have been formed on the street and operate throughout the United States. Two of the most notorious today are the Crips and the Bloods.
- *Prison gangs* serve several functions. One is criminal enterprise within the prison system. They also serve as a form of protection for their members within the walls. Finally, there is usually a connection between the gang members on the outside and those in prison. In essence, the prison gang is an extension of a street gang.
- *Outlaw motorcycle gangs (OMGs)* are similar to street gangs in that they are criminal organizations that are formed on the street and operate throughout the United States.

- *One percenters* are a form of outlaw motorcycle gangs. The ATF defines a one percenter as any group of motorcyclists that has voluntarily made a commitment to band together and abide by the organization's rules, which are enforced by violence, and to engage in activities that bring the club and its members into repeated and serious conflict with society and the law (National Gang Intelligence Center, 2011, p. 7).
- *Neighborhood/local gangs* are confined to a geographic area within a neighborhood, with sale and distribution of narcotics as their primary criminal enterprise.
- *Hybrid gangs* are gangs that have multiple affiliations nationwide.
- *Juggalos* are loosely organized hybrid gangs. Many juggalo subsets exhibit ganglike behavior and engage in criminal activity and violence.

Many of the gangs are noted for drug trafficking and have ties to the drug cartels. The National Gang Intelligence Center (2011) noted that these gangs are increasing the diversity of their criminal activity to include prostitution, human trafficking, and alien smuggling (pp. 24–26).

CASE STUDIES

Take a moment and examine the two case studies provided in this section. They will give you a wealth of information concerning gangs and their origins. I chose these case studies because each is unique.

In Case Study 7.1, a man is faced with the choice to live or die, and he chooses self-preservation over anonymity, which is often the situation of new gang members, whether in prison or on the street. Sometimes they have no choice and are forced to join, after which there is no escape for the individual.

CASE STUDY 7.1   I BECAME A SKINHEAD TO SURVIVE

Mark Smith was a local drug dealer with whom I had dealt many times. He was loosely affiliated with a local gang that had a reputation for selling drugs. He was a mixed-race man, half African American and half Caucasian; his features were Caucasian, and he had curly brown hair. After several years of getting arrested on drug possession charges and released, he was arrested and convicted for *armed robbery,* receiving a five-year sentence. Before he went to prison on these charges, I had retired and was completing my clinical internship with the Florida Department of Corrections. Smith was assigned to my caseload as patient.

Each week when I met with Smith, he was frantic and appeared to be in crisis because he had been threatened by two different gangs of inmates: a group of Black Muslims that threatened to rape him if he did not become Muslim, and a group of Skinheads who became angry with Smith because he was associating with the Black Muslims. The Muslims were unsure whether he was of mixed race, but suspected he was based on his mannerisms, body language, and vocabulary. The Skinheads knew that he was Caucasian and were calling him a race traitor.

Smith was torn because all of his life he had identified with African Americans, and he felt very uncomfortable with the Skinheads and their doctrine. Initially Smith attempted to remain neutral, but both groups pressured him. This went on for several weeks until the Black Muslims cornered him and stated that if he did not join the group, they would make an example of him. When he asked what that meant, Smith was advised that he would be gang-raped by all twenty members of the Black Muslims. The leader told Smith that he was a pretty boy and that even if he joined the group, he would become their "bitch."

Prior to making the decision to join the Skinheads, Smith attempted to resolve the matter by asking for help from the guards. They told Smith they would intervene only if Smith would snitch and identify the members of both groups. Smith felt that this would be a death sentence.

Smith believed that he was left with only one choice, and that was to join the Skinheads. As a member of the Skinheads, he received protection; in return, he sold drugs and participated in enforcement activities. This was not any different from his life on the street. Several years later, I ran into Smith on the street and he told me that he had sold drugs until he got out of prison, and the Skinheads had protected him. He also stated that it was a difficult time because he struggled with his racial identity. However, he was glad that he had a choice because most people do not (Thomas, 2003).

CASE STUDY 7.2   GANG OR MURDERERS?

Seath Jackson was a 15-year-old high school student who dated Amber Wright, another 15-year-old. The couple was described as being madly in love one month and hating each other the next. Their hatred turned into a battle of words on Facebook. Amber accused Seath of physical abuse, while Seath denied that it had ever happened. The Facebook battle led to Seath's murder. The incident that most angered the participants in the murder of Seath was one where Seath had pushed Amber and spit in her face. The participants in the murder were Kyle Hooper, Amber's brother; Michael Bargo, Amber's new boyfriend; Justin Soto, Bargo's friend; and Charlie Ely, Bargo's friend and the owner of the trailer where the murder occurred.

The incidents leading up to the murder were as follows. After Seath and Amber broke up, Amber began seeing 18-year-old Michael Bargo. Seath became aware of the relationship between Bargo and Amber and began challenging Bargo to a fight. On more than one occasion, he even showed up at Bargo's parents' house, yelling that he was going to burn it down, and threatened to kill the occupants. To make matters worse, after Amber and Seath broke up, Seath had been seen out with Hooper's girlfriend as well as at her house.

One of the Facebook messages written by Amber read: "I got so tired of you treating me like I was nothing. If you're so perfect, why don't you get over your jealousy and get a new girl you can hurt. . . . You know I cared deeply about you. I stuck with you through a lot of stuff. . . . It takes a real man to accept the fact he got broken up with."

Prior to April 17, 2011, the group had hatched a plan to kill Seath. On Sunday April 17, 2011, Amber began texting Seath under the guise of getting back together. Amber sent text messages for several hours before Seath finally relented, leaving a friend's house to meet Amber. Amber then took him to Charlie Ely's home where the group had been waiting to ambush Seath.

Hooper stated that each of the participants had a role in the attack on Seath. Amber walked in the door first, with Seath following. Hooper and Soto were waiting there with pieces of a wooden door frame. As Seath entered the house, each began beating Seath with the boards. Once the attack began, Hooper yelled a code word and Bargo came out with a gun. Hooper admitted that he wanted to hurt Seath for the acts of violence he had perpetrated against Amber and the fact that Seath had been with Hooper's girlfriend. However, he never thought that Bargo was serious when he spoke of killing Seath.

Seath fought until he was knocked to the floor. Once on the floor, Hooper and Soto held Seath down while Bargo pulled a gun and shot Seath. At that point, Seath was able to break free; he ran to the yard where he was tackled and shot in the head. Hooper, Bargo, and Soto dragged Seath's body back into the house and into the bathroom. They placed his body in the bathtub, only to discover that he was still alive, so Bargo shot Seath again. Then Bargo broke both of Seath's kneecaps. Bargo, Soto, and Hooper hog-tied Seath, stuffed his body into a sleeping bag, and threw the body into a raging fire in a firepit, where the body burned for the night.

On Monday April 18, Bargo shoveled Seath's remains into several five-gallon paint cans, and the group threw the cans in a local gravel pit where they often went to swim. After disposing of the body, they played basketball (Marion County Clerk of the Court, 2011).

Questions for Reflection: Do the two case studies presented here illustrate any of the theories discussed in this chapter, or do they fall outside of what has been defined as a gang? Since both studies are situational, ask yourself: What would I do if I were in a similar situation?

In Case Study 7.2, the Seath Jackson case, the group was not a formal gang; however, it was a group motivated by two things: jealousy and hatred. Seath was perceived to be a threat by the male members of the group. If you believe Hooper when he stated that he just wanted to hurt Seath, then why didn't he stop the attack when Bargo came out with the gun? There were several other opportunities to stop the attack because Seath had to be shot multiple times before he was killed.

The argument that I will pose in connection with the second case study is that leadership matters; if other people believe whatever the leader is telling them, then the leader will have followers. Although groups like this are not gangs in the formal sense, these types of incidents are growing in popularity with teenagers and young adults. In these situations, groupthink plays a role; one member poses an idea, and the group develops a series of distorted thoughts that provides justification for their criminal act. Again, with group action come both anonymity and absolution.

CONCLUSION

When I review the theories regarding street gangs, I find the story is the same. Gangs have changed and risen in popularity as a result of a number of events coming together—what Thomas (2013) described as the perfect storm: loss of unskilled laborer positions, poverty, and the change from an industrial economy to a prison-industrial economy; the influx of heroin and later crack cocaine; the incarceration of male heads of households and sometimes mothers; and a poor education system. One who is placed in such an environment has limited choices, and yet he or she has needs that extend beyond mere survival. The following quote says it all: "A 15-year-old boy recently walked into a suburban Mercedes Benz showroom, pointed at a black 500 SEL and announced, 'I'll take it.' He paid $62,000 cash from a brown paper bag. In the Jefferies Housing Project on the eastside, teenagers are driving new Corvettes, as Christmas bonuses for a job well done" (Blum, 1984, p. A1). The goal of every American is to achieve success by achieving wealth, and many gang members are doing just that.

Such success, however, comes at a price. In interviews with gang members, I have discovered that they clearly understand their situation: They will probably die at an early age or end up in prison. They figure that, in either instance, they will have had fun and developed a reputation. They look at the end result as the cost of doing business. As one young gang member told me, "It's just business: live, die, or prison. It's the cost."

REFERENCES

Alvesson, M. (2002). *Understanding organizational culture.* Thousand Oaks, CA: Sage.

Bandura, A. (1973). *Aggression: A social learning process.* Englewood Cliffs, NJ: Prentice-Hall.

Battin, S. R., Hill, K. G., Abbott, R. D., Catalano, R. F., & Hawkins, J. D. (1998). The contribution of gang membership to delinquency beyond delinquent friends. *Criminology, 36,* pp. 93–112.

Bennett, W. W., & Hess, K. M. (2007). *Management and supervision in law enforcement,* 5th ed. Belmont, CA: Thomson-Wadsworth.

Blum, H. (1984, January 28). U.S. helps Detroit attack drug rings that use young. *New York Times,* A1, A6.

Blumstein, A. (1995). Youth violence, guns, and the illicit-drug industry. *Journal of Criminal Law Criminology, 86,* pp. 10–36.

Bouchard, M., & Spindler, A. (2010). Groups, gangs, and delinquency: Does organization matter? *Journal of Criminal Justice, 38,* pp. 921–933.

Bowlby, J. (1940). The influence of early environment in the development of neurosis and neurotic character. *International Journal of Psychoanalysis, 25,* 154–178.

Bureau of Labor Statistics. (2012). *Occupational employment and wages—2012.* Washington, D.C.: Author.

California State Legislature. (2013). *Participation in a criminal street gang: California State Statute 186.22.* Sacramento, CA: Author.

Cameron, K. S., & Quinn, R. E. (2006). *Diagnosing and changing organizational culture.* San Francisco: Jossey-Bass.

Cooper, E. F. (2002). *The emergence of crack cocaine abuse.* Hauppauge, NY: Novinka Books.

Cork, D. (1999). Examining space: Time interaction in city-level homicide data: Crack markets and the diffusion of guns among youth. *Journal of Quantitative Criminology, 15,* pp. 379–406.

Dantzker, M. L. (1998). *Police organization and management: Yesterday, today, and tomorrow.* Boston: Butterworth-Heinemann.

Decker, S. H., Melde, C., & Pyrooz, D.C. (2013). What we know about gangs and gang members and where do we go from here? *Justice Quarterly, 30*(3), pp. 369–402.

Druckman, D., Singer, J. E., & Van Cott, H. P. (1997). *Enhancing organizational performance.* Washington, D.C.: National Academy of Science.

Egley, A., & Howell, J. C. (2013). *Highlights of the 2011 national gang youth survey.* Washington, D.C.: Office of Juvenile Justice and Delinquency Prevention.

Florida State Legislature. (2013). *Street terrorism enforcement and prevention: Florida State Statute 874.* Tallahassee, FL: Author.

Fuller, J. R. (2009). *Juvenile delinquency: Mainstream and crosscurrents.* Upper Saddle River, NJ: Pearson Prentice Hall.

Gibson, D. D. (2008). *The impact of parental incarceration on African American families. Praxis, 8,* pp. 23–29.

Gilley, J. W., Quatro, S. A., Hoekstra, E., Whittle, D. D., & Maycunich, A. (2001). *The manager as change agent: A practical guide to developing high performance people and organizations.* Jackson, TN: Perseus.

Grogger, J., & Willis, M. (1998). *The introduction of crack cocaine and the rise of urban crime rates.* Cambridge, MA: National Bureau of Economic Research.

Grossman, D. (1996). *On killing: The psychological cost of learning to kill in war and society.* New York: Little, Brown.

Gutman, H. G. (1977). *The Black family in slavery and freedom, 1750–1925.* New York: Random House.

Harms, P. D., & Snyder, H. N. (2004). *Trends in murder in juveniles: 1980–2000.* Washington, D.C.: Office of Juvenile Justice and Delinquency.

Hersey, P., Blanchard, K. H., & Johnson, D. E. (2001). *Management of organizational behavior: Leading human resources*, 8th ed. Upper Saddle River, NJ: Prentice Hall.

Howden, L. M., & Meyer, J. A. (2010). *2011 age and sex composition.* Washington, D.C.: U.S. Census Bureau.

Jankowski, M. S. (1991). *Islands in the street: Gangs and American urban society.* Berkeley: University of California Press.

Kirchhoff, S. M. (2010). *Economic impacts of prison growth.* Washington, D.C.: Congressional Research Service.

Klein, M. W., & Maxson, C. L. (2001). *Gang structures, crime patterns, and police responses: A summary report.* Washington, D.C.: National Institute of Justice.

Kurke, M. I. (1995). Organizational management of stress and human reliability. In M. I. Kurke & E. M. Scrivner (Eds.), *Police psychology into the 21st century* (pp. 391–416). Hillsdale, NJ: Lawrence Erlbaum.

Lacourse, E., Nagin, D., Tremblay, R. E., Vitaro, F., & Claes, M. (2003). Developmental trajectories of boys' delinquent group membership and facilitation of violent behaviors during adolescence. *Development and Psychopathology, 15*, pp. 183–197.

Marion County Clerk of the Court. (2011). *Case number 42-2011-CF-001491, Amber E. Wright, Capital Murder.* Ocala, FL: Author.

Maslow, A. (1943). Theory of human motivation. *Psychological Review, 50*(4), pp. 370–396.

Ministry of Justice. (2011). *Understanding the psychology of gang violence: Implications for designing effective violence interventions.* Kew, London: Author.

Moynihan, D. P. (1965). *The Negro family: The case for national action.* Washington, D.C.: U.S. Department of Labor.

National Gang Intelligence Center. (2011). *National gang threat assessment emerging trends 2011.* Washington, D.C.: Author.

New York State Legislature. (2013). *Gang assault in the second degree: New York State Statute 120.06.* Albany, NY: Author.

Opportunity Nation. (2013). *Zip codes continue to determine upward mobility in America.* Retrieved October 22, 2013, from: http://www.opportunitynation .org/news/entry/zip-codes-continue-to-determine-upward-mobility-in-america

Panzarella, R. (2003). Leadership myths and realities. In R. Adlam & P. Villiers (Eds.), *Police leadership in the twenty-first century* (pp. 119–133). Winchester, UK: Waterside Press.

Rosenberger, L. R. (1996). *America's drug war debacle.* Brookfield, VT: Ashgate.

Rothbart, M. K. (2007). Temperament, development, and personality. *Current Directions in Psychological Science, 16*(4), pp. 207–212.

Schein, E. H. (2004). *Organizational culture and leadership,* 3rd ed. San Francisco: Jossey-Bass.

Schroeder, D. J., & Lombardo, F. A. (2004). *Police sergeant exam,* 4th ed. Hauppauge, NY: Baron's Educational Series.

Texas State Legislature. (2013). *Compilation of information pertaining to criminal combinations and criminal street gangs: Texas Code of criminal procedure 61.* Austin, TX: Author.

Thomas, D. J. (2003). *Mental health case files.* Gainesville, FL: Author.

Thomas, D. J. (2010). *Professionalism in policing: An introduction.* Clifton Park, NY: Delmar Cengage Learning.

Thomas, D. J. (2013). *Review of drug arrest case files 1992–1994 Gainesville Police Department.* Unpublished raw data.

Time magazine. (1971). Heroin shooting war. *Time Magazine, 97,* p. 20.

Unnever, J. D., & Gabbidon, S. L. (2011). A theory of African American offending. Race, racism and crime. *Journal of Theoretical and Philosophical Criminology,* 5(1), pp. 96–98.

Whitfield, K., Alison, L., & Crego, J. (2008). Command, control, and support in critical incidents. In L. Alison & J. Crego (Eds.), *Policing critical incidents* (pp. 81–91). Portland, OR: Willan Publishing.

Wildeman, C., & Western, B. (2010). Incarceration in fragile families. *Future of Our Children, 20*, pp. 157–177.

Robbery

When you think of violent crime, which one scares you the most? Throughout this book we have discussed a number of serious crimes. The one crime that is universal, to which anyone can become a victim, is robbery. The act of robbery takes place in many forms, including carjacking and home invasion, and victims may be a business or a person. Examination of the varied locations reveals that anyone can become a victim at any time. Robbery has no boundaries; it even happens in schools, where kids are robbed of their shoes and jackets. In 2011, there were 354,396 robberies, and robbery ranked second as the most often committed violent crime in the United States. The only violent crime committed with greater frequency was aggravated assault, with a total of 751,131 incidents (Federal Bureau of Investigation, 2011).

Many Americans have a difficult time differentiating between the crimes of *robbery* and *burglary*. These terms have been used interchangeably in the media, as well as by victims of crime. Burglary is a property crime and is defined as illegally breaking and/or entering into a home, business, or conveyance with the intent to commit a crime therein (Florida State Legislature, 2013a). Simply put, breaking or entering alone does not constitute burglary; there has to be an intent to commit another crime such as theft, rape, murder, or property destruction as well. Robbery is a crime against a person or an establishment, such as a bank or a business. Although a business can be a victim of robbery, the employees of the business become victims as well. Robbery is defined as the taking of money or property, with the intent to permanently deprive the victim of the property, where force, violence, assault, or threat is used in the commission of the crime (Florida State Legislature, 2013b).

This chapter will dissect the crime of robbery and examine its etiology. As you read about the etiology, classification systems, and motives, and as you review the case studies in the chapter, compare and contrast the behaviors of a robbery suspect to those of murderers, rapists, and child abusers.

Questions for Reflection: Is the etiology of all criminal behavior the same? Or are the logic and motivations unique to the specific criminal? Is a robbery suspect different from other criminals? If so, how—and why do you suppose that is so?

ETIOLOGY OF ROBBERY

To understand robbery, it is important to understand its etiology. In the previous chapters, I have argued that the deficits in our personalities are directly related to three systems that intersect: environmental, psychological, and biological. This is also known as a biopsychosocial model. Each of these systems interacts with the others; in many instances, we have no idea to what degree unless an individual is diagnosed with a disorder such as schizophrenia, which is biologically based. Although there are a number of theories about why people commit violent crimes, the literature provides few theories on the etiology of robbery. There are, however, a number of theories regarding the motivations of robbery suspects. Therefore, as in the previous chapters, I will provide you with a sampling of the theories on the subject, and let you apply them singularly or in tandem to your understanding of the acts of robbery suspects, using the case studies in this chapter as a reference.

Merton (1938) argued that social structures apply pressure on some members of society to engage in criminal activity. Central to Merton's argument are the elements of social and cultural structure. The elements of cultural structure are the goals, purposes, and interests that provide the framework by which aspirations are defined. Social structure defines, regulates, and controls the acceptable methods of achieving those goals (p. 672). If a society is separated by class and allows only a certain number of individuals to acquire wealth, then that structure will lead to frustration and demoralization among other individuals. Merton argued that the response of those others is what is known as illegitimacy adjustment, meaning that their goals remain the same, but the means by which they attain them will become illegal.

Differential association also contributes to our understanding of robbery. This idea is grounded in learning theory. Sutherland (1947) argued that differential association provides that criminal behavior is situational and occurs when the criminal deems the situation and conditions are present. He also argued that criminal behavior is learned through small group interaction. The indoctrination includes methods, motives, and the adoption of distorted belief systems and attitudes. Bandura (1977) argued that except for elementary reflexes, all behavior is learned; responses are acquired through direct experience and/or observation (p. 16). Learning through direct experience is nothing more than the concept of reward and punishment. In the case of criminal behavior, positive reinforcement and inducements include the satisfaction of committing the crime, not being apprehended by the police, increased self-esteem, increased stature within a respective peer group, and the benefits of any financial or other reward as it relates to the commission of the crime.

Another theory is known as the conditioning or modeling process. Theorists in this field have argued that attitudes toward criminal activity are a learned condition response. Criminal behavior, such as robbery, is positively reinforced by both the monetary rewards and the thrill and excitement associated with the act of robbery (McGuire, Carlisle, & Young, 1965).

Laws and Marshall (1990) argued that deviant behavior is learned through the same mechanisms that are used to learn all human behavior. The theory proposed by these authors is closely associated with the concept of *operant conditioning*, which is a system of learning in which behavior is reinforced through reward and punishment. Skinner (1953) argued that the only way to determine whether an event has been reinforced is to observe whether there is a change in the frequency of the event. Skinner described two types of reinforcers:

- *Adding something,* or *positive reinforcement,* which is associated with necessities like food and water as well as monetary gain
- *Removing something,* or *negative reinforcement,* which can be associated with that which makes us uncomfortable, such as punishment, loud noises, bright lights, extreme cold or heat, or electric shock

If a child is taught that robbery is fun and exciting by peers or an adult, and that behavior is positively reinforced through rewards such as praise and monetary gain from the act, then it is easy to see how this behavior could be viewed as normal by the individual even though this belief system is contrary to social norms. It is through this process that acceptance of criminal behavior and distorted cognitions are developed. The reality is that this conditioning process is same one experienced by those who abide by the social contract and obey the law.

Conditioning and reinforcement are supported by both Seligman (1971) and Mineka and Ohman (2002). These researchers also argued that behavior is learned and theorized that when one is exposed to unprepared conditioning/fear, as opposed to prepared conditioning/learning, the unprepared exposure will have a greater impact on one's psyche. In the context of robbery, unprepared learning might take place in one event when a perpetrator experiences excitement, power, control, and/or pleasure during the act of robbery. Such an act is selective in nature, meaning that we have a choice to accept or reject the criminal act. The acceptance or rejection is contingent on the nature of the reinforcements—whether they are positive or negative. Keep in mind that the criminal act and the outcomes are resistant to extinction and may be associated with our basic needs, as described in Maslow's hierarchy of needs, which become embedded in the amygdala, the part of our brain that is responsible for our survival.

A review of two other theories discussed in Chapter 1, in the context of subculture violence and the code of the street, is essential to this discussion because they address the concepts of poverty, aggression, and pride. The subculture violence theory was introduced by Marvin Wolfgang and Franco Ferracuti in 1967. The theory was designed to explain spontaneous assaults and homicides. Subculture violence draws from the disciplines of the Chicago school of criminology, which examined medical, biological, and psychological factors contributing to crime. Wolfgang and Ferracuti (1967) theorized that subculture violence is only partly different from the state of the parent culture—that violence is, in fact, an integral component of the parent culture. The act of violence is learned and facilitated by positive reinforcement. Since violence is learned and positively reinforced, controls such as interpersonal conflict and guilt are obviated (Ferracuti & Wolfgang, 1973; Wolfgang & Ferracuti, 1967).

Two other studies tested the theories of Ferracuti and Wolfgang. Ball-Rokeach (1973) completed the first empirical study of the subculture violence theory and came to the conclusion that the values established by the subculture play little or no role as determinants of interpersonal violence. Bernard (1990) tested a variation not rooted in violence and suggested that angry aggression develops among the truly disadvantaged as a consequence of racial discrimination and low social position—that is, as part of the parent culture—as first theorized by Wolfgang and Ferracuti in 1967.

An extension of the subculture of violence theory was presented by Anderson in 1999 in *A Code of the Street*, which is a narrative ethnographic exploration of a low-income African American neighborhood in the city of Philadelphia. The basis for Anderson's research was rather simple; he wanted to know why inner-city youth are willing to perpetrate violence and acts of aggression toward each other (p. 90). Anderson (1999) defined the *code of the street* as a set of informal rules that govern relationships, behavior, and specifically violence (p. 33). Interestingly, those who have adopted middle-class values and live in these communities also have to adopt a duality in their personality: one that allows them to address their contemporaries in the neighborhood, and the other that allows them to be accepted by mainstream America.

Anderson (1999) argued that central to the code of the street and the violence is being treated with respect; he described respect as an external entity, "one that is hard-won, easily lost, and must constantly be guarded" (p. 31). The concepts of respect and credibility rest on the need for safety and security, and to be disrespected is a challenge to one's sovereignty. This need for self-preservation has grown out of a distrust of the police and the criminal justice system, so this same code extends to concepts such as "stop snitching campaigns," where those who have adopted the street code will resolve their own conflicts and are willing to die or kill in so doing.

Finally, Becker (1968) argued that people who commit crime do so because they choose to, and the choice is made by weighing the rewards and risks. Becker's theory is known as rational choice theory. In this view, one's decision to commit a criminal act is no different from someone else's decision to purchase food or clothing, because the same thought process or analysis is used for both. Becker believed that these decisions involve a detailed thought process in which the person examines the benefits of legitimate employment versus participating in criminal activity, and decides the latter will have the greater reward and better meet the individual's needs. In addition to evaluating the rewards, the person assesses the negative consequences for participating in criminal activity if caught. Becker argued that previous theories have no value because free will and choice are primary in the human decision-making process.

Several theories have been presented here. In Chapter 2, I made the following statement: "Everyone is capable of committing murder." Given the right set of circumstances, anyone can kill. Yet, when it comes to other acts of violence such as rape, crimes against children, arson, and robbery, that statement does not hold true; not everyone is capable of committing those acts.

Questions for Reflection: Why are other violent crimes different from murder? Is Becker correct in claiming that decisions regarding crime are rationally analyzed by an examination of the concepts of reward and punishment? Is the answer to this question in the motivations for the crime? What are some motivations for robbery?

MOTIVATIONS TO COMMIT ROBBERY

If we use the theories as a foundation for explaining why someone commits robbery, then I would say that each theory has a basis for explaining the motivations behind the commission of robbery. Besides being motivated to perform the act of robbery itself, a suspect can use robbery, like arson, to cover up the commission of another crime such as murder. I have been to a number of crime scenes where the motive was murder, and yet the victims were missing personal items that they would never have been seen in public without, such as a wedding ring, gold watch, diamond necklace, money, and/or credit cards. The suspect took them in order to mislead the police into believing the motive was a robbery gone bad, when in fact, all along, the motive had been murder. Good investigators examine every possible motive to determine the true motive behind a crime such as robbery.

CASE STUDY 8.1   MURDER OR ROBBERY GONE BAD?

Timothy Thomas was a 16-year-old African American male who lived in a local project. He was walking down Sixth Street at 11:00 P.M. on a Wednesday night. A car pulled alongside Tim, and the occupants called him over to the car. Tim turned the music on his boom box down, and an argument ensued between the occupants of the car and Tim for several minutes. At some point, neighbors heard the shouting, with Tim yelling, "Fuck you." As Tim turned to run from the vehicle, the neighbors heard a single gunshot and heard a car speeding westbound on Sixth Street. The next thing the neighbors heard was a knock on the door and someone yelling for help.

The neighbors had already called the police when they first heard the disturbance, and the police arrived on the scene in less than a minute. Tim had one gunshot wound to the back and was conscious and breathing. While waiting for the fire rescue team, Tim described the incident. He did not know the suspects and had never seen them before. All he knew was that the vehicle was occupied by four black males. When police asked why the occupants of the car shot him, Tim stated: "They wanted my box. When I said 'no,' they pulled the gun and told me to give it up. I worked too hard for this and wasn't giving it up. I ran; they shot."

Tim died in surgery three hours after the incident. Tim was shot with one 45-caliber bullet that severed his spinal cord. Once shot, Tim had run approximately 50 feet to the neighbors' front door where he collapsed. The boom box was destroyed when Tim dropped it. Police canvassed the neighborhood on numerous occasions, but never produced any leads. The word on the street was that shooting Tim was part of a gang initiation and that the perpetrators were from another city (Thomas, 1996).

Questions for Reflection

1. What was the motive for the shooting?
2. If Tim had given the suspects his boom box, would he still be alive?
3. Which theory do you believe applies to this case, and why?

Wright and Decker (1997) completed a study of eighty-six active armed robbers in an attempt determine their motivations. Prior to that study, most if not all studies had been done with incarcerated subjects. Wright and Decker cautioned that the results of the data collected from those who were incarcerated imposed limitations on the previous studies. I also advise caution in using data collected from self-reporting, only because the reporter is in control of divulging the information he or she wants the researcher to know. In fact, there are limitations to all data; it is important to determine what they are whenever we examine research.

Wright and Decker's (1997) study was conducted in St. Louis, Missouri. The armed robbers ranged in age from under 18 to over 40 years of age. The greatest concentration was between the ages of 18 and 29, which accounted for 41 percent of the sample population. These researchers attempted to determine the number of robberies the robbers had committed, both individually and collectively. They estimated the following numbers: 25 offenders committed fewer than 10 robberies; 30 offenders committed between 10 and 49 robberies; and 31 offenders committed more than 49 robberies (pp. 11–13). These findings are consistent with police data in that most burglars, robbers, and car thieves are serial in nature; if one such crime is solved, usually it turns out that ten or more other crimes are also cleared because they were committed by the same individual.

To obtain a better understanding of those who committed robbery, the Wright and Decker (1997) sample included offenders who did not just commit street robberies, but who also committed other types of robberies: seventy-three committed street robberies, ten committed commercial robberies, and three committed both commercial and street robberies (p. 16). It should be noted that although their crime of choice was robbery, most of the offenders in this study (eighty-two) were actively involved in other crimes, such as theft, burglary, assault, and drug selling, as well.

In the Wright and Decker study, eighty-one of the robbers spoke to the immediate need for money, and it should be emphasized that this was not about greed or the accumulation of wealth, but a matter of survival. However, the group was also cognizant of the fact that even if they had money and if the right opportunity presented itself, they would take advantage of it. Also, even though the offenders professed that they committed robbery as a means of survival, fifty-nine of the eighty-six offenders stated that they had spent the money on pleasurable activities such as substance abuse and gambling, which is a direct contradiction to the claim of needing money immediately in order to survive. In answering the question of why someone would commit robbery, Wright and Decker determined that the offenders' motivations "grew out of a sense of frustration and anger because the offenders found themselves locked into a cycle of events leading to nowhere" (1997, p. 46).

Another interesting aspect of the Wright and Decker study was that the offenders' victim selection was closely associated with the offenders' motivation. The offenders chose victims who flaunted their wealth through an overt display of material items such as cars, clothes, jewelry, and homes. The researchers pointed clearly to the fact that these offenders were isolated and had developed distorted thought processes, which they used to justify their decisions to commit robberies as well as other crimes, which is something we have seen in offenders of all the different violent crimes throughout this text.

In another study of motivation for robbery, Feeney (1986) completed interviews of 113 incarcerated California robbers in 1971 and 1972 and noted some interesting facts. This author discussed at length the process of rational choice and the thought process that a robber goes through before deciding to commit a robbery. His findings contradict the findings of Becker, who claimed that robbery involves a rational choice. Feeney found that 60 percent of the offenders in his study gave little thought to the act of robbery, meaning that there was no preplanning or thought of the possible consequences. Finally, fewer than 60 percent in this study robbed for money. Instead, Feeney found the following motivations in his population:

1. When money was the motivating factor, of the 113 offenders,
   a. 17 needed it for drugs
   b. 8 needed it for food and shelter
   c. 16 needed it for other specific items
   d. 16 desired it
2. When the robbery was motivated by something other than money, emotional needs became apparent; of the 113 offenders,
   a. 6 robbed for excitement, to relieve boredom, or because they were unhappy
   b. 6 robbed because they were angry or upset

    c. 6 robbed to impress friends or to prove they could do it

    d. 6 robbed because they were on drugs or drunk

    e. some were unsure about why they robbed

3. Those who generally were not robbers but had robbed did so for other reasons; of the 113 offenders,

    a. 5 did so to recover money owed

    b. 4 did so because the victims interrupted the offender during the commission of a burglary

    c. 4 did so because a fight turned into a robbery

    d. 6 did so because their partner started a robbery without their knowledge (pp. 55–57)

After reviewing the data associated with the motivations for robbery, I went back and evaluated fifty cases in which I made arrests and interviewed the suspects. The reasons for their actions varied and often depended on the situation. Fifteen of the offenders were street-level drug dealers; most often they robbed their clients with the belief that they were excellent victims, since they were seeking illegal drugs—thus the police would not consider the act as robbery, nor would the victims be bold enough to call the police. The dealers felt no remorse and viewed their clients as trash and a waste of life. In fact, they knew that if they lost a client, there would always be more to take that one's place. Also, the robbery enhanced their credibility on the street, making others think twice before attempting to rob or kill the street-level dealer. Most, however, did it for fun, power, and the thrill of humiliating a human being. Even when an arrest was made, it was not long before the charges were dropped because of the victim's refusal to prosecute.

Another common motivation in the population I studied was robbery to purchase drugs. Of the fifty, ten offenders in my population fell into this group. These offenders functioned haphazardly, meaning that they would rob indiscriminately and were easy to catch. It was not unusual on my police beat to receive a dispatch of a robbery that just occurred and, ten minutes after arriving at that location, receive another dispatch of a second robbery five miles away. In the interviews, the suspects' descriptions of their motive for these robberies were the same: money for drugs. Given the time line and locations, usually convenience stores or gas stations, in almost every instance the offender was "jonesing" and in need of a hit of crack cocaine. During interviews with these offenders, they stated that they just wanted to get high. Many of them sought to go on a binge, and that is why they needed so much money; and thus, robberies were committed one after the other. The drug dealer and the drug abuser are two of the most violent offenders with whom I have dealt. Dealers are violent because they want to establish their superiority. Abusers are violent because they become desperate, both physiologically and psychologically, and will do anything to get money for drugs.

CASE STUDY 8.2   HERO OR ROBBER?

Patrol officers responded to a robbery at a local convenience store. The owner stated that a black male walked into the store sweating and had what the owner described as a crazy look on his face. The man was talking to himself as he went to the cooler, picked up a 16-ounce Budweiser, and brought it to the counter. After the owner had rung up the beer and advised the man of the price, the man pulled a revolver from his front pocket and stuck it in the store owner's face. The suspect demanded all of the money from the cash register.

As the owner opened the cash register, the suspect moved the gun from his face and placed the gun against the store owner's chest. Once the owner handed over the money, the suspect stated: "I am sick and tired of you bastards moving into our neighborhood with your businesses, taking our money, killing us with the alcohol and cigarettes, and fucking our women. You bastards are bleeding us dry, and every one of these stores that I can rob is a victory for my community." The owner stated that the suspect then pulled the trigger on the gun, but nothing happened, and the suspect, looking shocked, fled the store on foot.

The officers taking the statement were stunned by this description of events and asked the owner exactly where the gun had been placed when the suspect pulled the trigger. The suspect had placed the gun against the left breast pocket of victim's shirt. The officers asked the owner whether he had felt pressure, saw a flash, or felt anything from the gun; and the owner replied that he had felt nothing and that there had been no bang. One officer noticed what he believed to be powder burns on the owner's shirt and asked the owner to remove the items from his pocket. The owner removed a notebook he used to record merchandise needed for the store. When he reached into the pocket again, he recovered a 38-caliber bullet. The suspect had actually fired the gun, but the muzzle flash could not be seen because the barrel was directly against the owner's chest. The owner could not recall anything other than witnessing the suspect pull the trigger because he was in fight-or-flight mode, which the body adapts in a crisis to protect itself.

The suspect was caught several days later, and in his interview, he stated the following: "First the white man and Jews owned these stores, taking us for everything. Now the Muslims have moved in, dealing the same poison to our people. The only way to hurt them is to take their money and kill them; it is the only thing they understand. My motivation was to save my community. It wasn't about the money; it was about the people." The suspect was asked about the shooting and he admitted to pulling the trigger. In fact, the suspect heard the gun go off, felt the recoil, smelled the gunpowder, and was confused when the victim remained standing and the victim's expression never changed. The suspect ran from the store confused and did not understand what had happened (Thomas, 1986).

The third category of robber I found in the review of my own robbery cases was one who robbed commercial establishments, such as banks and pharmacies, out of desperation. Fourteen of the fifty cases I examined fit this category. Most if not all of these offenders had fallen on hard times; they had lost their jobs, were losing their homes, their cars were being repossessed, and they needed money to feed their families. The schemes were grand: Five of the offenders robbed more than one bank. Much like serial killers or rapists, when robbers are responsible for robbing more than one financial institution, they become wise through experience. They learn about the dye packs and electronic locaters, and their demands move from just wanting money to asking for very specific things.

The amateurs, however—those who robbed financial institutions only once or twice—fell victim to the dye packs, which explode, emit tear gas, burn some of the money, and leave dye on the suspects' hands as well as on the money. One suspect took the money home and placed it in a washing machine with spot remover and poker chips in an attempt to remove the dye. Once the stains were faded enough, he took the money to a local bank to make his car and house payment, not realizing the serial numbers of the money from the dye pack had been recorded. He was arrested within two days of passing the marked money. From a psychological standpoint, amateurs pose a unique danger to the victims of robberies because in fact many of them are just as afraid as their victims during the encounter. In one such case, a suspect entered a local bank with a cocked revolver and ordered the clerk to hand over the money. The teller complied with every demand, but as the suspect reached for the money, he accidentally pulled the trigger, killing the teller instantly.

Four of the offenders I examined had robbed local pharmacies more than once, with the motivation of obtaining prescription pain medication. Unlike the bank robbers, there was no learning curve for those committing robbery for pain medication. These offenders more closely resembled those who were hooked on crack cocaine; they exhibited the same desperation, which made them both dangerous and vulnerable.

The final category in my examination was that of street robbers. This group is undoubtedly the most dangerous of all robbers because, in many instances, the robbery is committed on a whim or on the spur of the moment. These robberies occur when offenders feel they have the advantage, for example, when they spot an innocent party walking down the street at night, or when they lurk in a parking garage until an unsuspecting victim passes by and then jump out and beat their victim into submission before robbing him or her. Fear, alarm, and surprise are central to a street robber's ability to overcome a victim's resistance. Victims of street robberies describe the suspects as appearing out of nowhere and disappearing in a similar fashion. In these interviews, the suspects' motivations were many: money, fun and excitement, anger, and to prove a point. None of the suspects in these cases suffered hardship; their motivation was driven by distorted thoughts designed to boost their egos, which is consistent with much of the research on the motivation for robbery.

Questions for Reflection: Why do you think people commit robbery? Is it because they are angry, poor, and disadvantaged, or because of the excitement and power associated with the crime? Can you imagine a situation in which you might be willing to rob another person or an institution?

TYPOLOGY OF ROBBERY

Theorists have developed many classification systems based on empirical data like that provided in this chapter and in Chapter 1 in the discussion of what causes crime. Classification systems are rarely used from a law enforcement perspective, since the goal of law enforcement is to articulate the facts of the crime in painstaking detail. From a clinical perspective, however, classification systems are important because they help in the development of a treatment plan as well as in designing treatment programs. From the clinical perspective, then, one size does not fit all. Here I provide some of the classification systems that theorists have developed for robbery suspects.

A simple classification system for robbery is to classify robbers based on the instrumentality (weapon) used by the suspect and the location of the crime. This type of classification system is usually defined by state statutes. In addition, there are robberies that occur during particular seasons.

1. Typically, when speaking of instrumentality, the suspect is either armed or unarmed:

   a. *Armed robbery:* Many different weapons are used by armed suspects. Most common are guns, knives, and items that can be used as a bludgeon (baseball bat, bottle, tire iron, etc.).

   b. *Unarmed robbery:* Unarmed robberies can become even more violent than armed ones. Victims recognize the inherent danger of a weapon, but when they are threatened without a weapon, they may be less fearful and compliant. Usually in unarmed robbery, victims are physically assaulted and beaten to instill fear and to gain compliance.

2. Location is the second determinant in this classification system:

   a. *Home invasion robbery* occurs inside the home. Here the victims are brutally assaulted to obtain compliance as well as because the robber can show some form of superiority. The suspects in home invasion robberies are usually armed or become armed once in the home.

   b. *Carjacking* occurs on the street and the vehicle is occupied. This crime is usually violent, and sometimes the driver is taken hostage during the incident. Carjacking suspects are usually armed.

   c. *Commercial or business robberies* usually involve suspects who are armed or imply that they are armed. The goal is either money, drugs, or a combination of both. These crimes may be violent; often whether they become so is determined by two things: the confidence of the perpetrator or group (as they become more successful, they escalate in violence) and how the victims respond to the offender's demands.

   d. *Street robberies* involve suspects who may or may not be armed, and these robberies may or may not be violent. The offender may get away by making simple demands. The key here is the suddenness of the attack.

3. *Seasonal robberies* is a unique classification only because it is not usually included in the typical typology or classification. Seasonal robberies are robberies that usually start at the beginning of the Christmas holiday season, around Thanksgiving, and run until Christmas. These are crimes of opportunity; offenders are aware that during this season, shoppers carry more money, are distracted, and are easy prey when walking in mall parking lots and on the street. Businesses usually have more money on hand to meet consumer demands. Even with enhanced security at this time of year, offenders see targets of opportunity. If offenders were to do a risk analysis, they would have no choice but to believe that the odds of success would be in their favor at that time of year.

Canter and Youngs (2009) argued that from a psychological perspective, what defines robbery is the willingness of offenders to confront their victims, establish control, and impose their will on the victims. These authors described robbery as an expressive act with an intensity and drama that demands confidence by the offender (p. 270). They developed the following classification system:

- The *professional suspect* is described as an adaptive adventurer—one who influences the environment to complete the robbery (p. 272). Here the offender has addressed every aspect of the offense utilizing a cognitive process so that there are no surprises. The victims are treated as objects. This approach is very similar to that taken by the perpetrators of predatory violence, as discussed in Chapter 3, where the offense is cognitive in nature and the victims are a means to an end.

- The *victim suspect* is described as a case of integrative irony, where the offender is driven to relieve some internal conflict such as lack of self-worth or self-esteem, or impotency (p. 273). The behavior here is similar to that in reactive violence, as discussed in Chapter 3, in that the offender behaves impulsively, with no plan in place, and usually reacts violently if the victim offers any resistance or challenge to the offender's commands.

- The *hero suspect* is described as being on an expressive quest, in that the offender is attempting to have an impact on the external world (p. 273). This suspect is similar to the offender in Case Study 8.2, where the goal was to rid the black community of purveyors of poison. These types of suspects usually attack high-value targets, with risk-taking behavior, regardless of the targets' security measures (p. 273). The actions of these robbers are similar to those of a terrorist in an attack, such as that perpetrated by Timothy McVeigh.

Finally, another typology has been offered by Przemysław Piotrowski (2011), who argued that robbers should be classified based on their level of rationality prior to and during the offense. Although Piotrowski's classification system was limited to his analysis of street robbers, it is very similar to the one offered by Canter and Youngs, who addressed the broad spectrum of robbery offenders. Piotrowski developed the following classification system:

- The *rational street robber* is one whose actions are premeditated. These robbers act in a professional manner with planning; they are material-oriented and complete a cost–benefit analysis (p. 447). This category is similar to Canter and Youngs's professional suspect and the type described by Becker's discussion on rational choice. Again, this robber is similar to the predatory criminal discussed in Chapter 3, with the primary basis of functionality being the cognitive process.

- The *bounded rationality street robber* is heavily influenced by peers. These robbers act mostly under the influence of alcohol, with a need to correct an injustice (p. 448). They use distorted rationalizations to support their actions, and they are similar to Canter and Youngs's hero suspect as well as the suspect described in Case Study 8.2.

- The *irrational street robber* acts on a sudden impulse. This robber does not use a cost–benefit analysis, and often there are limitations to this offender's thinking

(p. 448). Here, there is a correlation between arousal and emotion. This offender's actions correspond to those of Canter and Youngs's victim suspect and to those whose behavior was categorized under reactive or spontaneous violence in the discussion in Chapter 3.

ADDITIONAL CASE STUDIES

You have had an opportunity to examine a number of the theories associated with robbery. The two cases in this section were chosen not for their notoriety but because of the insights they offer in regard to the distorted cognitive processes and justifications used by criminals. It is important to note that both robbery suspects are unique in their motivations. As you examine these two case studies, review the theories and typologies and determine which of them best fits each offender.

CASE STUDY 8.3   JEALOUSY OR ROBBERY?

Thomas Mitchell was a 16-year-old black male who had just left a party at 12:00 A.M. As he began to walk home, he walked past a local housing project. He was approached by two black male suspects, one of whom was armed with a handgun. The suspects robbed Mitchell at gunpoint, taking his Air Jordan basketball shoes and his Jordan leather jacket. The victim knew both suspects from school, could identify them, and could identify the apartment to which they ran.

Police were called to the scene. During the initial interview, Mitchell reiterated that he knew the suspects by name because he went to school with both of them and that they were in some of his classes at the local high school. Their names and physical descriptions were as follows:

- *Suspect 1*: Daron Ford, B/M, 16/17 years old, 5 11 , 190 lbs, short brown hair, brown eyes. He was wearing a black hooded ski parka, blue jeans, and wheat-colored Timberland boots. Daron was armed with a semiauto pistol believed to be a Glock. Daron pointed the gun at the victim's head and stated, "I want the coat and the shoes. If you don't give them to me, I will kill you. If you call the police, I will kill you. I never liked you anyway."
- *Suspect 2*: Michael Smart, B/M, 16/17 yrs old, 6 2 , 200 lbs, brown hair worn in a large afro, and brown eyes. He was wearing a Chicago Bulls Jacket, blue jeans, and black Timberland boots. Michael took the jacket and shoes as the victim removed them. Mike stated, "If you call the police, you and your family are dead."

The following is the description of the stolen property:

1. Pair of Air Jordan 21 shoes, size 13, black in color. Value $140
2. One Jordan leather jacket, size XL, black in color. Value $200

Once the suspects took the property, they ran upstairs to apartment 3B of the housing project. Police went to apartment 3B and, when they knocked on the door, heard the voices of two males. A suspect fitting the description of Daron Ford answered the door. In fact, he was wearing the same clothing that the victim described. Standing behind Daron was the second suspect, also fitting the description of Michael Smart. Police could see the Jordan leather jacket lying on the living room floor. The suspects immediately screamed, "Oh shit, it's the police," and attempted to slam the door shut.

The police officers forced the door open, and both suspects ran. Suspect Ford ran to the back of the apartment and was tackled by one officer. As he was tackled, Ford grabbed a jacket on the floor. After a short struggle, he gave up and was handcuffed. The officer searched the jacket Ford was reaching for and found a 9-millimeter Glock pistol in the pocket. The Glock was loaded with seventeen rounds, with one in the chamber. It was the same gun that the victim, Mitchell, had described. The second suspect was tackled in the living room and gave up without incident.

During the interview, Ford stated that he hated the victim. When asked why, if the victim had offended or assaulted Ford, the answer was "no." Ford said that the victim had always been nice and acted as a friend, but Ford looked at the victim's kindness as a way for the victim to show he was superior to Ford and those who lived in the projects. Ford felt that the victim had disrespected him by befriending him, because Ford thought that was the way the victim could show his superiority over Ford. He hated the victim because he had everything. The victim's parents had great jobs, nice cars, and a beautiful house; and the victim always had the best of everything.

Since the robbery could have happened at any time, police asked Ford why he and Smart chose that particular night. Ford advised that he and Smart were at the same party and left early after seeing the victim. They knew that the victim was walking and would have to walk by their place to go home, so they waited. They saw the victim was wearing the new leather coat and shoes, so they wanted the victim to feel humiliated. They knew if they took his shoes and his coat, he would have to walk home in the cold without them. The victim would feel what they had felt for years. What they did not count on was the victim going to the nearest house and calling the police, nor did they expect the police to respond as quickly as they did, especially since they had threatened to kill the victim and his family if he called the police.

The police then asked Ford what would have happened if he had been able to pull the gun from the jacket. Ford replied, "I was going to shoot both of you fuckers; I hate the police more than I hate Thomas. You stand for everything that I stand against. Both of my parents are in jail because of you, so this would be my revenge. It's a good thing that you did not say "police" at the door, because I would have gotten my gun and fired through the door. That's how much I hate you" (Thomas, 1995).

An analysis of Case Study 8.3 leaves one wondering how many robberies occur, as in this case, simply out of anger and hatred. The mentality of the suspects, Ford and Mitchell, included the belief that they were entitled, because they did not have much, to take from those who did. Jealousy is a powerful motivator. In interviewing the victim, it was clear that he had nothing but respect for both suspects and considered them friends. He stated that up until the robbery, he had no idea how the suspects felt about him.

If I were going to classify the two suspects in Case Study 8.3, I would consider them to be *victim robbers*. Both had a number of issues that extended beyond the victim, and they hated the police. Ford made it clear that if he had been given a chance, he would have killed the officers. Interestingly, Ford refused to admit that his parents had done anything wrong, and both were in prison on drug and robbery charges. If we examine the distorted thinking patterns of Ford and Smart, we can see that they never thought past the robbery, and that Ford had absolved his parents for their misdeeds and blamed the police.

An analysis of Case Study 8.4 makes it apparent that the gang evolved. It is clear from the interview that the group started committing the robberies in the hope of making some money and that they did not have any goals. It was only after the first two robberies that they began to take ideas from movies and learned to case businesses to determine the nuances of how they closed and when they could gain the most money. The beatings were employed in the beginning as a form of control; later they enjoyed them. In the interview, one of the suspects stated, "I loved watching them squirm, wondering if I was going to shoot them. Man, that is power." Ultimately they wanted money; the lifestyle of the rich was their dream. They never envisioned getting caught because they thought that changing the type of establishment would keep the police guessing.

CASE STUDY 8.4 'TIS THE SEASON

Police responded to a robbery at a local pharmacy. What was unusual about this robbery was that there were four suspects instead of one, and all they wanted was money; they did not want drugs. In this robbery, the suspects did take the pharmacist's class ring, which was unusual as well. A week later, another local pharmacy was robbed by the same four suspects, with one difference: That time, they brutally beat the pharmacist for no apparent reason. Again, all they took was money, emptying the cash registers both at the front of the store and at the pharmacy. The only description of the suspects in both robberies was four black males between 17 and 25 years of age. In each pharmacy, the suspects took approximately $1,000. Police had no leads, and there were no other robberies by this group.

Two weeks later, the suspects emerged, committing a third robbery of a large supermarket chain store. The robbery was at night after the store was closed. Apparently the suspects had been watching the supermarket and had learned the habits of the employees, especially those who stayed after closing time to clean and stock shelves, and secure the store for the night. The robbery was on Saturday night, meaning that no bank drop had been made and the store had cash on hand from Friday as well as Saturday. In their observations of the closing employees, the suspects had noticed that the store's doors were not secure because employees went in and out while getting carts and cleaning. The suspects entered the store just before the final three employees left. Their violence escalated once again; this time, they immediately began to beat the store manager and threatened to shoot the employees if the manager did not open the safe. The take from that third robbery was $15,000.

Three days later, the same suspects robbed a local movie theater. They had observed the theater over time, just like they had the supermarket. They robbed the movie theater on a Sunday night for the same reason they had chosen Saturday for the store: There had been no bank drop. They beat the manager and terrorized the employees until the safe was opened. The haul was $3,500 for less than ten minutes of work.

As the police department put together a task force, the suspects hit another large supermarket chain store. Again they observed the store in advance, and nothing had changed except, with this supermarket, the employees were aware of the previous robberies and locked the door every time they went outside to get carts or during cleaning. The suspects took an employee hostage and forced the manager to open the door. Once inside, the gang beat the manager as punishment for making them take a hostage. This robbery, like the movie theater, was on a Sunday, since after robbing the movie theater, the gang had realized that they could get the entire weekend's take if they waited until Sunday night as opposed to Friday or Saturday. In this robbery, they netted over $30,000.

Once the task force was in place, police set up surveillance at every potential target. It was two weeks before one unit observed a car occupied by four black males at a local pizza restaurant. The car was circling the block, and then one member got out of the car and went into the restaurant. The suspects left and came back on several occasions. The officer called for backup, and the task force stopped the suspects based on their suspicious behavior. Upon getting each of the suspects out of the car, in plain view the officers observed an AR-15 assault rifle loaded with a 20-round magazine and a sawed-off shotgun, and recovered two Glock 9-millimeter pistols from two of the suspects. The car was new and still had the temporary tag on it. In fact, as the investigation continued, it was discovered that all four suspects had purchased new cars, paying cash for them at a "buy-here, pay-here" lot.

During the interview, the suspects stated that after the first robbery, everything else was easy because they had gained confidence. They beat the victims to show them who was in control, and they felt that if they beat at least one person, everyone else would comply. For them, it was about the money and material things; they said they also wanted money to buy gifts for their families, which was something they had not been able to do because they were poor. The robberies began November 1, and the suspects were arrested one week before Christmas. They did not think that the police would ever catch on because they kept changing the type of establishment they robbed, which is why the pizza restaurant had been chosen. When they were stopped by police, they were on their way home to finalize their plans to rob the restaurant and change cars (Thomas, 1994).

The group in Case Study 8.4 did a lot of things correctly in terms of getting away with their crimes, but they made one big mistake. They only committed the robberies where they lived. This simplified police efforts and did not require obtaining help from or sharing information with other jurisdictions. In the interview, when asked why they took the pharmacist's ring, they said they took it as a trophy so they would remember their first robbery, where it all began. When they were stopped by the police, their first thought was that they had a headlight out; it was not until they saw all the firepower that they realized they had been caught. Although their violence had escalated, they had no desire to shoot it out with police, so they gave up.

If I were going to classify the group in Case Study 8.4, I would put them in the rational and professional category. Their discussion concerning poverty was not sincere, because none of the money had been used for anything except their own enjoyment—to party and to purchase cars.

CONCLUSION

In 2011, robbery ranked second of all the violent crimes reported in the United States. It is the one crime to which anyone can become victim, given the right set of circumstances: walking alone at night, working as a clerk in a convenience store or a bank teller, or being part of a family asleep in a home at night. In many instances, this is a stranger-on-stranger crime, and often the attacker threatens bodily injury or death and brandishes a weapon. Sometimes the offender beats the victim because the offender is unarmed and needs to establish control.

We may want to believe that robbery happens because the offenders are poor, and yet the data support a different hypothesis. Most offenders rob because of a need to party along with their friends, as well as for a host of other reasons that make sense to them, but none of which are defensible, socially acceptable, or rational to the rest of us. As with every other crime discussed in this book, the motivations for robbery—such as a sense of entitlement, and jealousy or anger—are built on, and justified through, distorted thought processes.

REFERENCES

Anderson, E. (1999). *Code of the street: Decency, violence and the moral life of the inner city.* New York: W. W. Norton.

Ball-Rokeach, S. J. (1973). Values and violence: A test of the subculture violence thesis. *American Sociological Review, 38*, pp. 736–749.

Bandura, A. (1977). *Aggression: A social learning process.* Englewood Cliffs, NJ: Prentice-Hall.

Becker, G. S. (1968). Crime and punishment: An economic approach. *Journal of Political Economy, 76*, pp. 169–217.

Bernard. T. J. (1990). Angry aggression among the "truly disadvantaged." *Criminology, 28*, pp. 73–96.

Canter, D., & Youngs, D. (2009). *Investigative psychology: Offender profiling and the analysis of criminal action.* Chichester, U.K.: Wiley & Sons.

Federal Bureau of Investigation (FBI). (2011). *Crime in the United States 2011.* Washington, D.C.: Author.

Feeney, F. (1986). Robbers as decision makers. In D. B. Cornish & R. V. Clarke (Eds.), *The reasoning criminal: Rational choice perspectives on offending* (pp. 53–71). New York: Springer-Verlag.

Ferracuti, F., & Wolfgang, M. E. (1973). *Psychological testing of the subculture of violence.* Rome: Bulzoni.

Florida State Legislature. (2013a). *Burglary, Florida State Statute 810.02.* Tallahassee, FL: Author.

Florida State Legislature. (2013b). *Robbery, Florida State Statute 812.13.* Tallahassee, FL: Author.

Laws, D. R., & Marshall, W. L. (1990). A conditioning theory of the etiology and maintenance of deviant sexual preference and behavior. In W. L. Marshall, D. R. Laws, & H. E. Barbaree (Eds.), *Handbook of sexual assault: Issues, theories, and treatment of the offender* (pp. 209–230). New York: Plenum Books.

McGuire, R. J., Carlisle, L. M., & Young, B. G. (1965). Sexual deviation as conditioned behavior: A hypothesis. *Behavior Research and Therapy, 3,* pp. 185–190.

Merton, R. K. (1938). Social structure and anomie. *American Sociological Review, 3,* pp. 672–682.

Mineka, S., & Ohman, A. (2002). Learning and unlearning fears: Preparedness, neural pathways, and patients. *Biological Psychiatry, 52,* pp. 927–937.

Piotrowski, P. (2011). Street robbery offenders: Shades of rationality and reversal theory perspective. *Rationality and Society, 23*(4), pp. 427–451.

Seligman, M. E. P. (1971). Phobias and preparedness. *Behavior Therapy, 2,* pp. 307–320.

Skinner, B. F. (1953). *Science and human behavior.* New York: Free Press.

Sutherland, E. H. (1947). *Principles of criminology,* 5th ed. Philadelphia, PA: Lippincott.

Thomas, D. J. (1986). *Robbery case files, Grand Rapids Police Department.* Grand Rapids, MI: Author.

Thomas, D. J. (1994). *Robbery case files, Gainesville Police Department.* Gainesville, FL: Author.

Thomas, D. J. (1995). *Robbery case files, Gainesville Police Department.* Gainesville, FL: Author.

Thomas, D. J. (1996). *Homicide case files, Gainesville Police Department.* Gainesville, FL: Author.

Wolfgang, M. E., & Ferracuti, F. (1967). *The subculture of violence: Towards an integrated theory in criminology.* London: Tavistock.

Wright, R. T., & Decker, S. H. (1997). *Armed robberies in action: Stickups and street culture.* Lebanon, NH: Northeastern University Press.

Victimology

Victimology is far from being a mundane topic. My original plan had been to provide an academic view in this chapter, as I have done in the other chapters, focusing on law, police interaction with victims, suspect–victim relationships, how victims are chosen, and victim typologies, and also to provide several case studies. In addition, I had planned to do what I generally do as an author, which is to avoid discussing my personal biases and the impact of policing on my psyche. Generally, I prefer to ask you to reflect on information and make your own decisions, rather than impose my views on you.

In this chapter, however, I decided to offer a perspective that is rarely discussed: how the interaction of victims and suspects influences the decision making of law enforcement officers. I will be basing the discussion on my own experience, as well as that of other officers with whom I have worked with over the years.

Let's take a moment to categorize the types of victims. In this book alone, we have encountered victims of homicide, rape, serial murder, child abuse, human trafficking, arson, gang violence, and robbery. This list is actually very short, because with every crime comes a victim. *Victimology* is the study of the interactions between the victim and the offender before, during, and after the commission of a crime (Burgess, Regehr, & Roberts, 2013; Talwar, 2006).

For the police, victims of crime are a resource: They provide information, their bodies are probed and prodded for evidence, and they are potential witnesses to a crime. Often they are forced to relive some of the most terrifying incidents that a human being can experience and survive. If the victim dies, family members fill in as surrogates and are forced to experience the horror through the testimony of witnesses and forensic experts—not to mention the attacks of defense attorneys who question the credibility and honor of a rape or murder victim.

Reflect on this statement: "A victim is a necessary evil in the investigation and prosecution of a criminal case." This statement, made by Sgarzi and McDevitt (2002), emphasizes that in a criminal case, all the attention is placed on the offender, and very little attention is given to the victim (pp. 1–2).

THE LAW

Historically, the first mention of victims' rights was outlined in the *Code of Hammurabi* 4,000 years ago in the discussion of proportionality in sentencing, meaning that a sentence or punishment had to be fair in relation to the crime (International Narcotics Board, 2007; Office for Victims of Crime, 1998). The law recognized that victims have a right of retributive justice, but only if it is fair and equal to their loss—in other words, "an eye for an eye."

Let's reflect again on the statement that in a criminal case, victims are a "necessary evil." Then it is important to also note, as I did in Chapter 2, that in terms of legislation, the United States demonstrated value for its animals long before it did for its children or women. Now we can list victims of crime, chronologically, at the end of this list. The sequence of legal developments is as follows:

1. *Animal abuse laws.* The first animal abuse laws in the United States were enacted in 1828 (Schlueter, 2008).
2. *Laws to protect children.* It has been argued that children are our most precious resource, and yet, as a country, we have been at a loss when it comes to protecting them. The first federal legislation that recognized children was not enacted until 1935. That legislation provided grants to states funding welfare services for children where their environment would impair their physical and social development, and services for maternal and child health (Seventy-Fourth Congress, 1935). The 1935 legislation, however, did nothing to protect children from acts of violence. It was not until 1962 that the *battered child syndrome* became recognized as an official form of abuse in an article published in *The Journal of the American Medical Association* by Dr. C. Henry Kempe and colleagues. The term *battered child syndrome* is all-encompassing, describing every form of abuse that a child might experience, including emotional, physical, and sexual abuse; malnourishment; and death. Despite Dr. Kempe's efforts, it was not until 1967 that forty-four states had passed legislation to protect children from abuse (De Cruz, 2010; Myers, 2006).

3. *Laws to protect women.* These laws were slow to evolve and are best described based on a timeline like that offered by Salimbeni (2010):

   a. 1975—The National Organization of Women established a task force to examine battered women and domestic violence.

   b. 1979—The United Nations held its first convention titled "The Elimination of All Discrimination Against Women."

   c. 1981—President Carter held the first National Women's History Week.

   d. 1983—The Police Foundation did its first study and determined that arrests reduce the likelihood of repeat offenses of domestic violence.

   e. 1984—The first federally funded program was established to assist victims of domestic violence through legislation known as the Family Violence and Prevention Act.

   f. 1988—*State v. Ciskie* (1988) empowered the victim of domestic violence to press charges, and if police were reluctant, the victim could take action against the agency and/or officers.

   g. 1991—*State v. Ciskie* became the landmark case by which state legislatures passed legislation requiring mandatory arrests in cases of domestic violence nationwide.

   h. 1996—The Lautenberg Amendment established that if a law enforcement officer was convicted of domestic violence, the officer would be stripped of the right to possess or own a firearm (pp. 15–19).

4. *Victims' rights legislation.* This legislation can best be defined as a series of laws that granted victims certain guarantees as victims of crime. Although every state has some form of these laws in place, they vary greatly from state to state. In general, the guarantees include the right to information; the right to be present at criminal justice proceedings; the right to due process, which includes the right to notice of and opportunity to be heard at important criminal justice proceedings; the right to financial recompense for losses suffered as a result of a crime, such as restitution and/or compensation/reparations; the right to protection; and the right to privacy (National Crime Victim Law Institute, 2011).

In my experience, the one victims' right that has many meanings or is defined differently by the courts and prosecutors is the right of participation. I have watched prosecutors make deals in cases where the victims would rather go to trial. In many instances, the victims are never consulted, and yet their participation is a prescribed right under the law. I have heard prosecutors offer the following excuses for excluding victims: "If we go to trial, we might lose"; "the defense is going to besmirch the character of the victim"; "if we accept a plea, the penalty will be the same, even though the offender is pleading to a lesser charge"; and "this will save taxpayers money."

In 1982, President Reagan appointed the first Task Force on Victims of Crime, which offered sixty-eight recommendations regarding the treatment of crime victims in order to improve that treatment. One of the task force's recommendations was to amend the Sixth Amendment to the U.S. Constitution to guarantee that victims would be present and would provide a victim's impact statement (Presidents' Task Force, 1982). Today all fifty states have some version of a law incorporating the guarantees suggested by that recommendation.

In 1991, the U.S. Supreme Court reversed its long-held position that victims' impact statements would adversely impact the rights of the accused during sentencing. In *Payne v. Tennessee* (1991), the Court reversed its decision by a vote of 5 to 4. Earlier, in *Booth v. Maryland* (1987), Justice Scalia had stated that victims should be allowed to produce an impact statement, noting that many feel the courts do not take into account the harm that an offender has caused to innocent members of society. In *Payne,* he also noted that the defense is allowed to parade a number of witnesses before the court "to testify to the pressures beyond normal human experience that drove the defendant to commit his crime, with no one to lay before the sentencing authority the full reality of human suffering the defendant has produced—which (and not moral guilt alone) is one of the reasons society deems his act worthy of the prescribed penalty" (*Payne v. Tennessee,* 1991).

It would be safe to say that we have come a long way when it comes to victims of crime and how they are treated. Many jurisdictions provide victim advocates, and they have been members of the court, prosecutor's office, and/or law enforcement agencies. The role of the advocate is to ensure that the victim's needs are met and to act as a liaison between the victim and the criminal justice system. However, when we look at the criminal justice system, we need to look at where victims get their first impression of the system and a sense of how they will be treated in the future.

POLICE AND THE VICTIM

The police personality is unique within American culture and also is responsible for the development of certain traits that are ostensibly found in policing. Skolnick (2004) offered an analysis of the police personality, stating that it consists of two elements: danger and authority. Danger is associated with potential violence and law-breaking; as a result, the police officer is suspicious and becomes isolated socially because of his or her role. The element of authority is associated with enforcing laws and regulating public activity (p. 101).

Jones (1995) expanded the discussion of the police personality by asserting that there are at least six attributes that are unique to the police subculture: conservatism, machismo, mission orientation, pragmatism, prejudice, and suspiciousness. At face value, each of these could interfere with successful victim interaction, and especially when a victim does not fit the mind-set of an officer. For instance, can a prostitute be raped? Can a drug addict be wronged if sold the wrong substance? The following paragraphs look at each of these attributes in more detail.

Conservatism. Police are generally more conservative than the general population. This is not necessarily negative; however, the profession is often seen as being closed-minded, with traditional views of the world and American culture (p. 209). This belief system is reinforced in training, when enforcing the law, and in interactions with peers.

Machismo. Policing is a profession that requires the ultimate in physical and mental toughness (p. 209). This aspect of the personality can hamper the application of empathy, and an officer's lack of empathy can prolong the victim's suffering and place the victim in a position where he or she refuses to cooperate.

Mission orientation. Police view themselves as protectors or guardians of society (p. 209). As such, there is sometimes a disconnect between police and victims; although dealing with victims is a necessary part of the police job, the greater part of the job is catching offenders. Police officers are often heard making statements like: "I am not a social worker; that is why we have victim advocates. My job is to catch the bad guys." How can an officer with a tendency to think that way effectively address the needs of a victim? *Pragmatism.* Because of the nature of the profession, police are very practical, look for functionality, and are response-oriented. By being pragmatic, the mission is less complicated. However, being pragmatic can lead police to overlook such concepts as innovation, experimentation, and/or research (p. 209). In police organizations, change is very difficult and slow. In the past, changes often have not taken place until prompted by a tragedy. All you have to do is examine the history of victimology and victim services to see clearly how much change is hated in the police profession. *Prejudice.* The issue of prejudice is hotly debated, and police organizations are constantly attempting to defend their actions in minority communities. The issue is not limited to one particular agency or community. It is important to understand that the community's perception, not the agency's, is the reality for community members. I have been to calls where victims strike out and state: "You don't care about me. All I am is a report to you. The bastard will have to kill me before you do anything. I bet if you were on the white side of town, you would arrest that bastard."

Suspiciousness. Law enforcement officers are the first to respond to every violent crime and are the first to interact with the victims and witnesses. When I first started my career, my training officers were cynical and mistrusted everyone they encountered. I remember that during my first night in patrol, one of my training officers asked me a profound question: Why do you want to be a cop? My answer was "I want to help people." I have asked that question a thousand times when training police recruits and doing psychological evaluations of new applicants for agencies. The answer is always the same as mine: "I want to help people." All I can do is laugh because I now realize that they will become that poor cynical bastard I encountered during my first night in a patrol car.

Most police officers enter the profession with the noblest of intentions, unaware of the impact the daily grind will have on their psyche. When I began my career, I did not really understand the danger of the job or the violence that occurs between humans, nor did I appreciate the loss and grief that victims and survivors experience. Today, some thirty-five years later, I can recall each of the calls that pushed me farther and farther away from humanity, allowing me to become increasingly detached and providing me with a psychological barrier behind which to hide all emotion. The end result was that my judgment remained rational—grounded in law, and not emotion. Although that is a positive outcome, the negative aspect of developing that psychological barrier was that I became disconnected, meaning that I had very little empathy for victims, with a few exceptions such as children, victims of rape, and survivors of brutal attacks.

Following are two examples of incidents that affected me deeply. I experienced these situations during my first three weeks of training. Keep in mind that it was not until years later that I understood their significance in terms of their impact on my psyche:

- We received a call of a pedestrian being struck by a car. When we arrived, we discovered the victim was a 7-year-old boy who rode his bike in front of an approaching traffic. The little boy sustained a skull fracture and was bleeding from his ears. I provided first aid until the paramedics arrived and assisted them until he was transported to the hospital. I remember seeing parents on the sidewalk as we worked on their son, and I interviewed them after the paramedics took over on the scene. It was then that I realized that the father was one of our detectives. I remember talking to my training officer about the case and my performance. I was told two days later that the parents removed the little boy from life support and he had died. I never gave the case or the family a second thought; to me, it was a job, and we had done all that we could do. I look back on the incident now and wonder how I could have been so detached.

- The second case involved a 75-year-old man. Someone had stolen his moped. On this day, I was with another training officer who had as many years in the department as I was old. He had asked me why I became a police officer, and my response had been "to help people." During our shift, we made it a point to try to recover the moped. Just before the shift ended, we observed the moped and gave chase. The suspect dumped the moped, and we caught the suspect and recovered the moped. The moped was returned to the victim that day. My training officer made the following comment: "You helped somebody and took some scum off the street. It was a good day."

- The very next day we received a call of a motor vehicle accident. On arrival, we discovered it was the old man. He had lost control of the moped and drove in front of a dump truck. There was nothing left of him. My training officer asked how I felt, and I could not speak. I blamed myself. Had we not found the moped, the old man would not have been killed. In a very cynical voice, my training officer told me: "We did our job, and this is something that we have no control over. You will see this time and time again, but God or fate or some higher being has another plan. Your job is to do what you can and go home at the end of every shift. This is not your fault."

I lived by that mantra for years. I also made it a point not to have friends on the job after losing a friend and mentor, Trooper Norman Killough of the Michigan State Police, who was killed just before I entered the police academy. Oddly, all I could see at the time of Norm's death was the honor, and not the pain and suffering of his loved ones and the organization. Ironically, and in contrast to Trooper Killough's death, as I was growing up in Detroit, a number of my friends fell victim to the heroin wars of the 1970s.

My experiences are not unusual to law enforcement officers. Each officer addresses the issues differently. Sometimes officers remain psychologically disconnected throughout their entire careers, and other times life-changing events force officers to connect with and trust others again. I fell into the latter category. Three life-changing events happened to me, ironically, at intervals of five years:

- The first was the death of my mother. She died during my fifth year of policing. After I returned to work and to the academy to teach, many people commented that I had changed and become more human.
- The second incident, five years later, was the murder of Officer Joseph Taylor of the Grand Rapids Police Department. He was a dear friend and fellow SWAT team member. In that tenth year of policing, the profession was no longer fun.
- The third incident, five years after that, involved a gunman who barricaded himself in his car. After three hours of negotiation and having established a bond with the gunman, I witnessed him take a gun and shoot himself in the chest.

These three events forced me to reevaluate the psychological effects policing had on me. Although painful, they removed some of the psychological detachment that had kept me from feeling empathy for others.

The police personality is complex, and there are no absolutes. From the perspective of victims and witnesses, the police provide the first impression of the criminal justice system. Sometimes it seems that a victim gets victimized twice, once by the offender and again by the police. The point of police–victim contact may also be the point where a victim may choose not to participate or refuse to offer any assistance because of what he or she perceives as an officer's inability to connect or show concern.

Many officers do what I did as a means of survival: create a psychological barrier. In so doing, however, they fail the public that they are meant to protect. Much like the criminal with a distorted thought process, the officer's cognitive process is distorted as well, but for different reasons.

> **Questions for Reflection:** Examining the police personality and my early experiences as an officer, do you believe that I was capable of connecting with victims? Do you believe that the emotional distance I developed was a necessary evil for survival? How might a police officer maintain both the detachment necessary for dealing with the harsh reality of police work and the empathy needed when dealing with victims?

TYPOLOGY OF VICTIMS

Theorists have developed many classification systems of victims based on empirical data. As noted previously, classification systems are rarely used from a law enforcement perspective, since the goal of law enforcement is to articulate the facts of the crime in painstaking detail. Victimology, however, is the exception to this rule, because classification systems may provide some insight into offenders' target selection. From a police perspective, victimology requires that police examine a victim's habits, associates, hangouts, and facts that only close friends would know in order to obtain an accurate picture of the victim. One thing that investigators learn through experience is that we never really know a person completely, not even if we are married to them.

In addition to the needs of the police, classification systems are important in victimology because they help in the development of treatment plans as well as in designing treatment programs for both victims and offenders. From the clinical perspective, then, one size does not fit all.

One theory that has been around for years is that of victim-precipitated violence, which is based on the concept that the victim played a role in the act of violence. More specifically, the offender and victim were partners in the crime. Associated with this relationship is the concept of proxemics, meaning that the closer one is to the crime, the more likely one is to elicit a response. What this theory does not take into account are the cases where offenders hunt their prey and the victims are completely innocent.

This theory of victim-precipitated violence has been a part of police bias for years, especially in dealing with the crime of rape. A woman's claim of rape is often viewed with some degree of skepticism based on the way she dresses, the location of the rape, or the time of day. All of these factors may be seen as insinuating that the victim got what she was looking for and/or deserved. The end result is complaints and claims from women who have not been taken seriously and women being discouraged from filing complaints of rape.

Mendelsohn (1940) interviewed victims and determined that a number of victims either consciously or unconsciously played some role in their victimization. Victims were classified as ranging from being 100 percent innocent to the imaginary victim. This author's six categories are self-explanatory: completely innocent victim, victim with minor guilt and responsibility, victim who shares equal responsibility, the victim is slightly guiltier than the offender, victim who is solely responsible for the victimization, and the imaginary victim.

Von Hentig (1948) described the relationship between the perpetrator and the victim as a duet; as the perpetrator and victim draw close, a number of interactions take place. For offenders, it is sizing up the victims (prey) and assessing whether they can establish control; for victims, it is determining whether the offender is friend or foe. It is here that von Hentig describes the assessment as being filled with repulsions as well as attractions, and it is during this assessment period that a series of interactions are set into motion. The relationship is that of a subject (the offender) and object (the victim), as opposed to two people entering into a causal relationship or viewing each other as equals. The object is a thing that is not a human and has no value, which is why the offender can attack with anonymity. Von Hentig classified victims based on their risk factors and created three broad typologies. Within each typology are a number of subclassifications. The three typologies are the general classes, the psychological types, and the activating sufferer. Ultimately, von Hentig believed that in most cases, the behavior of the victim was the cause of his or her victimization.

Hindeland, Gottfredson, and Garofalo (1978) believed that victimization occurred because of lifestyle exposure. This goes back to the concept of proxemics and demographics, meaning that if a victim's lifestyle—that is, where the person lives, works, goes to school, shops, and so on—places him or her in harm's way, then that person has a greater chance of being victimized.

As discussed in Chapter 2, researchers have argued that murder should be considered in terms of a situation or cause and effect. In most cases of murder, the offender and victim have had some form of relationship, and each of the actors (offender and victim) contributed to the escalation of the incident (Canter & Youngs, 2009; Luckenbill, 1977; Wolfgang, 1958). Roberts, Zgoba, and Shahidullah (2007) examined 336 homicide offenders and created the following classification system:

- *Altercation- or argument-precipitated homicides:* In this classification, the homicide occurs following an argument or altercation. Such disputes are often over insignificant amounts of money or property and/or disrespect. They usually start as verbal disagreements and escalate to fighting; ultimately they are resolved through shooting or stabbing, with murder being the end result (p. 500). As one of my clients stated in a therapy session: "I had no choice but to kill him. He disrespected me, and everyone knew it. If I did nothing, I would spend my remaining time in prison fighting everyone off. This way I get respect." My client pounded the victim's head into the floor until he was dead, and my client had ten years added to his thirty-year sentence for the murder of a drug dealer on the street. When I asked my client whether either murder was worth it, he replied yes, stating that in each case it was about respect (Thomas, 2001).

- *Felony homicide:* In these cases, the homicide is committed during the commission of another crime such as robbery, rape, burglary, kidnapping, or theft (p. 500). In some instances, the homicide may be the primary crime and another crime is committed in addition to the intended homicide. Other times the homicide occurs when the victim attempts to intervene in the offender's actions; the victim surprises the offender while the offender is committing a felony; the victim refuses to comply with the offender's demands; or the offender kills the victim and/or witnesses because they are considered a liability and can identify the offender. In an example of a case where the victim was considered collateral damage, the offender stated: "It was fate. The old bitch was going to die whether we killed her or not last night. Look, we broke in her house, to steal her money and whatever else we could find. We figured that she would be there, but she is an old lady so she wasn't a threat. Once in the house we found the old bitch asleep, so Tommy suggested we have some fun, so we decided rape her. Man, could that old bitch scream. Once we both had our way with her, we took turns beating her until she was dead. Think about it, she was going to die last night whether we killed her or God took her life naturally" (Thomas, 1981).

- *Domestic violence or intimate partner–induced homicides:* These homicides occur due to familial relationships, and offenders and victims may include intimates, family members, current or ex-spouses, and current or ex-boyfriends and girlfriends (p. 500). In this type of incident, often there is no logical reason for the murder in the eyes of an outsider. An example of the lack of logic is apparent in this excerpt from a 911 call made by a 14-year-old boy named Noah Crooks after he shot and killed his mother: "I shot my mom and I don't know why I did it. I tried to rape her, but I couldn't. She took my *Call to Duty* video game, and something just came over me. My life is over and it all goes down the drain now. I have to move and I'm going to jail" (Senzarnio, 2013). Noah had fired more than twenty rounds into his mother's body after his mother took his video game because he had received bad grades on his report card.

- *Accident homicides:* In this type of homicide, offenders cause death through the use of an automobile (p. 500). We understand that drinking and driving do not mix, and yet millions of Americans still partake in both activities at the same time. Drunk driving is responsible for a large number of fatalities annually. Here is a statement made by a drunk driving suspect after an arrest: "I was driving home minding my own business. I heard a thump and my car went up and my car shook like I hit the curb and ran over something in the road like a dog. I didn't think anything of it until you came to my house and told me that I killed someone. I had no idea it was a person that I hit. Now I understand that I was driving on the sidewalk and hit the guy. Come on, I could not have been that drunk" (Thomas, 1979).

As you examine these classifications, do you agree that the victims may have played a role in their own demise?

I will argue that there is a cause and effect in every encounter; however, in many cases, there is no provocation by the victim. As discussed earlier in this book, child rapists will say that a child enticed them. How can that be when a child knows nothing about sexuality until he or she is taught about it? If you accept the typologies that hold the victim responsible, then you will see victims as nothing more than a necessary evil to assist in the prosecution of a criminal case. To really understand victims, however, I think that it is necessary to understand the trauma and horror that they endure.

Questions for Reflection: Can you think of any circumstance in which a victim might be considered culpable in his or her victimization? What influences a police officer's behavior when he or she interacts with a victim? Is it the officer's own belief system regarding victims? Do you think the victim's status, profession, behavior, race, or a combination of some or all of these characteristics makes any difference?

THE PSYCHOLOGICAL AFTERMATH OF VICTIMIZATION

The road to understanding victimology is difficult at best. I am not so naive as to believe that the attitudes of the criminal justice system have changed completely and that victims are now always seen as more than a necessary evil. Victims have a unique position in society in that they are actors in a play in which, in many instances, they did not choose to participate; as such, if they survive, they can provide a firsthand account of man's inhumanity to man.

Herman (1992) paints a picture of psychological trauma that everyone needs to understand:

> [Trauma makes us] come face to face both with human vulnerability in the natural world and with the capacity for evil in human nature. To study trauma means bearing witness to horrible events. When the events are natural disasters or "acts of God" those who bear witness sympathize readily with the victim. But when traumatic events are of human design, those who bear witness are caught in the middle between victim and perpetrator. (p. 7)

In examining Herman's statement regarding trauma and its aftermath, it is important to note that all that is left are dead bodies, victims of rape, fatalities in car accidents, child abductions and murders, murder-suicides, and domestic violence (Regehr & Bober, 2005). No matter the level of preparation, the human psyche is not designed to handle such incidents, as evidenced by the difficulties experienced by police, firefighters, and members of the military, all of whom have the best training in the world.

To understand the impact that trauma has on the victim, we must look at the tactics of the offender and his or her goals, beginning with ideas like: Was the offending done in secrecy? Did the offender hide the crime? The answers to these questions are often yes in the case of domestic violence, child abuse, and, in many instances, sexual assault. Offenders often use bribes, promises, and, when all else fails, threats of physical harm to enforce secrecy. Herman (1992) argued that when all else fails, the credibility of the victim is attacked (p. 8). In court this is a very common tactic in homicide cases—defense attorneys will attack the credibility of the victim and, in many instances, make it appear like the offender had no choice but to kill the victim. Again, we face the conflict between valuing victims versus seeing them as a necessary evil.

Trauma destroys our sense of well-being and creates a sense of powerlessness in which our ordinary systems are overwhelmed. Even in well-adjusted individuals with a balanced lifestyle and excellent coping mechanisms in place, the impact of a traumatic event will have long-term effects (Herman, 1992; James & Gilliland, 2005). If I were speaking to a group of police officers about the trauma they suffer while working, they would say, "It goes with the job; just suck it up." The reality is, however, that no one's psyche is designed to handle such events. The mind, however, does have mechanisms in place that allow people to survive even the trauma associated with brutal attacks, such as the brutality of a gang rape. The literature describes one mechanism as the dissociative state, meaning that the victim's mind disconnects from his or her body. Victims in this state are often described as having a blank stare or appearing to be in shock.

Victims who have suffered through acts of violence experience an aftermath. Often they exhibit symptoms of anxiety, depression, hyperarousal, an inability to sleep, loss of appetite, a flat affect, intrusive thoughts, and disturbing dreams. What I have described are symptoms of *posttraumatic stress disorder* (PTSD) as outlined in the *Diagnostic and Statistical Manual of Mental Disorders, IV-TR* (American Psychiatric Association, 2000). The features of PTSD are brought on by exposure to an extremely traumatic event that involves actual or threatened death, or the witnessing of such an event. The victim/witness experiences intense fear, helplessness, or horror during the event. As a result, in the aftermath, the victim/witness seeks to avoid similar stimuli and experiences the symptoms of PTSD, which is one of the most common disorders resulting from trauma.

In providing this discussion of trauma, I wanted to make you aware that the victim/witness is more than a necessary evil. Victims are not objects or things, which is the way offenders often see them. They are people who suffer deeply because of the actions of offenders and sometimes, unfortunately, the secondary trauma they experience at the hands of the criminal justice system.

Questions for Reflection: How would you handle being the victim of a violent crime? How would you handle it happening to one of your loved ones? How might such an incident impact your household, daily life, and quality of life?

CONCLUSION

As I close this chapter, I am still shocked by some of what I learned during my research on victimology. I am still shocked by how little, as a society, we value human beings. I am still dumbstruck by how our legal system valued animals long before children, women, and victims of crime. I am still dumbfounded by my discovery that the Supreme Court denied the use of victim impact statements, based on the belief that they would unfairly prejudice the jury, because it accepted the argument that an offender could not have foreseen the impact of his actions before committing the crime.

There is no doubt that the system is moving in the right direction. However, it is a system with many flaws, and one so bound by politics that often there is no problem with restricting the rights of victims when it is to the advantage of the system to do so.

Because of the nature of violent crime, and our need for a reminder about what it means to be a victim, I am closing this chapter by repeating the Herman (1992) statement quoted earlier:

> [Trauma makes us] come face to face both with human vulnerability in the natural world and with the capacity for evil in human nature. To study trauma means bearing witness to horrible events. When the events are natural disasters or "acts of God" those who bear witness sympathize readily with the victim. But when traumatic events are of human design, those who bear witness are caught in the middle between victim and perpetrator. (p. 7)

REFERENCES

American Psychiatric Association. (2000). *The diagnostic and statistical manual of mental disorders, IV-TR*, 4th ed. Arlington, VA: Author.

Booth v. Maryland, 482 U.S. 496 (1987), Supreme Court Justice Anthony Scalia's dissenting opinion.

Burgess, A. W., Regehr, C., & Roberts, A. R. (2013). *Victimology: Theories and applications*. Burlington, MA: Jones and Bartlett Learning.

Canter, D., & Youngs, D. (2009). *Investigative psychology: Offender profiling and the analysis of criminal action*. West Sussex, United Kingdom: Wiley & Sons.

De Cruz, P. (2010). *Family law, sex and society: A comparative study of family law*. New York: Routledge.

Herman, J. L. (1992). *Trauma and recovery*. New York: Basic Books.

Hindeland, M. S., Gottfredson, M., & Garofalo, J. (1978). *Victims of personal crime*. Cambridge, MA: Ballinger, Hirschi, & Travis.

International Narcotics Board. (2007). *Report of the international narcotics control board for 2007*. New York: United Nations.

James, R. K., & Gilliland, B. E. (2005). *Crisis intervention strategies*, 5th ed. Belmont, CA: Thomson.

Jones, J. W. (1995). Counseling issues and police diversity. In M. Kurke & E. Scrivner (Eds.), *Police psychology into the 21st century* (pp. 207–254). Hillsdale, NJ: Lawrence Erlbaum.

Luckenbill, D. F. (1977). Criminal homicide as a situated transaction. *Social Problems, 25*(2), pp. 176–186.

Mendelsohn, B. (1940). Rape in criminology. *Giustizia Penale* [magazine].

Myers, J. E. B. (2006). *Child protection in America, past, present and future*. New York: Oxford University Press.

National Crime Victim Law Institute. (2011). *History of victims' rights*. Portland, OR: Author.

Office for Victims of Crime. (1998). *New directions from the field: Victims' rights and services for the 21st century.* Washington, D.C.: U.S. Department of Justice. *Payne v. Tennessee,* 501 U.S. 808 (1991), footnote 4/1.

Presidents' Task Force. (1982). *President's task force on victims of crime.* Washington, D.C.: Author.

Regehr, C., & Bober, T. (2005). *In the line of fire: Trauma in emergency services.* New York: Oxford University Press.

Roberts, A. R., Zgoba, K. M., & Shahidullah, S. M. (2007). Recidivism among four types of homicide offenders: An exploratory analysis of 336 homicide offenders in New Jersey. *Aggression and Violent Behavior, 12,* pp. 493–507.

Salimbeni, M. C. (2010). *Law enforcement officers' understanding of domestic violence amongst their colleagues.* Boca Raton, FL: Dissertation.Com.

Schlueter, S. (2008). Law enforcement perspectives and obligations related to animal abuse. In F. R. Ascione (Ed.), *The international handbook of animal abuse and cruelty: Theory, research, and application* (pp. 375–392). West Lafayette, IN: Purdue University Press.

Senzarnio, P. (2013, May 2). First deputies on scene testify in Crooks trial. *Waterloo-Cedar Falls Courier,* A1.

Seventy-Fourth Congress of the United States. (1935). *The social security act, title IV-B.* Washington, D.C.: Author.

Sgarzi, J. M., & McDevitt, J. (2002). Introduction. In J. M. Sgarzi & J. McDevitt (Eds.), *Victimology: A study of crime victims and their role* (pp. 1–5). Upper Saddle River, NJ: Prentice-Hall.

Skolnick, J. (2004). A sketch of the police officer's "working personality." In B. W. Hancock & P. M. Sharp (Eds.), *Criminal justice in America: Theory, practice, and policy.* Upper Saddle River, NJ: Prentice-Hall.

State v. Ciskie, 110 Wn. 2d 263, 271, 751 P.2d 1165 (1988).

Talwar, P. (2006). *Victimology.* Adarsh, Delhi: Isha Books.

Thomas, D. J. (1979). *DWI traffic investigation, Grand Rapids Police Department.* Grand Rapids, MI: Author.

Thomas, D. J. (1981). *Homicide case files, Grand Rapids Police Department.* Grand Rapids, MI: Author.

Thomas, D. J. (2001). *Inmate case files, Gainesville Police Department.* Gainesville, FL: Author.

von Hentig, H. (1948). *The criminal and his victim.* New Haven, CT: Yale University Press.

Wolfgang, M. E. (1958). *Patterns in criminal homicide.* New York: Wiley & Sons, Science Editions.

Conclusion

As the reader, you have had a chance to view violent crime through the eyes of the criminologist. You have learned about the history of crimes and criminal law, and about various theories regarding the causes of and motivations for crime. You have examined specific criminals and their crimes, including murder, rape, serial murder, crimes against children, human trafficking, arson, gangs, and robbery. You also have been introduced to victimology—the study of how victims are affected by the crimes against them, and how victims are treated by the criminal justice system.

Questions for Reflection: What have you learned? Have you found one theory to be better or more useful than the rest? What kinds of limitations have you found in the theories? Do you believe that the only real place to learn about criminals is on the street, through interacting with them, or do you think the study of crime can provide important information as well?

OVERVIEW OF VIOLENT CRIME

Acts of violence shock the conscience of the society, and yet we often become desensitized to such acts. For example, when the Columbine school shooting happened, as a society we were shocked; we reacted the same way when the Sandy Hook school shooting occurred. However, mass shootings are almost an everyday occurrence now; we no longer wonder if one will happen, but when. This means that no one is immune to being a victim of such a crime.

Other violent crimes that have been discussed in this text, such as robbery, rape, murder, and serial murder, are also all too common. Many people believe that if they live in the right neighborhood, work in a safe environment, and choose their friends wisely, they will not become a victim of such a violent crime. This belief is especially common among those who subscribe to the theories associated with victimology, in which it is the relationship between the offender and the victim that dictates the probability of victimization. This belief, however, is not founded in reality. Anyone can be a victim of violent crime.

Murder

Everyone is capable of committing murder. When we examine the concept of murder, it is difficult for many to comprehend how an individual can take the life of another without there being some form of special circumstance. The reality is that murder is closely associated with human emotions, needs, and actions such as jealousy, revenge, money, sex, insanity, anger, commission of other crimes, fear, boredom (just because), or any combination (Falk, 1990; Ghiglieri, 1999; Wille, 1974; Wilson, 1993).

The family plants the seed of future acts of violence: This statement became a theme throughout most of the text. Gelles and Straus (1979) made the following observation concerning family violence:

> With the exception of the police and the military, the family is perhaps the most violent social group, and the home the most violent social setting, in our society. A person is more likely to be hit or killed in his or her home by another family member than anywhere else or by anyone else. (p. 15)

In examining this quotation, I was struck by the fact that the family also appears to be the basis of learned behavior. Remember, behavior is not learned in a vacuum; there are many contributing factors. I would also argue that the family may well be the foundation not only for acts of violent behavior but also for the cognitive distortions that allow one to perform violent acts—that is, how one responds to perceived transgressions along with a lack of coping mechanisms.

Murder has many motivations, and there are a number of classification systems for murderers. Research indicates that we learn acts of violence as we develop from infants to adulthood and experience a number of disappointments. Those of us who do not murder usually acquire coping skills and learn how to manage disappointment, anger, rage, jealousy, and resentment.

Rape

Rape, a crime with many monikers, is defined by state statute. Each state may have a different way of defining it. In the state of Michigan, it is called *criminal sexual conduct* and has four degrees, which include behaviors ranging from something as simple as touching to sexual penetration. The state of Florida calls it *sexual battery*, which by its very nature describes the crime as touching, union with, and penetration of sexual organs.

With the crime of rape, it is important to understand the relationship between the victim and offender as well as the way society views each. The question that we in the United States have struggled with for many years is: When a victim says "no," does that equate to forcible rape? With that question in mind, consider the following: There is no particular profile of a victim. Victims range in age from infant to senior citizen; they are not of a specific gender but may be either male or female (rape is not limited to females and children); and, finally, victims come from every socioeconomic background.

The problem of rape, as well as the misperceptions surrounding it, not only is an issue in society as a whole, but also has been a major problem in specific areas of society. For example, the U.S. military ignored the problem for years until it was brought to the forefront in 2012 by former secretary of defense Leon Panetta, who provided the following data in a press conference: In 2011, there were 3,191 sexual assaults reported in the military, but this number is only a fraction of the actual crimes committed. Panetta reported that he believed the true number of sexual assaults to be closer to 19,000 for that same year, and that 56 percent of the victims were men (Parrish, 2012).

Anyone can become a victim of sexual assault. Groth and Birnbaum (1979) noted that any discussion of provocation is ridiculous, since the assaults can and do happen in every conceivable location, at all times of the day, and no person is immune from becoming a victim (p. 7). If you consider the data regarding male soldiers who have been victims, it is clear that anyone has the potential to become a victim in any circumstance.

The actions of a rapist, serial killer, or violent criminal are built on a faulty foundation. This faulty foundation is developed early in life and forces the individual to find a form of escape, which is most often bound in fantasy. As Leo Boatman, the fledgling serial killer, stated in his interview with police after his arrest:

> When I was growing up my life was miserable and I had no control. The state of Florida is responsible for raising me and I escaped the abuse in foster homes and juvenile detention by reading murder mystery books and placing myself in the role of the killer. It was there that I was in control and it was there that

I learned to manipulate others to get what I wanted. (Marion County Sheriff's Office, 2006)

The question will always be: How can someone attack another human being and literally take the one thing that is so closely associated with the victim's dignity—the right to refuse? If you review the reasons for sexual assaults and the typologies of rapists and sexual serial killers, in each case, the same thing is missing: a sense of humanity. In addition, all the offenders lack empathy.

Crimes Against Children

Children are victims of violent crime far too many times, and those who are supposed to be their protectors are usually the violators. The discussions of crimes against children and of serial rapists and sexual serial killers were separated because to offer both in the same chapter would diminish the importance of acts committed against children. It is important to acknowledge that children are often a forgotten lot and have had very little value as victims under the protection of the law. Throughout this text, I outlined the impact of negative environments on personality development: The end result is the creation of monsters.

Conditioning and modeling theorists have argued that the relationship between children and sexual excitement by adults is a learned condition response. The behavior is associated with an experience the offender may have had in childhood with an adult. The behavior is learned, and as a result, the child's fantasy is associated with other children. Since this is the model to which they were introduced, during masturbation, these people as adults become fixated on children and associate pleasure and orgasm with the image of a child (McGuire, Carlisle, & Young, 1965).

Laws and Marshall (1990) argued that deviant behavior is learned through the same mechanisms by which traditional sexual behavior is learned, which supports the theory presented by McGuire et al. The Laws and Marshall theory is closely associated with the concept of *operant conditioning*, which is a system of learning that is reinforced through reward and punishment. Skinner (1953) argued that the only way to determine if an event has been reinforced is to see whether there is a change in the frequency of the event. Skinner described two types of reinforcers:

- *Adding something*, which is *positive reinforcement* and is associated with food, water, and sexual contact.
- *Removing something*, which is *negative reinforcement* and can be associated with that which makes us uncomfortable, such as loud noises, bright lights, extreme cold or heat, and electric shock.

Seto (2008) stated that there is distinct difference between pedophiles and nonpedophilic offenders. Pedophiles are likely to have boy victims, multiple victims, prepubescent victims, and unrelated victims. These findings are supported by Abel and colleagues. In contrast, nonpedophilic offenders are more likely to have girl victims, single victims, pubescent victims, and related victims (p. 63). Finally, sex offenders of children use different techniques that include grooming, gifts, threats, attention, and force/coercion.

Human Trafficking

As Americans, we know that slavery no longer exists. We are reminded almost daily that this country was founded on principles of freedom and has been about change and moving forward since the Civil War and the signing of the Emancipation Proclamation. Supreme Court cases like *Brown v. Board of Education of Topeka* (1954), the civil rights movement of the 1960s, voting rights legislation, and finally the election of Barack Obama as the first African American president of the United States are all symbols that slavery no longer exists, right?

Human trafficking is modern-day slavery. It comes in many forms, from the homeless child snatched off the street and sold into the sex trade, to a family selling a daughter into domestic slavery or the sex trade to end their poverty, to the promise of freedom for domestic services, and finally to the indentured servant working in the field. The only common theme in human trafficking is that the victims in most instances have had no say regarding the terms of how they are used. Human trafficking is a transnational problem; it consists of crimes against persons and has no borders.

The number of people who fall victim to human trafficking is unknown, according to a U.S. State Department *Trafficking in Persons (TIP) Report* (2008), but it is estimated that annually between 600,000 and 800,000 men, women, and children are trafficked across international borders; approximately 80 percent of them are women and girls, and up to 50 percent of them are minors (p. 51). The U.S. State Department report articulated that the majority of the victims are trafficked into sexual exploitation.

There is clearly a world market for children who are missing and exploited. Many of the countries from which children go missing or are exploited are third world countries, and the children are homeless, begging, and on the street, which makes them easy prey (Montgomery, 2001; U.S. State Department, 2008). In the United States and in most modern societies, an additional variable that is not present in the third world is the Internet, which also makes children an easy prey.

Data from the National Center for Missing and Exploited Children (2006) offer insight into the problem in the United States. According to that organization, an estimated total of 58,200 children were abducted by a nonfamily perpetrator in 1999; of that number, an estimated 115 children were victims of stereotypical kidnappings; in stereotypical kidnappings, 40 percent of the children were killed; in only 21 percent (12,100) of these cases was the child reported missing and law enforcement became involved while the child was still missing; youths aged 15 to 17 were the most frequent victims of these nonfamily abductions (59 percent); girls were more frequent victims than boys in this study, making up about two-thirds all victims; and nearly half of these victims (46 percent) were sexually assaulted by the perpetrator (p. 53).

The United States has long had a posture of differentiating between its citizens and those who are not its citizens. In fact, the United States was founded on the principle of protecting the civil rights of its citizenry. The key words here are civil rights *of its citizens*—without that citizenship status, one has no protection under the Constitution. The first ten amendments of the U.S. Constitution guarantee U.S. citizens their rights; more specifically, the First, Second, Fourth, Fifth, Sixth, Tenth, and the Fourteenth Amendments spell out the limitations of the government and the rights of U.S. citizens. I would argue, however, that these guarantees are dependent on race, gender, sexual orientation, ethnicity, and/or religious affiliation. From a practical position, it could be argued that the concept of civil rights is in the eye of the beholder; here, as in other instances noted throughout this text, "one's perception is one's reality."

Arson

Arson is the one crime that most officers do not understand because it is not traditional in the way that robbery, rape, murder, burglary, and theft are—in the sense that they are more common, and therefore more familiar. In addition, investigating an arson requires the participation of other agencies and the expertise of fire marshals or the local fire department, and often police and fire departments do not play well together. From a practical standpoint, fire or arson is rarely discussed unless the loss of property and/or life is so devastating that it requires a multiagency response and the case makes the national news. The reality, however, is that arson is more common than one might think. The U.S. Fire Administration (2001) estimated that arson was the leading cause of fire in the United States and offered the following data: Of 267,000 arsons annually, arson is responsible for 475 deaths, 2,000 injuries, and $1.4 billion in property loss each year (p. 1).

Gaynor (2002) described fire behavior as learned and as part of our developmental process, which is sequential like all other forms of human development; through proper guidance in school and home, and proper social interaction, a child learns the appropriate responses (p. 1). However, negative social influences, family dysfunction, and stressors can lead to repeated intentional acts of fire-setting. Gaynor identified four distinct levels in the development of fire-setting behavior:

- *Fire interest*—between ages 3 and 5: Questions focus on the physical properties of fire.

- *Fire-starting*—between ages 3 and 9: The child experiments at least once with fire-starting material under the supervision of a parent or caregiver. It should be noted that the majority of children will engage in at least one unsupervised incident motivated by curiosity.

- *Fire-setting intentional, no psychological problems*—between the ages of 7 and 10: Children have learned the rules of fire. Although intentional, fire-setting in this stage may not represent a psychological problem, and the behavior can be stopped with parental involvement and intervention.

- *Fire-setting intentional, with psychological or social problems*—between the ages of 7 and 10: Some in this age group are motivated by psychological or social problems, and the fires have been planned for weeks or months. Motives for this fire-setter may be anger, revenge, attention seeking, criminal mischief, crime concealment, or an intent to destroy property or people.

In reviewing the literature, we find that there is very little that differentiates the etiology of arson and the arsonist from that of other criminals. One similarity between arsonists and other criminals and those who have been victims and then committed violent crime is that they have chosen to retaliate through their crimes. In this sense, arsonists are exhibiting the same behavior as students who have been bullied and retaliate in the form of a school shooting; workers who feel they have been wronged through job termination and retaliate through mass murder, killing their supervisors and coworkers; and students or workers who use arson as a form of retaliation by burning down their school or place of employment, or the principal's or CEO's home. I argue that in each of these cases, the perpetrator has become so angry about perceived wrongs, a system's failure to protect him or her, or actual wrongs that he or she feels like there is no recourse but to retaliate violently. Such acts do not happen in a vacuum, but through a series of events. As those events are processed, there is a failure of the offender's coping mechanisms, coupled with distorted or delusional thinking. The offender finds, through his or her cognitive process, that the only recourse is retaliation through an act of violence or property destruction.

Robbery

The act of robbery takes place in many forms, including carjacking and home invasion, and victims may be a business or a person. Examination of the varied locations reveals that anyone can become a victim at any time. Robbery has no boundaries; it even happens in schools, where kids are robbed of their shoes and jackets. In 2011, there were 354,396 robberies, and robbery ranked second as the most often committed violent crime in the United States. The only violent crime committed with greater frequency was aggravated assault, with a total of 751,131 incidents (Federal Bureau of Investigation, 2011).

Ferracuti and Wolfgang theorized that subculture violence is only partly different from the state of the parent culture—that violence is, in fact, an integral component of the parent culture (Ferracuti & Wolfgang, 1973; Wolfgang & Ferracuti, 1967). Ball-Rokeach (1973) completed the first empirical study of the subculture violence theory and came to the conclusion that the values established by the subculture play little or no role as determinants of interpersonal violence. Bernard (1990) tested a variation not rooted in violence and suggested that angry aggression develops among the truly disadvantaged as a consequence of racial discrimination and low social position—that is, as part of the parent culture—as first theorized by Wolfgang and Ferracuti in 1967.

An extension of the subculture of violence theory was presented by Anderson in 1999 in *A Code of the Street,* which is a narrative ethnographic exploration of a low-income African American neighborhood in the city of Philadelphia. The basis for Anderson's research was rather simple; he wanted to know why inner-city youth are willing to perpetrate violence and acts of aggression toward each other (p. 90). Anderson (1999) defined the *code of the street* as a set of informal rules that govern relationships, behavior, and specifically violence (p. 33). Interestingly, those who have adopted middle-class values and live in these communities also have to adopt a duality in their personality: one that allows them to address their contemporaries in the neighborhood, and the other that allows them to be accepted by mainstream America.

Anderson (1999) argued that central to the code of the street and the violence is being treated with respect; he described respect as an external entity, "one that is hard-won, easily lost, and must constantly be guarded" (p. 31). The concepts of respect and credibility rest on the need for safety and security, and to be disrespected is a challenge to one's sovereignty. This need for self-preservation has grown out of a distrust of the police and the criminal justice system, so this same code extends to concepts such as "stop snitching campaigns," where those who have adopted the street code will resolve their own conflicts and are willing to die or kill in so doing.

Becker (1968) argued that people who commit crime do so because they choose to, and the choice is made by weighing the rewards and risks. Becker's theory is known as rational choice theory. In this view, one's decision to commit a criminal act is no different from someone else's decision to purchase food or clothing, because the same thought process or analysis is used for both. Becker believed that these decisions involve a detailed thought process in which the person examines the benefits of legitimate employment versus participating in criminal activity, and decides the latter will have the greater reward and better meet the individual's needs. In addition to evaluating the rewards, the person assesses the negative consequences of participating in criminal activity if caught. Becker argued that previous theories have no value because free will and choice are primary in the human decision-making process.

In a study of eighty-six robbers completed by researchers Wright and Decker (1997), eighty-one of the robbers spoke to the immediate need for money, and it should be emphasized that this was not about greed or the accumulation of wealth, but a matter of survival. However, the group was also cognizant of the fact that even if they had money, if the right opportunity presented itself, they would take advantage of it. Also, even though the offenders professed that they committed robbery as a means of survival, fifty-nine of the eighty-six offenders stated that they had spent the money on pleasurable activities such as substance abuse and gambling, which is a direct contradiction to the claim of needing money immediately in order to survive. In answering the question of why someone would commit robbery, Wright and Decker determined that the offenders' motivations "grew out of a sense of frustration and anger because the offenders found themselves locked into a cycle of events leading to nowhere" (1997, p. 46).

So, I have to ask: Is robbery about needs, jealousy, pleasure, power, or greed?

Gangs

Gangs have been around since the beginning of time. They are not limited to humans. All animals are territorial, hunt in packs, and protect themselves from predators in large groups. If you examine the behavior of animals, we as humans are not so different. Society as a whole is based on the concept of a social contract where we give up our free will for protection by government. Giving up free will means that we agree to not violate the law and, if we choose to do so, accept that we will be punished. Yet, the term *gang* does not make us think of the civility of society based on a social contract; instead, it conjures up pictures of Al Capone and famous movies such as *The Godfather* and *Scarface*.

What is the definition of a gang? When I think of the word *gang*, I define it as a group of three or more who are involved in criminal activity. In examining a number of state statutes, I found that each used similar language to define a gang as follows: a formal or informal ongoing organization, association, or group of three or more persons with a common name or identifying signs or colors whose primary activities are the commission of criminal or delinquent acts (California State Legislature, 2013; Florida State Legislature, 2013; New York State Legislature, 2013; Texas State Legislature, 2013).

Bouchard and Spindler (2010) offered an analysis of gangs, arguing that rather than using membership or structure to identify a gang, we would be better served if we defined a gang based on its level of organization. These authors argued that organizational sophistication defines organizational behavior in gangs, much as it does in business. In essence, the organization creates a culture that supports criminal activity, and in so doing, the acts of criminal activity become more violent over time. Organizational culture and behavior are an extension of the organization's leadership and are supported by the value system that the leaders espouse.

Researchers have determined that there are a host of risk factors that can lead one to select gang membership over all else. Most are attached to developmental domains that influence our behavioral patterns. As discussed in previous chapters, central to the core of an individual is the interaction between the psychological, biological, and environmental influences; one, two, or all three can predispose an individual to be susceptible to a life of delinquency and crime. Environment seems to have the greatest influence regarding the decisions and needs of an individual. On a daily basis, a child is bombarded with influences, both positive and negative, from a number of sources. The family is the first source, and the environment that it provides is hugely influential—whether it is loving, supportive, and nurturing; or cold, distant, and fraught with acts of violence.

When I review the theories regarding street gangs, I find the story is the same. Gangs have changed and risen in popularity as a result of a number of events coming together—what Thomas (2013) described as the perfect storm: loss of unskilled laborer positions, poverty, and the change from an industrial economy to a prison-industrial economy; the influx of heroin and later crack cocaine; the incarceration of male heads of households and sometimes mothers; and a poor education system. One who is placed in such an environment has limited choices, and yet he or she has needs that extend beyond mere survival. The following quote says it all: "A 15-year-old boy recently walked into a suburban Mercedes Benz showroom, pointed at a black 500 SEL and announced, 'I'll take it.' He paid $62,000 cash from a brown paper bag. In the Jefferies Housing Project on the eastside, teenagers are driving new Corvettes, as Christmas bonuses for a job well done" (Blum, 1984, p. A1). The goal of every American is to achieve success by achieving wealth, and many gang members are doing just that.

Victimology

Victimology is the study of the interactions between the victim and the offender before, during, and after the commission of a crime (Burgess, Regehr, & Roberts, 2013; Talwar, 2006). For the police, victims of crime are a resource: They provide information; their bodies are probed and prodded for evidence; and they are potential witnesses to a crime. Often they are forced to relive some of the most terrifying incidents that a human being can experience and survive. If the victim dies, family members fill in as surrogates and are forced to experience the horror through the testimony of witnesses and forensic experts—not to mention the attacks of defense attorneys who question the credibility and honor of a rape or murder victim.

Reflect on this statement: "A victim is a necessary evil in the investigation and prosecution of a criminal case." This statement, made by Sgarzi and McDevitt (2002), emphasizes that in a criminal case, all the attention is placed on the offender, and very little attention is given to the victim (pp. 1–2).

Historically, the first mention of victims' rights was outlined in the *Code of Hammurabi* 4,000 years ago in the discussion of proportionality in sentencing, meaning that a sentence or punishment had to be fair in relation to the crime (International Narcotics Board, 2007; Office for Victims of Crime, 1998). The law recognized that victims have a right of retributive justice, but only if it is fair and equal to their loss—in other words, "an eye for an eye."

Yet, in the United States, there were laws against animal cruelty long before we began to protect children, women, or victims of crime. It was not until 1982 that President Reagan appointed the first Task Force on Victims of Crime, which offered sixty-eight recommendations regarding the treatment of crime victims in order to improve their treatment. One of the task force's recommendations was to amend the Sixth Amendment to the U.S. Constitution to guarantee that victims to be present and would provide a victim's impact statement (Presidents' Task Force, 1982).

Victims' rights legislation can best be defined as a series of laws that granted victims certain guarantees as victims of crime. Although every state has some form of these laws in place, they vary greatly from state to state. In general, the guarantees include the right to information; the right to be present at criminal justice proceedings; the right to due process, which includes the right to notice of and opportunity to be heard at important criminal justice proceedings; the right to financial recompense for losses suffered as a result of a crime, such as restitution and/or compensation/reparations; the right to protection; and the right to privacy (National Crime Victim Law Institute, 2011).

The road to understanding victimology is difficult at best. I am not so naive as to believe that the attitudes of the criminal justice system have changed completely and that victims are now always seen as more than a necessary evil. Victims have a unique position in society in that they are actors in a play in which, in many instances, they did not choose to participate; as such, if they survive, they can provide a firsthand account of man's inhumanity to man. Herman (1992) paints a picture of the psychological trauma that victims endure:

> [Trauma makes us] come face to face both with human vulnerability in the natural world and with the capacity for evil in human nature. To study trauma means bearing witness to horrible events. When the events are natural disasters or "acts of God" those who bear witness sympathize readily with the victim. But when traumatic events are of human design, those who bear witness are caught in the middle between victim and perpetrator. (p. 7)

CONCLUSION

Rather than reinvent the wheel, in this chapter, I provided the main points of each previous chapter so that you could reexamine them. I hope that you walk away with a sense that there is very little difference in the psyche of one type of criminal as opposed to another.

In Wille's (1974) analysis of the data on murderers and nonmurderers, he determined that, psychologically, the murderers overall spent less time thinking about anger, fear, and aggressive behavior, meaning that a great deal of their energy was spent on repressing such thoughts and feelings. However, if provoked, there was an expectation that the response would be sudden, violent, and destructive. Wille described two syndromes that he found present in every murderer:

- *Syndrome of repression and intense thought,* which allows the subject to function normally in his or her world, with one exception—the syndrome of expectancy
- *Syndrome of expectancy,* which can be described as the subject being always on edge and ready (pp. 33–34)

I interpret the syndrome of expectancy to mean that the person's body is always in a state of "fight or flight," ready to respond with aggression to the slightest provocation. In such a constant state of hypervigilence, the body is never able to relax.

I chose to close this chapter with a discussion of Wille's research because every type of offender we have examined has displayed a distorted cognitive process and failed coping mechanisms, both of which directly relate to Wille's syndromes of repression and expectancy. As you reflect back on the contents of this text, also keep in mind that victims are more than a necessary evil in the criminal justice system; they have endured a rare horror over which they had no control and have been firsthand witnesses to man's inhumanity to man.

REFERENCES

Anderson, E. (1999). *Code of the street: Decency, violence and the moral life of the inner city.* New York: W. W. Norton.

Ball-Rokeach, S. J. (1973). Values and violence: A test of the subculture violence thesis. *American Sociological Review, 38,* pp. 736–749.

Becker, G. S. (1968). Crime and punishment: An economic approach. *Journal of Political Economy, 76,* pp. 169–217.

Bernard. T. J. (1990). Angry aggression among the "truly disadvantaged." *Criminology, 28,* pp. 73–96.

Blum, H. (1984, January 28). U.S. helps Detroit attack drug rings that use young. *New York Times,* A1, A6.

Bouchard, M., & Spindler, A. (2010). Groups, gangs, and delinquency: Does organization matter? *Journal of Criminal Justice, 38,* pp. 921–933.

Brown v. Board of Education, 347 U.S. 483 (1954).

Burgess, A. W., Regehr, C., & Roberts, A. R. (2013). *Victimology: Theories and applications.* Burlington, MA: Jones and Bartlett Learning.

California State Legislature. (2013). *Participation in a criminal street gang: California State Statute 186.22.* Sacramento, CA: Author.

Falk, G. (1990). *Murder: An analysis of its forms, conditions, and causes.* Jefferson, NC: McFarland.

Federal Bureau of Investigation (FBI). (2011). *Crime in the United States 2011.* Washington, D.C.: Author.

Ferracuti, F., & Wolfgang, M. E. (1973). *Psychological testing of the subculture of violence.* Rome, Italy: Bulzoni.

Florida State Legislature. (2013). *Street terrorism enforcement and prevention: Florida State Statute 874.* Tallahassee, FL: Author.

Gaynor, J. (2002). *Juvenile firesetter intervention handbook.* Emmitsburg, MD: U.S. Fire Administration.

Gelles, R. J., & Straus, M. A. (1979). Violence in the American family. *Journal of Social Issues, 35*(2), pp. 15–39.

Ghiglieri, M. P. (1999). *The dark side of man: Tracing the origins of male violence.* Reading, MA: Perseus Books.

Groth, A. N., & Birnbaum, H. J. (1979). *Men who rape: The psychology of the offender.* New York: Plenum Press.

Herman, J. L. (1992). *Trauma and recovery.* New York: Basic Books.

International Narcotics Board. (2007). *Report of the international narcotics control board for 2007.* New York: United Nations.

Laws, D. R., & Marshall, W. L. (1990). A conditioning theory of the etiology and maintenance of deviant sexual preference and behavior. In W. L. Marshall, D. R. Laws, & H. E. Barbaree (Eds.), *Handbook of sexual assault: Issues, theories, and treatment of the offender* (pp. 209–230). New York: Plenum Books.

Marion County Sheriff's Office. (2006). *Leo Boatman interview: Case number 06001267.* Ocala, FL: Author.

McGuire, R. J., Carlisle, J. M., & Young, B. G. (1965). Sexual deviation as a conditioned behavior: A hypothesis. *Behavioral Research and Therapy, 2,* pp. 185–190.

Montgomery, H. K. (2001). *Modern Babylon? Prostituting children in Thailand.* New York: Berghahn Books.

National Center for Missing and Exploited Children. (2006). *Missing and abducted children: A law enforcement guide to case investigation and program management.* Alexandria, VA: Author.

National Crime Victim Law Institute. (2011). *History of victim's rights.* Portland, OR: Author.

New York State Legislature. (2013). *Gang assault in the second degree: New York State Statute 120.06.* Albany, NY: Author.

Office for Victims of Crime. (1998). *New directions from the field: Victim's rights and services for the 21st century.* Washington, D.C.: U.S. Department of Justice.

Parrish, K. (2012, January 20). *Panetta announces initiatives targeting sexual assault.* Retrieved August 28, 2013, from: http://www.army.mil/article/72243/

Presidents' Task Force. (1982). *Presidents' task force on victims of crime.* Washington, D.C.: Author.

Seto, M. C. (2008). *Pedophilia and sexual offending against children: Theory, assessment, and intervention.* Washington, D.C.: American Psychological Association.

Sgarzi, J. M., & McDevitt, J. (2002). Introduction. In J. M. Sgarzi & J. McDevitt (Eds.), *Victimology: A study of crime victims and their role* (pp. 1–5). Upper Saddle River, NJ: Prentice-Hall.

Skinner, B. F. (1953). *Science and human behavior.* New York: Free Press.

Talwar, P. (2006). *Victimology.* Adarsh, Delhi: Isha Books.

Texas State Legislature. (2013). *Compilation of information pertaining to criminal combinations and criminal street gangs: Texas code of criminal procedure 61.* Austin, TX: Author.

Thomas, D. J. (2013). *Review of drug arrest case files 1992–1994 Gainesville Police Department.* Unpublished raw data.

U.S. Fire Administration. (2001). *Arson in the United States, 1*(8). Washington, D.C.: Department of Homeland Security.

U.S. State Department. (2008). *Trafficking in persons (TIP) report 2008.* Washington, D.C.: Author.

Wille, W. S. (1974). *Citizens who commit murder.* St. Louis, MO: Warren H. Green.

Wilson, A. V. (1993). *Homicide: The victim/offender connection.* Cincinnati, OH: Anderson.

Wolfgang, M. E., & Ferracuti, F. (1967). *The subculture of violence: Towards an integrated theory in criminology.* London: Tavistok.

Wright, R. T., & Decker, S. H. (1997). *Armed robberies in action: Stickups and street culture.* Lebanon, NH: Northeastern University Press.

Index

About the Author

David J. Thomas, PhD, currently serves as an associate professor in the Department of Professional Studies at Florida Gulf Coast University where he teaches in the Forensic Sciences Behavioral Analysis Program. He holds PhD in forensic psychology and a master's in education. His research interests include police, police/forensic psychology, serial homicide, victimology, violence, and terrorism.

Dr. Thomas served as a police officer in Michigan and in Florida, retiring from the Gainesville Police Department after twenty years of service. During his tenure as an officer he has held assignments in Patrol, DUI Enforcement, Detectives, Narcotics, Training, Community-Oriented Police Team, Hostage Negotiation, and served as a Field Training Officer. Training is his specialty, where he has been certified to train police recruits and in-service officers for the last twenty-nine years. He is a certified expert, in the Florida courts, in the use of force. In addition to his academic pursuits, Dr. Thomas is the CEO of Police Counseling Services, LLC where he provides consulting and counseling services to several law enforcement agencies in Florida.